ENDORSEMENTS FOR LOVE AND TIME

A wonderful and unique book. A series of brief but profound contemplations on the twin mysteries of love and time, as lived by one man with the heart of an artist and the soul of a poet. Take time to savor it.

> Connie Zweig, Ph.D.,
> Author of *The Inner Work of Age: Shifting from Role to Soul.*

I have never read a book on aging like *Love and Time*. Filled with heart-opening stories, poetry, and reflections about the journey into the later chapters of elderhood, this book gave me a visceral experience of what it can mean to be fully, passionately present to all the painful losses and the shining gifts that accompany this precious stage of life. For those of us seeking to deepen our ability to love others, ourself and our lives amid the profound inevitable changes that aging brings, Richard Matzkin's powerful personal testimonial provides hope, inspiration, and practical guidance from a courageous elder whose wisdom has been forged in the fire of experience.

> Ron Pevny,
> Author of *Conscious Living, Conscious Aging,*
> *and Director of the Center for Conscious Eldering.*

Richard Matzkin's *Love and Time* is an exquisitely heart-felt meditation on the paradoxes of love and death, devotion and despair. If this were simply a love letter to the long-lived life, it would be enough. But there's a love story woven into the pages that is so deep and passionate, it would make even younger readers aspire to someday experience the greatest joy of all: growing old together. Highly recommended.

Carol Orsborn, PhD,
Author of *The Making of an Old Soul: Aging As The Fulfillment Of Life's Promise*

Love and Time is a rich mosaic of reflections, memories and stories -- the summation of one man's journey through life. The book includes many images of the author's sculptures, a compelling addition to the reader's experience. As a teacher and writer on Elder issues, Richard Matzkin offers us his unusual book, a variation on a memoir and a valuable resource on the deeper dimensions of aging.

Olivia Ames Hoblitzelle,
Author of *Aging with Wisdom: Reflections, Stories & Teachings*

Richard Matzkin's book, *Love and Time*, is a deeply nourishing feast of information, inspiration, and hard-earned insights for those of us who are sincerely committed to the process of spiritual maturation. A powerful and creative blend of personal stories, classical wisdom teachings, visual art, well-chosen quotations, and straightforward honesty about the realities inherent in the aging process, this book invites the reader to fully recognize what Buddhist teachings call "the preciousness of a human birth." I strongly encourage you to accept Richard's invitation and to trust that doing so will teach you a great deal about living fully and loving well.

David Chernikoff,
Author of *Life, Part Two - Seven Keys to Awakening with Purpose and Joy as You Age*

Love and Time is a book I've been waiting for, not like any other book on aging I've read (and I've read lots of them.) A voice of lived experience, rendered thoughtfully, profoundly, provocatively. Indispensable.

> Harry R. Moody, PhD,
> Author of over 100 scholarly books and articles on aging and former
> Vice President of AARP

Love and Time is a captivating read, wrapped in prose, poetry and sculpture. A unique view into past, present and future lives.

> Gail Zelitzky,
> WomenOver70: Aging Reimagined Podcast

Also by Richard Matzkin

THE ART OF AGING:
Celebrating The Authentic Aging Self
With Alice Matzkin

LOVING PROMISES:
The Master Class For Creating Magnificent Relationship

MANifesto:
A Call For Men To Become Warriors For Kindness

BECOMING LOVE Able:
How A Man Can Grow To Be A More Loving Partner

JOURNEY INTO ADULTHOOD:
A Young Person's Initiation For Navigating The Seasons Of Their Life

LOVE and TIME

Embracing Change, Growth And Mature Relationships In The Winter of Life

by Richard Matzkin

Forewords by Alice Matzkin and Harry R. Moody

To my beloved Alice, and to the beloved memory of my parents, Ruth and Jack, and Baba Muktananda. And to Roameo, the cat.

CREDITS

THANKS TO: Cousin Pam Grau for executing the cover art, Jose Ramirez of Pedernales Publishing for putting it all together, Donna Summerville for correcting my bad spelling and punctuation, Rene Norman for the back cover photo, Alice Matzkin and Michael Butler for photos of the sculpture, Alice Matzkin and Harry R. Moody for their Forewords, Rick Moody for inspiration.

ACKNOWLEDGMENTS

LAYING IN BED THIS MORNING, I am overcome with gratefulness. My heart is overflowing, thinking about all the many people who have generously contributed to my life. Some of these were through personal contact, and some through books and media. Some were present with me for a fleeting moment, and some for an extended period. With some, our connection was with ease and joy, and some with difficulty and pain. Some are alive, and some are no longer here. By helping me open my mind, uncover my feelings, and come in contact with spirit, they have all contributed to make me who I am.

Thank you.

CONTENTS

FOREWORD—LOVE
Alice Matzkin

A LOVE LETTER

I HAVE BEEN GIVEN THE GIFT by my darling husband, Richard, to write the Foreword about LOVE for LOVE AND TIME. Since he has already written heartfelt pages about love in action in this book, and Harry Moody has so graciously written his Foreword about TIME, I feel that I can only write a personal love letter to Richard about the love we have shared for the past 41 years.

   We married in India when he was 39 and I was 43…Now he is 80 and I am 84. We have lived half our lives together.

Dear Richard,

   You are my dearest, sweetest, darlingest human person in the universe, love of my life, captor of my heart, man of my dreams…

   You are everything to me…. husband, lover, father, brother, mother, best friend, teacher, student, child, super hero…soulmate.

   Your loving self always sees me and treats me as if I am a beautiful precious jewel at all times, in spite of my wrinkles and grey hair. Your hand is always there waiting when I reach out to its warmth. Your body is always available to cuddle and hug. Your touch is always gently loving.

Your love has embraced my children, family, and friends with the utmost sweetness, care, concern and generosity of spirit.

Your loving has opened my heart and my eyes to the love that exists within me and everywhere.

I appreciate that you treat everyone with loving kindness, honesty, compassion and good humor.

I feel safe walking through this lifetime with you. You have always been there with me for the good times as well as the difficult ones. We have had lots of adventures, tons of laughs and fun at home and all over the world. Now in our 80's, watching with shock and awe, the decomposition of our old bodies, life is more and more poignant and precious, beautiful, and mysterious. We realize that our time together in this incarnation is getting shorter and shorter. The sadness is so deep.

Everything comes to an end... and a beginning. Hopefully, we will pick up where we left off, as we did in this lifetime and probably many others. Time (or whatever it is) will tell. In the meantime, it has been an exquisite run!

I love you with all my heart and soul.

Alice

FOREWORD—TIME
Harry R. Moody, PhD

TIME AND THE RIVER OF MEMORY

"HAVE YOU GOT THE TIME?" someone asked me. I wanted to reply, "What is time?" But I held my tongue and said nothing until I just looked at my watch to satisfy the questioner. What is time? The author of this book invites us to go deeper, and we need some guidance on this journey, don't we?

Modern philosophers, from Immanuel Kant to Henri Bergson and Martin Heidegger, have offered pronouncements about time. But gerontologists hardly ever do. Then again, even while they are looking for biomarkers, the gerontologists can't even find agreement to tell us what aging is, let alone what time is. What they do say, and what they don't say, about it reminds us of a famous statement by Supreme Court Justice Potter Stewart, who was asked to define pornography. He answered: "You know it when you see it." St. Augustine in his Confessions wrote the first work of autobiography. Augustine said much the same thing about time: "I know what it is until you ask me what it is and then I can't say." So get used to the evasions. Evasions are familiar territory when it comes to defining what time is.

Before Augustine, in the ancient world, others ventured deeper into these waters. Speaking of deep waters, we find it hard to escape the idea that, somehow, time is a river—perhaps the fourth dimension as Einstein would say. The ancients got there first. Heraclitus (died 480 CE) is often labeled

"The Dark," not because of his complexion, but because of his oracular pronouncements. Heraclitus made a famous statement about time as a river: "No man ever steps in the same river twice, for it is not the same river and it is not the same person." But does the river analogy tell us something we didn't know before, or does it even tell us anything at all? May we have time to ponder this question. But answering the question may take even more time than we can have, should we live so long.

We sometimes use the phrase "in our time" to refer to the 20th or 21st century. The physicists want to take over the conversation about time, but they quickly find their own limits: Physicist Sean Carroll said, "Time is a label we stick on different moments in the life of the world." John Archibald Wheeler said that "time is nature's way of keeping everything from happening all at once." A strange statement? Wheeler claimed that he found this aphorism scrawled in a Texas men's room, and Woody Allen repeated Wheeler's aphorism, whether in agreement or in ridicule. Perhaps, like Einstein, Feynman and other physicists, we've stumbled on one more evasion just as Augustine did in the 4th century.

Humanists are sometimes more bold. Daniel Borstein said, "Time is the landscape of experience." While Vladimir Nabokov said, "Time is only memory in the making." Martin Heidegger wasn't sure about time, but he managed to write a whole book on the subject (Being and Time), which proved to be one of the most influential monographs in contemporary philosophy. Bold or evasive, physics or philosophy, it seems we've gone no further down the road. But we have identified memory as a crucial axis for our individual experience of time, and you, reader, will travel on this axis as you read this book and go down this road. Will you get far enough on the journey, even if you read all the chapters in this book? Or are you engaged in an impossible task by tracking both time and memory? Will this inquiry get easier, or harder as you grow older? As an elder myself, I see the pitfalls of memory all around me—above all I see it in myself.

Is it possible to venture further down this road? Sigmund Freud, founder of psychoanalysis, called psychoanalysis "the impossible profession." Freud offered this as a warning to us, and for you, too, as reader of this book. Freud was right to be cautious. In my case, I remember nothing from years of psychotherapy that I had, not even my analyst's name. What about spirituality? Yes, I've tried to go down that road for the redemption of time. But once more, I remember little from years of meditation. Does all this mean that both psychotherapy and meditation are worthless? No, both have their benefits, I believe, like reading this book has been a benefit for me and will be a benefit for you. But remember Freud's warning: an "impossible profession."

Pondering time and memory is a bit like body work. My body does its work, not only all day long, but at nighttime, too. The body does its work and I do mine. Stumbling along, reading this book, pondering time and memory, you will find many points of interest. But another caution: the Sufis, mystical exponents of Islam, said that "seeking comes from finding, not finding from seeking." You can venture to lots of places in the search for memory. Spiritual seekers begin with awareness that our time is running out.

In Denmark I visited the grave of Soren Kierkegaard and as I looked at the gravestone ("Here lies SK, in the arms of Sweet Jesu"), I noticed that he refused to put even his name on the stone. Kierkegaard also said, "Life can only be understood backwards, but it must be lived forwards." What he said was not an invitation to memory or autobiography, but an insistence that, whatever we learn in self-knowledge comes too late: we understand our life backward, but we must live it forward, requiring some sort of faith.

Like the author of this book, I keep searching, even in old age. Knowing the limits of rational understanding, as Kierkegaard did, I look for a more indirect approach: for example, the language of dreams. I sleep each night and write down my dreams, but then discover that I remember almost none of those dreams, except very few. But maybe it doesn't matter. My dreams do their work and I do mine. True for my pancreas, too. Dreams are like body work, as Jung understood.

Ever on the lookout, I have visited Dante's tomb in Ravenna. Dante has remained there in exile, as he did to the end of his life. Am I then like James Joyce, another exile, this time voluntary, mining his memory for what might turn out to be almost incomprehensible (Finnegan's Wake). Am I a grave robber, visiting tombs in order to find life stories?   But those in these graves are all dead. Could they have just told me I was on the wrong track? Looking for memory, my own or the exiles like Dante and Joyce, will lead me to evasions and illusions. Looking for truth in memory is like looking for water in the desert. You see only a mirage but it looks like water and that's a good thing to make you start walking. You keep walking toward water that isn't there. But eventually you arrive somewhere, if you live long enough, if you don't run out of time.

So now, dear reader, you need to walk away from this preface and start reading the book. It will offer you the author's memories, but not your own. You must walk through your own desert, eyes out for water ahead. And even your own search may be like my memory and my dreams—often inaccessible, but sometimes astonishing, as Proust understood and also insisted that we should understand, too.

LOVE AND TIME is a great book. What is offered here is neither guidance nor a warning. It is an invitation. Treat each fragment in this book like a dream. Treasure it, even read it out loud. (I read every word out loud to my wife.) Above all, ponder it. Do not worry about understanding it completely. It will do its work indirectly, just as dreams do.

INTRODUCTION—LOVE AND TIME

WHAT IS THIS STRANGE BOOK? Is it a philosophical treatise? A memoir? A love story? An art book? A self-help book? A collection of stories, quotes and essays? It is all these and more. LOVE AND TIME is one man's personal exploration, on entering his eightieth year, of the powerful influence of the passage of time on an aging person's life and relationships.

Love and Time—the two most important and valuable aspects of human existence. Time is the most precious commodity in a human life. It is a nonrenewable resource. The pursuit of love and passion is the most essential use to which we can devote our limited time on Earth.

Love evolves over time. As we mature, so does our love mature. The love, sensuality and passion we are capable of as adults is very different than what we were capable of when we were adolescents and young adults. And entering into our later years, with the ripening of our mind and heart, our ability to love has the potential to grow and deepen even more. This will be a central focus of the book—mature love—but not the garden variety. We will explore a kind of love that is profound, a love which has been burnished by the passage of time.

A recurring theme is intimate partnership, but this is not a book exclusively for old couples. Many elders, due to death, divorce or preference, find themselves living alone or without a partner. Of what relevance is the discussion of love for them? There is significant overlay. Love is love, and love includes the whole field of objects of love—the love of parents, children, siblings, friends, even thine enemies.

Though not always explicitly stated in the text, the truths about love we explore here remain true for whatever form love takes.

Warning. In reading this book and contemplating it's message, you will not be taking a leisurely stroll in the park with me. While it's more a personal book, based on my experience as an old lover, rather than a scientific or academic tome, it is still a difficult read. Be prepared to embark on a strenuous emotional trek at times, with some steep ascents, deep valleys and precipitous cliffs; a journey filled with both wonder and dread. Frightening, joyous, heartbreaking, uplifting, depressing, frustrating… loving and aging is all of this and more.

Don't expect the sweet, pink valentine variety of love. Intimate, generous connection to life partners, family and friends is not all butterflies and rainbows. Real love entails some difficult challenges. This degree of depth and width of love usually does not evolve on its own without our consciously investing ourselves—our time, energy, emotions, thoughts and resources. Living with love and passion takes dedication and sacrifice. It requires we show up with our best selves…always. Mature love is hard work.

It is also hard work to contemplate the passage of time. Time is constantly passing, yet rarely do we have thoughts about our impermanence. We do our laundry, feed the dog and complain about the weather, but how often do we give more than a passing glance to the reality of our ongoing physical deterioration or of the immanence of our own death? Yet these are real. Decline and death lives with us moment by moment. To unblinkingly stare into the face of the truth of our fragile body and limited time on Earth is not for sissies. While not easy, it is an invaluable undertaking. If we earnestly explore our impermanence, it will add immeasurably to the depth and meaning of our lives. This exploration is a path to our physical, intellectual, emotional and spiritual well-being. Embarking on that path of inquiry can deepen your ability to love. It *will* deepen your ability to love.

So, lend me your time and journey with me. Instead of trying to hide or deny or minimize the ongoing effects of time on our body and mind, we will endeavor to consciously embrace our aging with acceptance, openness and curiosity. Then, in spite of the considerable losses wrought by time (or maybe because of them), we will then have the possibility to embrace life in all its fullness and wonder and obtain the bountiful gifts our later years can offer. This is our life's purpose, this is what our life so far has prepared us for. Our destination is not stagnation, despair and dissolution, but rather aliveness, ripening and harvest. Ultimately, you will find, as I have, our destination is love.

Readers who enjoy receiving information through their mind will find lots of material to chew on. But don't expect a scholarly dissertation. I'm not a gerontologist, not an expert on aging. I'm just a guy who came to the realization that I needed to look into my aging in order that my remaining days will have more juice and more meaning. Throughout the book, in addition to information and theoretical excursions, you'll find many short stories, poems, quotes, personal ruminations and anecdotes from my life. Together they contribute what is an extended personal exploration of life and death, loss and gain, appreciation and regret, past and future and a celebration of love, passion and sensuality into old age. I hope that you'll be stimulated by these ideas, and I believe you'll recognize yourself in many of these personal stories and quotes.

Initially, I was very excited about the book. Love and time are meaty subjects. I thought long about it, chose the title, even designed and executed the cover art for the book. But then, when it came time to write, I found myself dragging my feet. Any excuse would keep me from sitting down and putting pen to paper. I realize now what the problem was. This book awakened my fears. It hits too close to home.

Writing is mental exploration. When authors set their mind to write, they are fated to learn about the subject they choose to write about. I came to learn that the subject of this book is myself, my hope for a wholesome and fulfilling future, but also my realistic fears, my profound sorrow, my sense of foreboding of the inevitable changes the coming years might bring. As I got more into gathering notes and writing, I became depressed. I'm an old man. During the process of writing this book, I celebrated my eightieth birthday. That's really old. Eighty has brought greater recognition that my time is running out. What losses might be lurking around the corner, what illness, what debilities, what helplessness, what suffering? What deaths might be laying in wait for my loved ones? And for myself? And how soon?

I persevered and brought the project to what I believe is a successful conclusion. I digested my difficult emotions, faced my fears as best I could, learned much about myself. I looked at where I had been, where I was headed, where I succeeded, where I had fallen short. Turning my thoughts inside and writing was highly beneficial. It was a rite of passage for me. I found purpose. I was profoundly deepened by the process. In so many ways I had been sleepwalking through life. Writing this book was my education and my therapy. It helped wake me up and it has positively influenced how I am living going forward. I'm different now than when I started. I appreciate my life so much more now. This is a good sign for the reader. Since writing this book has changed me for the better, my hope is that, in reading this book, you too might change for the better.

I made what was a difficult decision to write about Time before I write about Love. It was difficult because the issues connected with time—aging, impermanence, illness and death, are emotionally challenging and tough to grapple with. It's not a crowd pleaser or subject of casual conversation. And I didn't pull any punches. I fear that some readers might be turned away by reading the bad news about aging before they get to the good news about love. (Truthfully, if you contemplate deeply, it's all good news, all beneficial.) However, it seemed more appropriate to explore Time first. I urge you to push through the bitter tasting initial parts of the book because this will make the sweet parts taste even sweeter.

The contemplation of time is a prerequisite for opening to the realities of life. Life has its limits, its pain, its endings. Exploring these difficult challenges wakes us up, gooses us to not waste a moment, pushes us to be more who we're meant to be, do more what we're meant to do, so that when our time is coming to an end, and we look back at the life we lived, we won't be immersed in regret or wail about what could have been. Therefore, I see our tasting of Time's bitter truth as medicinal.

Exposing ourselves to this bitter truth also demands some degree of a spiritual awakening. Loss, illness and death that we are likely forced to face as we age are spiritual challenges, not just medical or psychological ones. We must engage not only our body, mind and heart, we must also delve into our soul. If we engage with our soul, our aging becomes our spiritual path, awakening entails our spiritual awakening. My past experiences in spiritual community and with spiritual teachers, and my present spiritual practices have informed much of the material herein. In many ways then, this is a spiritual book. The process of writing it has been an important part of my spiritual practice.

Take note that this is not a book about the second half of life or even the last third. It's not for what to do post retirement, or advice for those going through midlife crisis. It is about being old, the final quarter of life, seventies on up, the biblical "three score and ten." The differences between the issues faced by those in their sixties, and those in their seventies are significant. The additional ten or fifteen years can make a world of difference.

I would think the book would be of special interest for Baby Boomers, the post WWII generation bump, the oldest of whom have already entered into the door of old age and, as of this writing, are deeply into their seventies. As they have in the past, Boomers tend to explore new and nontraditional ways of living. The challenge of delving into mature relationships and conscious elderhood would be right up their alley. While Boomers are on the cusp of old age, and experiencing directly the effects of Father Time, LOVE AND TIME would also be valuable, and provide guidance and encouragement for readers of all ages. It is never too early to address the Winter of life and begin preparations for a good old age.

A word about me. I am not lying when I say that I am an expert on love. Becoming an expert lover is the one thing in my life of which I am most proud. My forty-plus-year relationship with my wife, Alice, has provided me the greatest joy and the greatest learning. It has been a long, painful road for me to gain my expertise—three failed marriages and numerous broken relationships caused by my immaturity, selfishness, affairs, hiding, lies and domestic violence. I am not proud of the path I had taken. I caused suffering and endured suffering. But I am happy to say that I grew through my experience, and in addition, partook of psychological and spiritual support, so that, when I met Alice, the love of my life, our love instantly blossomed into the relationship we had both been hoping for. Forty years on, our marriage remains the deepest, sweetest, most fulfilling humanly possible.

When I write a lot about the great relationship I have with Alic, I do so not to brag, though I am proud of what we have accomplished. I bring up our relationship often because it is inspirational. I feel that it's inspiring to the reader that a guy like me, who's had a long history of screwing up relationships, finally ended up with a great one. I offer this book in hope that the reader can learn from my experience. Maybe they can avoid some of the pitfalls I had fallen into and experience the joy that is possible in a mature, loving partnership.

You might find that LOVE AND TIME is not a practical book in the sense that there are not a lot of suggestions about actions you can take, like questionnaires, written exercises, meditations, visualizations or experiential processes. It is only near the end that I discuss tasks a person can engage with that can help lead to a good old age, and even then, without a lot of detail. I've chosen to go wide rather than to go deep, so what you find here is more of an owners manual for maintenance of an old body and mind, rather than a detailed repair book. The book is more about gaining perspective and understanding, with the idea that understanding can be a prerequisite to action. With understanding comes motivation. With motivation comes action. With action comes change.

The chapters are short, sometimes just a few sentences. Because the writing can be dense, and the thoughts can be highly condensed, more of your attention is required. There are some concepts in a paragraph or two that would take a full book to explore. See the short chapters herein as objects for contemplation. If you come upon a sentence or two that grabs you, give yourself permission to linger. I urge you to not rush through. Take your time and put in the effort to think about and digest what I've written. It's a hearty meal. I've seasoned the meal with ingredients that I believe will spark your imagination and stimulate your mind.

And don't neglect the art. There are sections throughout LOVE AND TIME where there is an interplay of words and art. The sculptures scattered throughout are an integral part of the reading experience. The combination of image and commentary conveys a far more impactful experience than words alone. For many years l used the medium of sculpture to delve into my fear and curiosity about my aging and dying. I tried to not be timid in my approach. Because I felt confronted by the subject matter, many of the sculptures illustrated here are confrontational. Viewing them can bring to awareness powerful emotions and painful realizations. The poignant images are selected from two of my sculpture projects that explored aging: "Naked Old Men," representing the effects of time on the body, and, "Old Lovers," representing aged love. Love and time.

The sculptures will move you—if you allow them. As a sample, take a moment now and look at the front cover of the book. Breathe in the image of the clock face and sense its meaning. Feel the caring in the old lover's embrace. See the expression of love on the elder woman's face. Note the gentle loving in their hands. This is a visual experience of love and of time.

I'm glad this book has found you. I wish you a good journey.

Richard
Ojai, California
6/20/23

THE CIRCLE

The life cycle – child, adult and elder

OPENING—SEASONS OF LIFE AND RELATIONSHIPS

To everything there is a season. Ecclesiastes 3

WATCH THE CYCLING PROGRESSION of the seasons of the year, from Spring, to Summer, to Autumn, to Winter, and again, to Spring. Experience, over time, the evolving of your human life, the lives of your parents, your children, your friends. Observe your body grow and change from child, to adult, to aged person. Feel your love as it grows and changes and ripens over time. Know that your life, your body, your relationships, your world evolves through a process that can be likened to the progression of seasons.

To be alive and human is to be living the seasons of life.

Seasons Of The Year

As it follows its elliptical orbit around the Sun, there are times of the year when Earth is closer, and times when it is farther away. This results in variations in temperature and length of days, and these variations produce the pageant of the four seasons, and effect all life on Earth.

In Spring, the earth is waking up from the slumber of the cold days of Winter. Seeds safeguarded in the depth and darkness of Winter soil germinate and are called to life. Sap flows and plants begin to sprout. Buds form. Animals become more active or emerge from their hibernation. Birds build nests and lay their eggs. Animals give birth, feed and protect their young. It is the time of growth and renewal.

The warm days of Summer follow, and is the time of year when animals, insects and plants are most active. Fruits are growing and ripening. Leaves, grasses, and flowers are in full glory. Food is plentiful and animals hunt and forage. Their young venture out on their own and seek to pair with a mate. At the end of Summer, temperatures begin dropping and hours of light decrease.

Activity slows as Autumn progresses. Animals pad their dens and gather what stores of food they can. Mammals gain fat and thick, full coat in preparation for the cold. Sap, the lifeblood of plants, recedes. The ground is littered with brilliant reds and golds, as some plants drop their leaves to better prepare for Winter. Autumn is the time of gathering in, a time of harvest. Late Autumn is also a time that initiates regeneration, as plants have finished maturing and drop their seeds in preparation for a new cycle of life in the coming year.

Due to cold weather and scarcity of food in Winter, animals and plants, in order to conserve their energies, have slowed down their activity and life processes. There are more hours of darkness. Some animals hibernate. It is a time of rest. Some plants, insects and animals, their life cycle completed, will weaken and their life will come to an end.

Seasons of a Life

The pattern of a human life can be seen to mirror the patterns of nature during the progression of the seasons.

Spring is the time for youth. In the Spring of the life cycle, a child is born and rapidly grows. It is a time where, under the nurturance and protection of the adults in the family, the child enjoys social play, reaches out for new learnings, new experiences, and begins to acquire knowledge and skills that will serve him or her in adult life.

The Summer of life, adulthood, like the time of the year, is the most active season of life. It could be said to begin in late adolescence. The young adult begins to navigate life in the big, wide world, increasingly separating from dependence on family, and finding ways of personal and financial self-support. They establish their personal identity, peer identity, career identity and sexual identity. Many form long-term intimate bonds and aim to create a stable family constellation of their own. For many during this period, focus is on family, home, career and finances. Optimally, as Summer wears on, equilibrium is established and stability achieved.

People respond in different ways as Autumn progresses. For some, as they move through middle age, the Autumn of life, ambition wanes and they are not so concerned with rushing around, doing and acquiring. Instead, by late middle age, they may want to slow down, adjust to decreasing energy and deal with the start of a physical debility or two. Maybe they retire, and with more time available, begin to enjoy the fruits of the Autumn season—leisure, travel, social relationships, etc. Others may become disturbed as they see Winter approaching. In Autumn, they might try to hold off Winter by trying to create endless Summer, through exercise, medical intervention or whatever the latest anti-aging fad is current. Still others may take a different route. Sensing loss of youth and seeing old age just around the corner, they reevaluate goals set in Summer and feel the push to pursue their dreams, accomplish altruistic goals or do the things they have always wanted to do before their time runs out. There is grieving to be done because those in Autumn recognize Summer is over and the previous self is in the process of dying.

The passage of years brings a person to the Winter of life—old age. People in Winter see their time drawing to a close. Their vital energy is ebbing, illnesses and debilities might be taking their toll. Often, their life slows down and contracts, with less travel, friends and social activities, and more concerns with health and diminishing comforts. People in Winter tend to look back at previous seasons and evaluate the life they have lived, with some combination of feelings of satisfaction and/or regret. A goal they may want to accomplish is to tie up loose ends and make peace with themselves and others. Some may seek to establish a legacy, with money, or good works, or by passing on knowledge they have gained over their lifetime, with intention to leave the world a better place than when they arrived. They might turn inward, seeking life's meaning, and upward, searching for solace in religion and the realm of the spirit. The challenges of Wintertime present an elder with the opportunity to deepen as no other season can.

Seasons of Relationships

As we move through the seasons of our lives, we evolve. Our personality and character changes. Our needs and circumstances change. Our view of life changes. The way we relate to others changes. How we love changes. The subject of this book is primarily the latter part of the seasons of the human lifespan, especially the Winter of life. Our interest is primarily on the effect of the Winter season on our life, and the effects Winter has on our intimate relationships and on the relationships we have with the people in our lives we care about.

PART 1.

BECOMING OLD

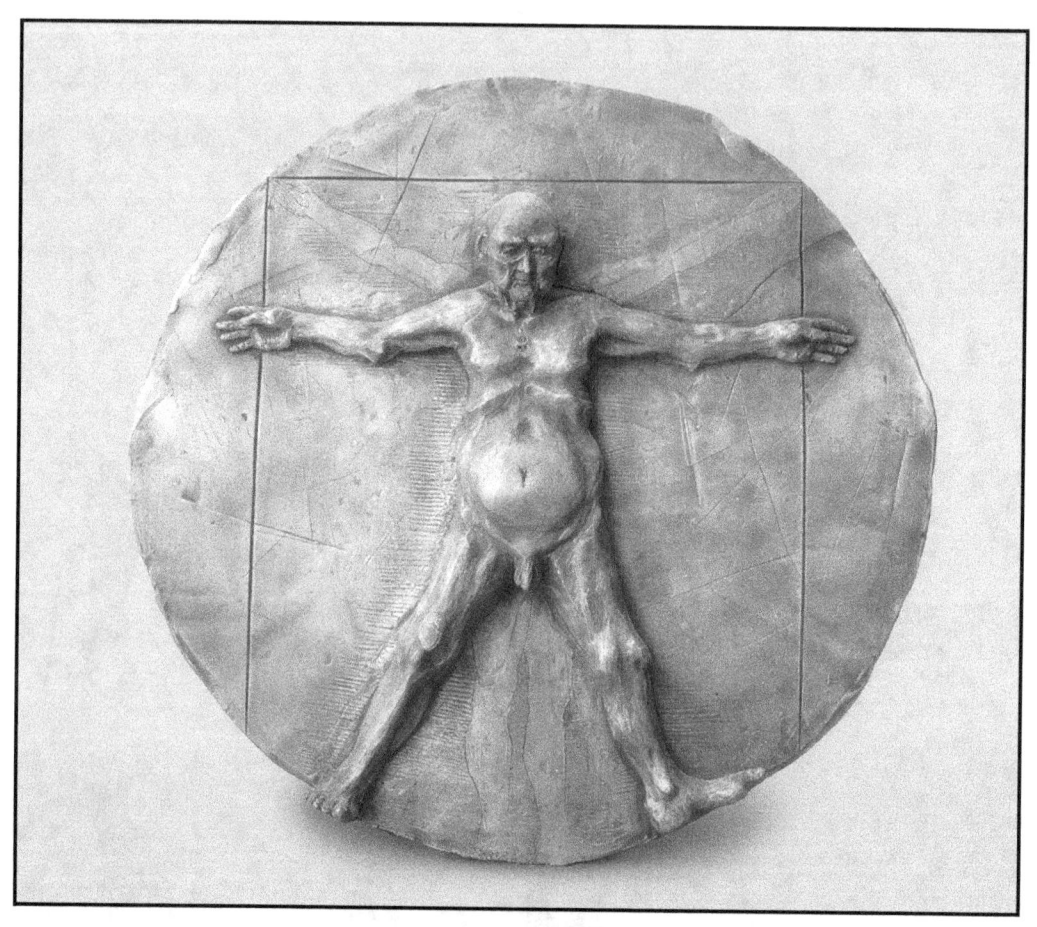

VITRUVIAN MAN: 40 YEARS LATER

A version of DaVinci's famous drawing, 40 years hence.
Drawing etched in background

ABOUT TIME

There is a mountain that is six miles high and six miles wide. Every hundred years, a bird flies by with a silk scarf in its beak. The tip of the scarf grazes the top of the mountain. By the time the entire mountain is worn down, that's how long each being has been working toward liberation.

Buddhist tale

What is Time?

TIME IS AN ARTIFICIAL CONSTRUCT. It doesn't exist. We humans created time so that when we want to meet Uncle Charlie for lunch at the restaurant in town, we need to make sure we'll both be there together.

Time is composed of the past and the future. The past is what has already happened. It is stored as memory. The future is what will happen. It is a fantasy. In between past and future, like the invisible line dividing air from water in a glass, is the present moment. This instant, the present moment, is timeless. It moves ever forward, never backward. NOW, the present moment, is infinite. It stretches from an infinite past to a future that goes on for eternity. It always was and always will be.

We can divide the present into discrete units. Those units are measured by movement. The most basic movement humans have always used for dividing time is planetary motion, the movement of the earth in relation to the sun. One rotation of the earth constitutes a day. One revolution of the earth around the sun constitutes a year. Eventually, humans developed more precise ways of dividing up time into finer and more refined fragments—the moving shadow on a sundial, the dropping of grains of sand in an hourglass, the swing of the pendulum, winding spring, cranking of gears and movement of hands around a clock face, or more recently, the progressing glow of the numerals on a digital clock.

We can also mark the progression of time by the changes in our bodies and the bodies of those around us. We look at our hands and see them gradually changing—taking on wrinkles, thin skin, age spots. Soon they turn into the hands of our parents, and eventually, if we're lucky, our grandparents. We watch our children, whose body we could once hold in the palm of one hand, overtake us and grow to be taller than we are.

Time flows forward and never ends. But it will temporarily end for us when we fall asleep or lose consciousness. Time ends permanently for us when we die. For all we know, in death, time is extinguished, like the flame of a candle that has burned out. Maybe.

A Clam

Years ago, we camped for a night on the Topatopa mountains in the Sespe Wilderness. The next day, as we trekked to near the summit of the mountain, I glanced to the side of the trail. There, among scattered rocks, was a fossilized clam shell. What? A clam shell? At the top of a mountain? Many miles inland from the ocean? How many millions of years ago must that clam have lived at the bottom of the sea? How many tens or hundreds of millions of years did it take for the ocean bottom to push up and become a mountain? The millions of years the clam has been around is nothing compared to the age of the earth, 4.54 billion years. And the time the earth has been around is nothing compared to 13.8 billion years, which is the estimated age of the galaxy. My lifetime of eighty years seems long to me, but it's a blip in time compared to that clam, or the mountain, or the earth, or the universe.

The Preciousness Of Time

Time is the most precious commodity a person can possess. A lifetime without love or money or a place to live would be hard, but you could survive, and some people do. Without food or water or even air, you can survive for a few weeks, a few days, a few minutes. But without time, nothing exists.

Time is the container for everything to exist. We have a limited time to live, maybe 10 or 60 or 100 or more years. Or maybe, as you maneuver your car into the traffic lane without seeing the truck bearing down on you, you have but a few seconds left to live. This is not given for us to know.

People who have experienced a life-threatening event often report a changed perception of their time. The genuine possibility that their time could be over is a sobering wake up call. It is an experience in the gut, not a concept in the mind. After I had a heart attack several years ago, my relationship to time radically changed. I felt as if I had been given the gift of a second life. Since then, I have been determined to make the most of my "bonus time" and am living with renewed verve, appreciation and gratitude. Total gratitude. This phone call with a friend…precious. This delicious meal…precious. This cuddle with Roameo the cat…precious. I honestly consider my heart attack to be a gift and one of the high points of my life.

Taking into consideration the uncertainty of our future, we would be smart to realize the preciousness of our time. We would not waste a moment. We would be thankful for every second.

After all, each moment that passes is one moment less of life we have to live.

Time Is Money

There is a saying, "Time is money." In a way, that's true—if you want to invest your time only in making money. But there are more valuable ways to invest your time.

What if you were to invest your time into creating something that was valuable and fulfilling for you. There are approximately 22 billion seconds in the average human lifetime. Some people spend most of their adult seconds trying to garner enough wealth so that they can enjoy retirement and do the things they put off doing. Later, later, later, they live life for later. But sometimes later never comes. I say that's a waste of valuable seconds. If you could invest at least some of those seconds in something that brings you and others joy and growth and meaning, those seconds would take on special value.

Time is the coin of your life. It is the only coin you have, and only you can determine how it will be spent. Be careful lest you allow other people spend it for you.

Carl Sandburg

A billion seconds, not counting sleep, equals 31 years. Would you trade those years for a billion dollars? I don't think so.

There are 86,400 seconds in a day. You cannot buy back your seconds. The time that has passed has already been spent. If you would treat your time as if it were your money, you would take care of how you spent it. You would be aware, very aware, of how you waste it.

Your life consists of the way you spend your time. Invest in your health. Invest in your happiness. Invest in what will help you grow—wiser, deeper, safer, more loving. Invest in what will help others grow to become wiser, deeper, safer, more loving. These would be wise investments that would pay huge dividends.

The Experience Of Time Is Flexible

Time is measured in precise intervals. Each second is exactly one second long, each hour, exactly one hour. However, as we live, time is experienced as flexible as a rubber band. Tell your young son on Thursday that you will be taking him to an amusement park on Saturday, and time will seem like an eternity to him. If you are in pain, getting a root canal in the dentist's chair, minutes will seem like hours.

Earlier in my life when I lived several years in a monastic environment, I had an interesting experience of the flexibility of time. Except for an occasional holiday celebration, days at the ashram were monotonously the same. Wake for meditation at 4:30 AM, followed by morning chant, work, noon chant, midday meal, rest, work, chanting, evening meal, evening chant, meditation or sleep. It was the same day after day. Days would dissolve into each other. Time became distorted. Hours would seem long, seem short. A week would go by in what seemed like a day, a day would seem endless.

When we are in a novel environment, filled with new experiences, it is not unusual for days to seem long. In our forties, Alice and I traveled around the world. We visited many exotic countries and experienced new people, new tastes, new and challenging situations that required our focus and engagement. Because the days were so full of "firsts," experiences we never had before, our waking hours seemed to go on forever. The thirteen and a half months we were away could easily have been several years.

The idea of "firsts" is a reasonable explanation of why time seems to pass more slowly for younger people. They have so many more firsts…first car, first relationship, first job, first semester in school. The young are more engaged and pay more attention to the unique details of these novel experiences, and time seems to expand. As elders, "been there, done that," and our attention tends to gloss over details. Time seems to fly by.

Past Within The Present

The past interpenetrates the present. Though we live in the present moment, this moment encompasses all of our past moments. I'm an adult, yet within me are all my experiences as an infant, a child, an adolescent, a young man. I'm still that shy little boy hiding behind my father's trousers, still that triumphant teenager who caught the pass in the end zone and won the football game, still that hurt husband, facing divorce, trying to make sense of a broken marriage. These past experiences and accompanying feelings are all alive in me, maybe not conscious, but somewhere available to be triggered and brought to awareness by an event or memory. In this sense, the past is timeless, alive in every moment.

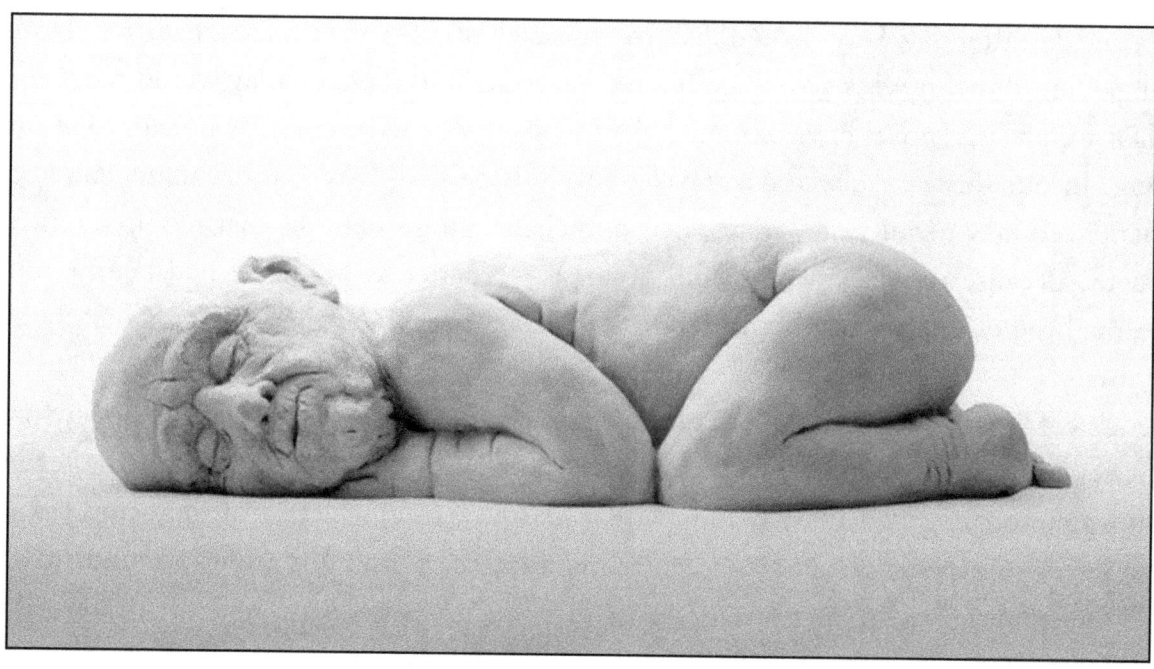

OLD BABY
A baby's body with an old man's face

Fleeting Time

Barely the day started and it's six in the evening
Barely arrived on Monday and it's already Friday
And the month is already over
And the year is almost over
And already 40, 50, 60 years of our life has passed
And we realize we lost our parents, friends
And we realize it's too late to go back

Wild Woman Sisterhood

As elders, it's a universal experience and a constant complaint. We would swear that time is actually moving more quickly the older we've gotten. It's like in the old black and white movies, when they want to indicate the passage of time, they show pages of a calendar rapidly flipping, or the hands of a clock spinning faster and faster. As we look back, it seems as if what happened a few days ago was actually a week, two weeks ago was actually a month. The illusion that time is moving faster the older we get is not what's most disturbing. What's most disturbing is the reality that with time speeding along so quickly, we are more rapidly approaching the end of our life.

This should be a reminder to us all to not put things off till tomorrow. Because tomorrow was yesterday. So don't wait to be kind, and don't wait to say "I love you."

Young Time, Old Time

When we are young, there is so much to do, so much to see, so much to become. We are not content. We are oriented to the future. We are on the move, rushing somewhere, somewhere new, somewhere else.

There is always something to look forward to in the next stage. As children, we are eager to grow up, as adolescents, we are eager to become independent, as adults, we are eager to be wealthy, secure, to be somebody. And then, as we get older and have lived our dreams, or given up on them, striving for the future becomes less important. We have less future. We begin to learn the meaning of "enough."

How did it get so late so soon?
It's night before it's afternoon.
December is here before it's June.
My goodness how time has flown.
How did it get so late so soon?

Dr Suess

As elders, with so much striving behind us, and less of a future ahead of us, we are more oriented to "now," the present moment. We are able to be immersed in being in the present, enjoying our precious *now*. (Unless, as some elders tend to be, we are stuck in the past.)

Without a busy schedule, we can spend our precious now by *being*, rather than by *doing*, being in the moment rather doing for the future. No rush. Being in the flower garden, leisurely pulling weeds, the morning sun warming our back and shoulders. Being seated at the kitchen table, enjoying the taste and aroma of a cup of coffee. Being with our beloved, reading in bed together, aware of the serenity and sweetness of this moment, the only moment there is.

What Is Old?

The age you consider "old" is related to the age you are. A 2009 Pew Research poll asked Americans what age they considered a person old. Those between the ages of 18 to 29 put the number at 60. Those 65 and older said 74.

When I was around thirteen, I was sitting on a bench at a park and a ball rolled up to where I was seated. I remember a boy of around eight came up to me asking for the ball. "Could you throw me the ball, mister?" He called me "mister." I was shocked. I never considered myself a "mister." To this little kid, I was a grownup. To an eight-year-old, a teenager is old.

In the Sixties, hippies made the viral statement, "Never trust anyone over thirty," as if a thirty-year-old was an old person. As a twenty-year-old, I would view a person of forty as an elder. A person aged thirty might think a sixty-five-year-old is ready for the garbage heap. I'm in my eighth decade and I don't feel old, not a day over forty. I'm sure that, if and when I will have reached my nineties, eighty will seem really, really young. I asked my Aunt Kitty, when she was in her early nineties, "How old do you feel you are?" Her response, "Maybe in my forties." It could be true that age is just a number.

A Living Calendar

When I was a kid, there was a store near us that had a giant slice of the trunk of an ancient redwood tree resting against the side of the building at the entrance. On the trunk of a tree, each light and dark ring, called an annual growth ring, represents one full year. This tree was old. There were little labels attached to the trunk, each representing a notable occurrence in history. Near the center, when the tree was young, was a label indicating the time of the discovery of America. There was one for the signing of the Constitution, Abraham Lincoln's presidency, World War I. I would contemplate this trunk every time I would visit the store. In front of me was a calendar that stretched back over hundreds of years.

Time Frozen

Before me is a stack of old photographs, remnants of the family history bequeathed to me by my parents and my Aunt Kitty. I'm looking with a magnifying glass at a faded sepia photo of my great grandparents, formal pose, painted background, taken by a professional photographer in 1893. Another of my maternal grandparents, faded colors, hand-tinted, dated 1903, by a photographer in New York City. Another, a black and white photo of my parents, smiling and embracing in the living room of the apartment I spent the first few years of my life in, taken in the early '40s, shortly before I was born. Another, myself at age 7, with friends, in the alley next to our old house that's not there anymore.

The magnifying glass pours over the figures and background, searching faces long turned to dust, looking at details: my grandfather's old fashion 3 piece suit with starched shirt collar, my mother's brooch, the old lamp in the living room, the antique table my great-grandmother's hand is resting on.

These old photos defy time and allow me to enter into the past, into a long-gone world inhabited by ghosts. Moments frozen in time.

Among the articles I discovered going through my parents possessions after their deaths was my mother's diary. It was a faux-leather binding, dated January 1925. The last entry, in my mom's neat script, was June 13, 1927. The yellowed pages contained the everyday experiences of a budding young girl, just entering her teens, opening to the newly discovered world of friends, school, boys, cultural icons of the time. My mother had always been "Mom" to me. Here was a picture of a person I never knew, an innocent, her secret feelings written in her own hand. After reading this slim diary, I would never know my mother in the same way. Moments frozen in time.

I'm listening to the tinny sounds of an audio tape recorded on an early reel-to-reel audio recorder. It preserved a day in 1949, a raucous party given for family by my parents, celebrating our new home. I'm about five years old. I hear the familiar voices of my parents, my maternal grandparents, other relatives long gone. My aunts, Kitty and Sylvia, are singing a popular song from that era, accompanied by the deep bass of Uncle Joe. My dad interviews me in his best radio announcer voice.

Listening to the high tones of my own 5-year-old voice, I picture that young, innocent boy who is me. A moment frozen in time.

An Archeological Dig

Having grown up during the Great Depression, and having experienced privation during that time, my mother was a hoarder. She never threw anything away, never knowing if she would need it in some difficult time in the future. She kept things organized, but there was a lot of stuff. Most of the house was neat and clean, but the shared bedroom where long ago my brother and I grew up, was where her hoarding tendencies played out most. Things were boxed and neatly piled 5 or 6 feet high throughout the room. There were narrow aisles, one leading to a closet, and on the other side of the room, an aisle leading to my father's desk and file cabinet, which served as his office.

Along one wall was the bed I had slept in when I was growing up. It was piled high with boxes and suitcases and folded clothes.

After my parents died, my brother and I went about cleaning out the house they had lived in for almost 50 years, in order to ready it for sale. We dreaded the prospect, both because it held sad remembrance of their absence, and because it was such a gargantuan task.

We worked our way around the room, sorting and piling stuff in containers outside—garbage, giveaway, thrift store, keep—but mostly garbage.

I finally came to my old bed, where things were piled so high I couldn't see over the top. As I worked my way from top down, I became aware of an ordered sequence. My mother had placed objects on the bed over time, as she needed to store them, newer objects on top of older objects. There were my notebooks and some college texts, below these, clothes I had worn as a teenager, below these, games I played when I was 8 or 9 years old.

This was an archaeological dig, and as I removed object after object, I was experiencing my life backwards in time, seeing objects I hadn't laid eyes on for more than half a century. I finally excavated the very bottom layer. There, folded and compressed by the weight of the items above, was my baby blanket.

The Value Of Time
author unknown

To realize the value of one year, ask a student who has failed their Final Exam.

To realize the value of one month, ask a parent of a premature baby.

To realize the value of one week, ask the editor of a weekly newspaper.

To realize the value of one day, ask a daily wage laborer who has a large family to feed.

To realize the value of one hour, ask lovers who are waiting to meet.

To realize the value of one minute, ask a person who has missed the train or bus or plane.

To realize the value of one second, ask a person who has survived an accident.

To realize the value of one millisecond, ask the person who has won the Silver Metal at the Olympics.

It's Later Than You Think

When Alice and I give workshops and interviews, we'll often end by singing an old song recorded by Guy Lombardo and his Royal Canadians. The refrain goes;

Enjoy yourself, it's later than you think
Enjoy yourself, while you're still in the pink
The years go by, as quickly as a wink
Enjoy yourself, enjoy yourself, it's later than you think.

IMPERMANENCE

Nothing is permanent. Nothing. All that appears must some day disappear. All that begins must end. All that is born must one day die.

A mayfly lives for only 24 hours, a fly, 15 to 30 days, a flea, 60 days, a butterfly, 1 to 2 months, a cockroach, 2 years, some wood-boring beetles have a life cycle of 50 years. The maximum lifespan of a rat, 4 years, a rabbit, 13 years, a crow, 15 years, a dog, 25 years, a goldfish, 25 years, a cat, 35-40 years, humans, up to 120 years, a tortoise, 150 years, a rockfish, 200 years. The oldest tree, a bristlecone pine, is almost 5,000 years old.

Life on Earth will end in about 1.5 billion years.
The Earth and our solar system will die in about 5 billion years.
The universe will come to an end in about 100 trillion years.

Nothing is permanent.

Trimurty

Years ago, Alice and I visited the Elephanta Caves. Situated on an island, six miles east of the city of Mumbai, India, the caves are a series of ancient temples carved out of solid basalt rock. In a prominent place in the main temple is a massive sculpture of three connected faces of the main Hindu gods. The sculpture stands over 20 feet high. On the right is the face of Brahma, the god of creation. In the middle is Vishnu, the preserver. On the left is Shiva, the god of destruction. These three processes, creation, maintenance, and destruction, represent the nature of every aspect of the visible universe, from the birth of stars and galaxies over billions of years, to the lifespan of a butterfly, over a period of days. Everything that exists is subject to these three cosmic functions. All that exists is born, stays for awhile, and then is destroyed. This is the nature of change.

Brahma, Vishnu and Shiva are of the nature of change. We become familiar with and are comfortable with growth and maintenance. But with Shiva, destruction disturbs us. And so we resist, and the very resistance, the fighting against change, is what causes us to suffer. Suffering is holding on, with all our might, to what is changing. Growing old and dying is the process of change. The god Shiva at work.

Thus it is with human life.

The days of our years are threescore and ten and if by reason of strength they be fourscore years,
yet is their strength labor and sorrow,
for it is soon cut off, and we fly away.

Psalms 90:10 KJV

Entropy

Entropy is a term used in chemistry and physics, but it is also descriptive of the process of impermanence. In this context, it is the simple statement that, over time, things progressively decline into disorder. "The degradation of matter and energy in the universe to an ultimate state of inert uniformity."

I watched a fascinating documentary on TV on the effects of the passage of time on man-made structures. It showed what buildings would look like if left untended by humans after weeks, months, years, centuries. It is amazing how soon decay begins to set in. Wood is the first to go. It decomposes or is devoured by termites. Even materials we consider "permanent," like concrete and metal, begin to melt away given enough time. Concrete cracks and dissolves into its components and flakes away. Metal rusts, becomes thin and brittle and disappears. Almost immediately, plant life begins to take over and cover up collapsing man-made structures, probing roots speeding along the process of disintegration. Given enough time, nature triumphs and traces of civilization are obliterated.

On practically every continent there existed thriving cultures that, for whatever reason, disappeared. The original walls and foundations of their buildings became walls and foundations for new structures built by ensuing inhabitants. The civilizations that followed created stories and, over time, the stories became myths. Or the jungle and forest reclaimed the city, like Angkor Wat, and it was forgotten, except for fables of the "Lost City" that were dismissed as a myth.

Sometime in the distant future, our descendants might be taking a tour to visit the ruins of the fantastic, fabled city of Las Vegas, or walk among the crumbled stones of the Statue of Liberty. They'll muse about the ancient civilization that produced such imposing structures.

Sparta

When we visited Greece, Alice and I took a bus from Athens through the Peloponnesian peninsula on our way to the island of Crete. The bus stopped at the ancient city of Sparta, and we decided to get off, look around for awhile, and take the next bus to continue on our journey.

In a class on world history, I learned about the Peloponnesian War, the series of battles between the powerful city-states of Athens and Sparta that took place beginning in 431 BC to 404 BC. This war was a highly historically significant event. The defeat of Athens marked the end of the Golden Age of Greece. The balance of power of Greece shifted after that defeat when Athens was absorbed into the powerful Spartan Empire.

Contemporary Sparta is a modest city of around 35,000 inhabitants. We followed the sign to the ruins on the outskirts of town. What we saw of the once powerful city-state on that sunny Spring day was a herd of sheep grazing amid ancient olive trees planted among scattered stones and columns.

There was a ruined and overgrown amphitheater, a remnant here and there of a wall or a foundation. That was all that remained of a great and powerful civilization that flourished for centuries.

The well-known ancient Greek historian, Thucydides, made a prediction when he wrote, "Suppose, for example, that the city of Sparta were to become deserted and that only the temples and foundations of the buildings remain, I think that future generations would, as time passed, find it very difficult to believe that the place had really been as powerful as it was represented to be." How right he was.

Disappearing Art

We are friends with a sculptor and owner of a concrete fabrication business, named Jud Smith, who lives and works in Northern California. Many years ago Jud gifted us with one of his sculptures, a large "thing" made of distressed plywood and pre-aged tin that resembled some sort of industrial object or part of an old piece of machinery. This was an outdoor piece that was to reside in our garden. The aim? The sculpture was designed to disappear. And it did. After years being exposed to the elements in our garden, the wood gradually rotted and the metal rusted. It eventually collapsed, and, as expected, became an unidentifiable mass taken over by weeds. An essential part of the "art" of the piece was for the viewer to experience the slow changes as the sculpture gradually disintegrated over time.

This is the process of entropy, and this is the same process we all go through as we age. We rust and rot, and, once buried in the ground, are eventually taken over by weeds.

Artistic Demonstrations Of Impermanence

Years ago we visited the Natural History Museum in Los Angeles when they invited a group of Tibetan Buddhist monks to create a sand mandala, an intricate geometric composition of colored sand. It is a sacred form of art whose purpose is to promote peace, purification and healing. Beginning in the center of a blank, sanctified circle, five or six feet in diameter, the monks meticulously "paint" the mandala using narrow metal funnels, filled with colored sand. They create their lines by tapping on the funnel to release a thin stream of a colored line. To completely fill in these beautiful, complex mandalas, it often takes weeks of intense, long hours work, several monks working at a time. When finished, the mandala is consecrated. Then, after all that artistic labor, the sand is swept up into an urn and thrown into a river or flowing stream of water. The act of the destruction of the mandala serves as a reminder of the impermanence of the world.

On the ground in front of the main entrance to the Ashram in India, artists would paint a beautiful circular design, using colorful powders. These beautiful, complex works of art, called *rangoli*, had a spiritual purpose. They were done in the early morning hours, long before visitors arrived. When the gates opened and people entered, they would track the powders throughout the ashram. At the end of the day, only a bare trace of the rangoli would still be visible. At night, the last of the powder would be washed away, ready for a fresh rangoli in the morning. The ephemeral aspect of the rangoli is a reminder of the fleeting nature of life.

Redwood Forest

Walking in a forest of redwoods is to experience the phenomenon of impermanence in action. In Northern California, where most of the redwood forests can be found, there is a thirty-one mile road, Avenue Of The Giants, that snakes through a State preserve. Along the route are numerous trailheads, each one leading to magical forest glens. As you enter any of these trails, you will be walking in deep shade amongst massive trees, some over 300 ft. tall and upwards of 3,000 years old.

The cycle of life is in full view. On the trail you'll see trees of all ages, from tiny saplings to venerable giants. Some of these ancient trees have fallen, many of them lying for decades. Time has taken its toll. The fallen trees are in various stages of decay. From the rotting bodies of these fallen trees, saplings can be seen, pushing their way up towards the dappled light, nourished by the organic matter in the decaying wood. This cycle has gone on for millions of years: growth, death, decay, and rebirth.

Flowers

Flowers are delicate and beautiful to look at, delicious to smell. They are used for all sorts of occasions, happy events, like weddings and Valentines Day, sad events, like funerals. But consider this—flowers are a perfect representation of impermanence. No matter how beautiful they are, as soon as a flower is cut, it begins to die.

On my desk in the office is a small blue vase with two beautiful flowers in it. Roses. They were given to me three years ago. They are dried, shrunken and darkened to a deep brownish red. They are long dead, but they are beautiful. Part of their beauty lies in remembrance of the love with which they were offered to me. And part lies in my recognition of the impermanence they represent.

Wabi-Sabi

In the West, we like our things new and shiny. Not so much in the East.

There is a Japanese aesthetic principle called Wabi-Sabi, which finds beauty in that which is old, transient and imperfect. Examples could be the beautiful reds, oranges and yellows of withered autumn leaves, the rough, asymmetric trunk of an ancient olive tree, the aged patina on an old wood table, the mottled, wrinkled hands and face of an old woman. These kinds of things encompass an object's history and character. They denote the passage of time and add a depth to its beauty.

In line with Wabi-Sabi, Japanese potters would often produce pottery that looked aged and well-used. In olden days, if a master potter produced a flawless cup, they would purposely put a crack or blemish in it. They saw the perfection in imperfection. So different from our country, where, if something is old, dented or tarnished, we immediately get rid of it and buy a new one.

Fire

Several years ago there was a devastating fire in our area. It spared our house, but burned a number of outbuildings. One of those buildings was the canvas storage room. Thirty years of Alice's paintings and drawings were consumed in seconds, along with the hopes for a traveling exhibition of both our work, "The Art Of Aging." My workshop, with tools and hardware collected over a lifetime, went up in smoke. Gone were photos and videos of joyous gatherings of family and friends, memorable vacations, family history. The entire front of our property was a tangled mass of twisted metal, shattered glass, and everywhere, a thick layer of grey ash.

The truth is, fire did the job time would have done eventually. It would have all disappeared over time. It just would have taken a bit longer. Everything burns in the fires of time.

Ozymandias

When we were in Egypt we visited the ancient city of Thebes. It was here, on the banks of the Nile, there once resided the mortuary temple of Ramesses ll, the powerful Egyptian pharaoh who ruled Egypt 1279 to 1213 BC. His Greek name was Ozymandias. When his temple was built, it was named "Temple of Millions of Years." Now, several thousand years later, not much remains.

A colossal statue fragment of the sculpture of Ramesses ll that was taken from the temple in 1816, created a stir when it was to arrive in London in 1818. (It didn't get there until 1824.) This event was the inspiration for the famous poem, Ozymandias, by Percy Bysshe Shelley, which documents the hubris and inevitable decline of even the most powerful.

Ozymandias

I met a traveler from an antique land,
Who said, "Two vast and trunkless legs of stone
Stand in the desert... .Near them, on the sand,
Half sunk, a shattered visage lies, whose frown,
And wrinkled lip, and sneer of cold command,
Tell that its sculptor well those passions read
Which yet survive, stamped on these lifeless things,
The hand that mocked them, and the heart that fed;
And on the pedestal, these words appear:
My name is Ozymandias, King of Kings;
Look on my works, ye Mighty, and despair!
Nothing beside remains. Round the decay
Of that colossal Wreck, boundless and bare
The lone and level sands stretch far away."

When we visited, few other tourists were there, picking their way among scattered remains. There was lots of sand that *"stretch far away."* There was silence. A warm wind was blowing.

The Illusion Of Permanence

In the Mahabharata, an epic Indian philosophical poem, a wise sage was asked, "What is the most amazing thing in life." His answer, "People see others dying around them, yet never remember that they too will die."

We may intellectually know that we are subject to pain and illness in our lifetime and that at some point our life will end, but somehow the reality of impermanence doesn't sink down into our gut. We may realize it to some degree when we get ill or someone we know dies, but the uncomfortable feeling eventually passes and we get on with our life, again subconsciously expecting that we have all the time in the world. We expect that whatever was bothering us will go away as it has in the past, and we will be as good as new in a short time. But as we get older, we don't bounce back as we had when we were young, and as the years add up, it becomes more difficult to hold on to the illusion of impermanence.

The progression of our physical and mental decline is ongoing. Today, if nothing happens to interrupt it, we will be less than we were yesterday, and tomorrow we will be less than we are today. Weaker, slower, less energy, less vitality. We can alter the decline a little bit, but it's only temporary, and it only puts off the inevitable ending. Entropy will have its way.

We all want stability, a permanent solid ground on which we can reside. We want to always to be safe and secure, yet that's not the way the world works. There is nothing permanent we can hold on to. The nature of the universe is constant change, and so also the nature of the body. Brahma, Vishnu, Shiva. Creation, maintenance…and dissolution.

No Guarantees

Our friend Terry was preparing for work one morning not too long ago, when a sudden headache came on, followed by blindness in one eye. Stroke. His life changed. Forced into retirement, no driving, dependent on his wife for many things he could formerly do with ease.

I was driving in Sicily, on a long awaited vacation with family, when I felt a pain in my jaw and chest. The "widowmaker" heart attack. If there hadn't been a hospital nearby, the family would have been flying home with the body.

The people who were busy boarding the United Airlines flight 175 at 8:14 AM on 9/11 had no idea that their life would come to an end in a few minutes.

At this very moment, though you may be feeling perfectly well, there might be a cancer growing in your body that will eventually kill you. You don't know.

Life has no guarantees. We have no control. There is no way to prepare for what might happen in the next hour, the next minute. All we can do is take care in this moment and be grateful that we are fortunate to have this moment. And remember…there are no guarantees. That thought will help us to be grateful.

Inshallah

When we traveled around the world, we visited many Muslim countries. When we would make arrangements to meet someone or attend a future event, the person we were speaking with would usually end their sentence with the word, "Inshallah." We asked Hamid about it, and he told us that it means, "God willing," or "It's in God's hands." It refers to events one hopes will happen in the future. Yet the future is uncertain. One never knows God's plan or what the future will bring. So it's God's will.

As I grow older, I find myself thinking, "Inshallah" when I make a date or appointment, especially if it's months off into the future. Planning a trip North in the spring? Inshallah. A book tour in the fall? Inshallah. A meal with friends in two weeks? Inshallah. Tomorrow? God knows if I'll be around tomorrow. God knows, I don't. Inshallah.

So Soon Forgotten

How long will it be before you are forgotten after you die? Probably not long. There will be sadness and grieving after you've passed on, and your loved ones will think about you. But thoughts of you will come to their memory less and less as time goes on. People get on with their busy lives. The world will forget you, unless you've done something very, very good, or something really, really bad. Even then, you'll probably be remembered after only a generation. Or two? And then it will be as if you had never existed. Just a headstone

Life is too short. Start with dessert.

Barbara Streisand

or a plaque in a cemetery. Or a footnote in an obscure history book. Or records kept somewhere in the archives of the Social Security Administration.

I won't be long remembered. I will be nobody's ancestor. I had no kids, my stepkids had no kids. My brother had no kids, Alice's brother had no kids. For me, the few books I've written, a short film or two, a few recordings with my band and some bronze sculptures are my material legacy. For Alice, two paintings hanging in the National Portrait Gallery of the Smithsonian Institution in Washington DC, with a label and the description, "By Alice Matzkin. Born November 18, 1939, died....."

In ancient Roman culture, when an emperor or general rode into the territory he had just conquered, or victoriously returned to Rome, a slave was assigned to stand behind him and repeatedly remind him, "Remember, you are mortal."

You will be remembered by those who knew you and cared about you when you were alive. And then they too will pass. You may be a faint memory of those who were children when they met you. Then…what remains? A few faded photos, your treasured possessions—the kitchen table you purchased as newlyweds? Grandma's antique vase? The lamp you bought at the antique store on your vacation in Virginia? You loved these objects. While you were alive they held the imprint of beautiful memories. Your possessions are passed out to family and friends, or head to the garbage bin, or go to the thrift store, or, if they have value, the antique store or sold online by your heirs.

Those who come to obtain these once treasured objects have no idea of their history and the feelings that were embedded in them. (Neither did you know of their history when you acquired them.) The new owners will go on to embed their own feelings in these objects, their own history, their own memories. And, in turn, pass them on to be forgotten.

Our Final Vow

Alice and I have been married a total of nine times. Five of those times have been to each other. A marriage is a happy occasion and a wonderful opportunity for a party and a chance to renew our wedding vows. Our first marriage was in India, a two-hour Hindu ceremony by a Brahmin priest, conducted in Hindi. Next, we were married by Alice's brother, a potluck wedding in our backyard. Our third marriage renewal was a Christian ceremony by a reverend wearing a Hawaiian shirt in Cupid's Chapel, an "over the top" garish pink wedding chapel in Las Vegas. Next, we had a traditional Native American wedding ceremony officiated by Grandpa Semu, a Chumash medicine man, complete with Indian drummers and native chanting. And finally, we were married by a rabbi.

Since we had been abiding by all our vows, we felt that in our final wedding, we should create a vow that we had never stated before. After much deliberation, the vow we decided on was, "May we always remember that today may be the last day we might have together." That vow continues to have deep meaning for us and has been an important guide in our marriage. It reminds us of the transience of life and the necessity for holding on tightly, and letting go lightly.

Past And Future

You and I are existing at one infinitesimal moment in the flow of time.

Visualize the following and you'll know it to be true. From the past, standing behind you, as far as the eye can see, are lined up hundreds of thousands, millions of your ancestors. Starting with your parents, and before them, each of their parents, and on down the multiplication of bloodlines, is a history of shared DNA spanning back over countless eons. You know the names and faces of only the most recent, a generation or two or three. The rest are anonymous, lost in history.

In the front of you, in an endless mass of humanity going forward, is your future, your descendants, your sons and daughters, then their sons and daughters, or your future relatives if you don't have children. The vista that lays before you stretches far and wide, and you cannot see an end to that sea of humanity. Eventually, not too long into the future, you will be among the ancestors. Eventually, you too will be anonymous, lost in history.

OLD MAN AND BABY
An old man looks with fascination at the baby that is himself

And here you are now, at this moment in time, a blip poised between thousands of generations past, and thousands of generations into the future, living your all-important life, complaining about the unseasonable weather, obsessed with the extra pounds you've gained, frustrated by the neighbor kid who practices trombone late into the night. These are important considerations, not to be dismissed. Yet against the backdrop of infinity, of what consequence are they?

These contemplations of our impermanence in this and ensuing chapters may seem depressing. Try not to see this as an opportunity to become sad or hopeless. Realizing, on a deep level, that you and everything and everyone will not endure, actually presents you with an opportunity to wake up. You can awaken to the beauty of the moment, awaken to the beauty of being alive right now. Knowing that your end may be near or far can help you treasure this precious, precious moment.

Yes, everything will be stripped away from you, everything. That will inevitably happen, *but not yet*. Right now, this present moment in time is holy. Realizing this is deserving of your deepest, heartfelt gratitude.

There is an app you can get on your computer that is called, WeCroak. It is based on an old Bhutanese saying, "You will become a happy person if you remember your death five times a day." The app automatically sends reminders to you through your computer that you will die. The reminders come at random times throughout the day. You never know when they will come. Just like death.

AGING

OLD MAN WITH CANE
Strong, but bent with age

The Riddle of the Sphinx—"What goes by four legs in the morning, two legs at noon, and three legs in the evening?"

Oedipus answered, "Humans. As babies they crawl on all fours, as adults they walk on two, and when they get old, they use a cane."

An Outline Of Aging

It might be useful here to sketch out a brief overview of what it might look like to get old. Psychologists Eric Erikson, Daniel Levenson and journalist Gail Sheehy, among many others, wrote about developmental stages in the human life-cycle, usually starting from infancy. I'll do it now, although in much abbreviated form, starting from middle age. It's just a sketch, and may not fit for you, but it will give you a sense of what might be in store for you, or what has been your experience, decade by decade, as you grow older.

Fifties

Your fifties are not too much different than your forties. You're still robust, still looking good and feeling good, though your energies are somewhat diminished from your forties. Though you might be feeling less competitive, you're still productive and at the top of your game at work, possibly in leadership function. Your kids are busy creating their own lives, so your active, hands-on parental roles are in the past. Your parents though, are needing more assistance. Socially, you're active and out and about. However, strands of grey and wrinkles appear, and aches and pains are beginning to happen with greater frequency, and energy is not as it was a decade earlier. Not to worry, old age is still a long way off, but that doesn't prevent you from more seriously taking care of your health.

Sixties

The reality that you are getting older is taking hold as retirement is just around the bend. You start thinking in earnest, "What am I going to do to occupy the rest of my life?" "Do I have a 'gift' I can offer the world?" Energy, strength and stamina is waning and chronic physical ailments have started making their appearance. You are becoming acutely aware that you are not going to live forever. You see it in your parent's decline or deaths. You see it when you look at your reflection in the mirror. You cringe at the vision of your wrinkles, expanded waistline and grey head of hair, or thinning remaining hair. Seeing the changes you are going through, you might experience some mourning for your lost youth. In earnest, you hit the gym, watch the diet, take those vitamins, in hopes of bringing back some of what you've lost.

Seventies

Sixties still feels young, but by the seventies, you feel like you've passed a milestone. Parents have probably passed away, leaving you an orphan. Friends too, have sickened or died, letting you feel your mortality more acutely and wonder, "Will I be next?" If family is in the picture, connection with your family takes on increased importance during this period. Your body has begun to give you problems and you watch with apprehension as the problems worsen. You spend more of your time in doctor's waiting rooms and you gobble down a variety of pills every day. Lots of changes afoot as you are retired and are trying to be productive or enjoy your leisure time. You spend time looking back, with pride if you've lived the life you wanted and accomplished what you set out to do, and with regret if you didn't. You may have the inclination to give back, to share with others what you have and what you've learned.

Eighties Plus

At eighty you're old, genuinely old. If you've reached your eighties, you are at or near your average lifespan. Increasing frailty, illness, increasing memory issues may be occurring at this time, leading possibly to changes in living arrangements. You might be moving to the protective environment of family, or to a smaller, safer, elder-friendly home or apartment, or if necessary, to a senior care facility. Roles become reversed as your children have taken on a parental, caretaking function with you. Physical and mental decline may have lead to dependency and shrunk your world, with few significant relationships remaining. You might become preoccupied with immediate bodily needs and few personal comforts. This might lead to despair and depression, and a lessening of your will to live. Confined to wheelchair or bed, living mostly within a single room, your last months or years might be spent simply existing, being kept alive and waiting for death to overtake you. Unfortunately, this is the reality for many elders in their eighties and nineties.

Conversely, even though facing physical and mental challenges, old age may have provided you the potential to grow wider and deeper and more wise. When you were younger, you thought about old age and spent some time in preparation for your last years. You've done the math and realize time is getting short, and you spend more of your quiet moments finishing up what remains unfinished, contemplating your life and making peace with death. You want the precious time you have left to be quality time. Ideally, you look back at your life with wide perspective and with a sense of completion, and hopefully, with a sense of acceptance and fulfillment. Your years enable you to see the world with perspective and wisdom, and to feel gratefulness for having been granted such a long and fruitful life. You are unwilling to die before you are dead. You are determined to live with as much consciousness and vitality as you are able to muster until your last breath. Depending how you live this last stage of your life, you can serve as an inspiration and example to younger generations.

This Is Aging—Common Bodily Changes With Age

Continuing our overview of the aging process, here is a brief sketch of how our bodies might change as we age. Every body is different, so this is just a general description.

Cardiovascular system—blood vessels tend to stiffen, forcing the heart to work harder. Heart muscles adjust to the increased workload. High blood pressure and other heart problems are common.

Skeletal system—bones tend to shrink in size and density, becoming weaker and more subject to fracture. Tendency to grow shorter because of bone shrinkage and compaction of discs and cartilage in the spine.

Muscles and connective tissue—muscles lose strength, flexibility, and endurance, affecting coordination and balance. Joints and cartilage wear down and can cause joint pain and arthritis.

Digestive system—weakened digestive acids. Structural changes in the large intestine can lead to irregularity and constipation.

Urinary tract—bladder can lose elasticity, leading to more frequent urination. Weakening bladder muscles can lead to urinary incontinence.

Brain—changes in the brain and associated vessels can lead to memory issues, dementia and Alzheimer's.

Senses—cataracts are common, as well as sensitivity to glare and difficulty focusing. Hearing often diminishes, especially in the higher frequencies.

Mouth—gums might shrink and pull back. There can be a higher risk for tooth decay and gum infections.

Weight—metabolism slows, as does physical activity, and if food intake remains the same, there is the tendency to gain weight. Tendency for increased belly fat.

Skin—skin thins, becomes less elastic, more fragile, resulting in more frequent bruising. Wrinkles, sagging, age spots and small growths are common.

Hair—hair commonly loses pigment and turns grey. Tendency for hair to thin and bald spots to occur.

Sexual organs—hormonal changes and tissue changes are common, leading to less desire and ability for sexual activity.

The physical effects of aging are not a pretty picture, but then the alternative is not very attractive either.

Varieties Of Aging

Aging is complicated. When we consider aging we usually consider the physical aspects, the aging body. But there are other dimensions of aging…emotional, mental and spiritual dimensions. And in a person, these don't necessarily age uniformly. An older person could be physically youthful and mentally alert, yet emotionally be childish. Or they could be a physical wreck, yet be emotionally and spiritually mature. You might find it interesting to give yourself an estimate of what you would consider your physical, emotional, mental and spiritual age, actually assign them a number, and compare them with your current chronological age.

Courage

Reading and absorbing the list of the effects of age on the body, being aware of the deaths of loved ones and other losses you will incur as you grow old, knowing the inevitable downward trajectory of your life that is ahead of you—this is heady stuff, not for everyone. Many people, overwhelmed by what the coming years might bring, want to shield their eyes from the reality of their aging. It takes courage to open your eyes.

At times I have been "a fly on the wall" of our art exhibits, wandering around anonymously, trying to capture people's true responses. Some can't wait to leave the exhibit, so fearful and emotionally impacted are they by some of the raw images. Some hang around, spending a long time in contemplation of each piece, allowing their thoughts and feelings to percolate.

To look directly at our fear of our future is a heroic act. My admiration goes out to those of you who are now reading this book. You exhibit courage.

September Song

Oh, it's a long, long while,
From May to December,
But the days grow short,
When you reach September.
When the autumn weather,
Turns leaves to flame,
One hasn't got time
For the waiting game.

From the 1938 musical, Knickerbocker Holiday, by Kurt Weil and Maxwell Anderson

Time is a Thief

For every one of us, time is a thief. Some will be stolen from sooner, some later. From some of us, time will take more. From some, time will take less. But we will all be robbed.

Time steals our strength, our energy, our health, our beauty, our independence, our memory, our friends and family, our relevance. Ultimately, time steals our life. An enduring characteristic that describes the effect of time in the aging process is *loss*. In our youth we don't experience a lot of losses. The peak for physical abilities like strength and endurance for men is in the mid-20s to early thirties, for women it is slightly later. It's downhill from then on. As we grow older, the years bring on greater decline and the angle of decline becomes steeper.

I've written a little poem that describes the process of loss in aging.

> *From cane*
> *To walker*
> *To wheelchair*
> *To bed*
> *Ashes*
> *Love now*

The poem is a warning. It describes what could be the likely trajectory of losses by old age on many people's body and limitations of the spaces they are able to occupy. But the last line is different. It describes a countermeasure that will allow us to obtain a gift that our conscious aging can confer. The losses can wake us up, inspire us to savor our present moment and spend that moment with an open heart. The losses can wake us to the preciousness of others, of self, of our own life. Losses can affect our body, but not our heart. They can wake us up to love now. We receive these gifts of aging, not despite our losses, but because of them. That is a priceless gift that aging can bestow.

A Self-Portrait

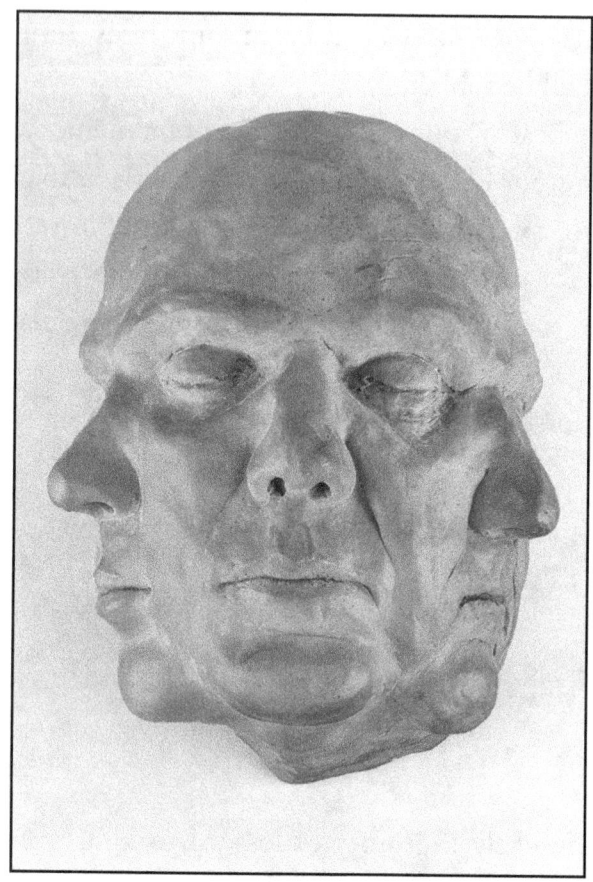

EVOLVING SELF PORTRAIT

A portrait of myself in clay in four quadrants, age 20, 40, 60 and (when the work was completed) and 80.

Around twenty years ago, at age sixty, I began a self-portrait in clay. It is a piece that shows what I looked like at 20, 40, 60, and what I might look like at 80. Though it seems to be three faces, it is actually in four quadrants, each two decades apart.

Sculpting the piece was very interesting for me. When sculpting, you caress the clay with your fingers. Here I was, caressing my own face as a young man, adult, middle-aged man, and imagining my face as I might look as an elder.

Milestone Birthdays

Every ten years, a milestone birthday rolls around. Sixty, seventy, eighty, ninety. They say age is just a number, and it is, but those years with zeros in them seem a bit more daunting now than when we were 10 or 20 years old. As we grow older, each ten years seems a lot more significant than the previous decade.

Even the years with fives in them, mini-milestones, are significant. On my 75th birthday, three quarters of a century, we had a big bash. Over sixty people showed up. We cooked a delicious meal for all, the dessert table was overflowing with goodies, a raucous "happy birthday" was sung as I blew out candles on my birthday cake. Our friend, famous pianist Roger Kellaway, celebrated bass player Chris Colangelo and I gave a jazz concert. A good time was had

Each ten years of a life has it's own fortune, it's own hopes, it's own way, it's own desires.

Goethe

by all. Later that night, laying in bed and recounting the wonderful events of the day, we realized to our horror that we had miscalculated. This had been only my seventy-fourth birthday, not my seventy-fifth. Embarrassed, we didn't tell anyone. Hopefully, our friends will not have done the math and discovered the missing year. Unless they read this book.

As I am writing this book, I turned eighty. Eighty is different from seventy-five. There is no doubt, eighty is old. Though I don't feel like I'm old, I AM old. I'm taking things more seriously now. Time could be short. If there are things that need to be done, they should be addressed and not put off for another day. At eighty, there may not be another day.

Old

"Old"—The word holds so many negative images and connotations—decrepit, stale, useless, decaying, passé. Contrast that with "young"— fresh, vibrant, new, active, passionate. Yet, there is the opposite. Youth can be naïve, immature, shortsighted, inexperienced. And, the old could be wise, dignified, venerable, enduring, authoritative, having depth of character and mature judgment. Without minimizing the legitimate merit of "young" as we age, we are coming to a greater appreciation of these positive values of "old."

From my book, THE ART OF AGING: *Celebrating The Authentic Aging Self*

A similar word that can have multiple connotations is "Elder." An elder can be elderly, old, infirm. But an elder can also be an individual who, because of their years, their experience, their insight and wise judgement, is seen as a person who is to be respected as a source of wisdom. In many cultures, elders hold the traditions of their people. They are venerated and conferred with when important decisions are to be made. "Elder" is a much more respectful term than "senior citizen," "oldster," or "elderly." I'd like to see "elder" used more often.

What It Is Like To Be Old

Years ago a group of experimenters devised a way to give people, especially young people, the experience of being old so they could have a sense of the trials and tribulations of aging and feel some empathy for older people.

They fabricated an "Age Suit" that created the experience of being old. There were glasses that reproduce faulty vision, earplugs that reduced sound and made hearing difficult, a back brace that kept the back bent over, weights on arms, wrists, ankles and chest that made movement difficult. (It would be a more accurate depiction of old age if they could somehow figure out a way to temporarily erase short-term memory.)

Those who wore the suit reported that they felt like they had aged 40 or 50 years. Walking was difficult and they quickly tired and needed rest and assistance. After donning the suit for just a few minutes, they said that for the first time, they had some inkling of how difficult being old might be.

How sad and difficult it is that we elders are forced to wear our age suit permanently.

Seeing Old People

They're around. We'll occasionally see them in restaurants, aided by their caretakers, slowly spooning food into their mouths. We'll see them on their walkers, inch by inch, making their way in the crosswalk, reaching the other curb long after the traffic light has turned red. We'll see them dozing in their wheelchairs when we visit relatives in their nursing home. Old people.

What thoughts go through our own minds, us not-quite-so-old persons, as we anxiously watch these quite-old persons? For me, it's at times a sickening feeling in my gut, a recognition that in five or ten years, or less, this could be me. I want to turn away. I don't want to be that person, weak, dependent. Yet I know I am not immune to age. How long will I be self-sufficient? Don't know. The future is not in my control. But for now, I'd rather see young people. It's more pleasant to close my eyes than face the future.

Irreversible Losses

There are times when the reality of your aging hits you between the eyes. For me, some of those moments come with the realization that, for the most part, what I've lost to age is gone and not coming back. I'll never again be the handsome dude I was when younger. It is too late for me to become a brain surgeon. The physical strength and endurance I had as a youth is gone forever. My sexual vitality will not return. I'll never again see my best friend who died a year ago. All lost to time.

The moving finger writes; and having writ, moves on: nor all thy piety or wit shall lure it back to cancel half a line, nor all thy tears wash out a word of it.

Omar Khayyam, 10th Century Persian poet. The Rubaiyat

When we're young, there's always another day, and with it, the chance for healing, for reconciliation, for renewal, for a new beginning. But when we're an old dog, new tricks are harder to learn and the opportunity to learn them is harder to come by or has passed. I feel saddened by this sense of finality. I know, as has been happening, this sense of so many things ending will continue and increase as time goes on. I can understand how the very old, feeling their life lacks a future, can fall into a paralyzing depression. Time moves on, and nothing can lure it back.

Second Childhood

Old age has been called "Second Childhood," and for good reason. The very old can be seen as sharing similar characteristics with the very young.

In Shakespeare's play, "As You Like It," there is a famous speech that begins, "All the world's a stage," and goes on to describe the Seven Ages Of Man. The last is Old Age.

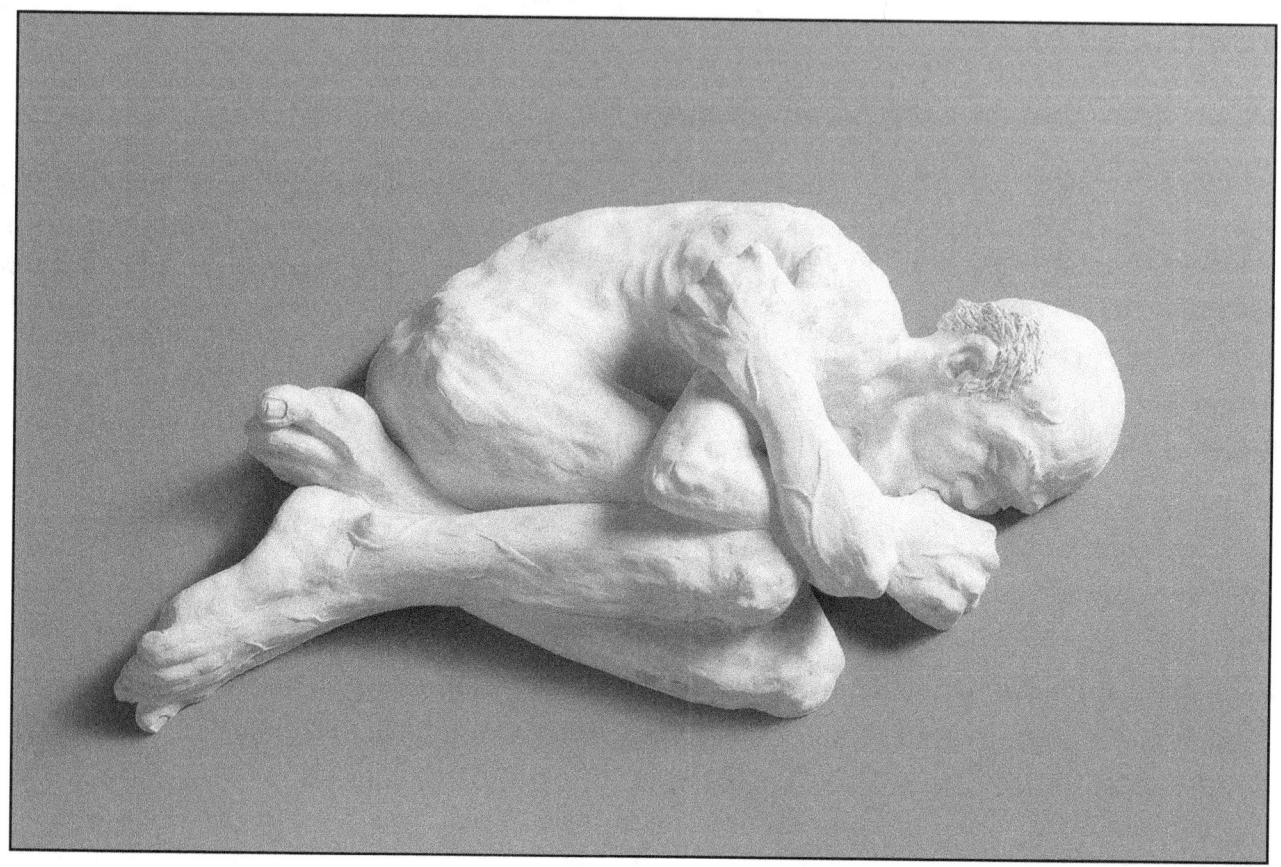

FETAL MAN
An old man regressed in fetal position sucking his thumb

If you've ever visited a facility where the very old are cared for, you will have seen residents who are in second childhood. As with young babies, they are dependent. They may need help getting dressed, being fed, (soft and easily chewed food), bathed and supported when they stand and walk. Like babies, they may be bald, lack teeth, don't speak, or speak in simple sentences. And many need to wear diapers. For them, the clock has run backwards.

Last scene of all
That ends this strange eventful history
Is second childishness and mere oblivion
Sans teeth, sans eyes, sans taste, sans
everything

William Shakespeare

This would be torture if this is to be the way I end my life. The worst would be the loss of my sense of dignity.

Slow Motion

When they got old, my mom and dad moved in slow motion. It would take the first quarter of the day just for them to get up and get dressed, and the last quarter for them to get ready for bed.

Going somewhere with my parents would take forever. Alice and I would come into town every week and bring my mom and dad to their favorite restaurant. They were in their nineties and moved as slow as snails. It was literally a half day affair getting to and from lunch. We would make sure they were properly dressed, hearing aids in, canes at ready, slowly guiding them to the car, Alice at dad's elbow, me with my arm around mom's waist. They moved as if they were wading through jello.

Push back car seats, ease them in, dad in front, mom in back, reaching around to get their seatbelts buckled. (Similar to what young parents go through getting their toddlers situated.) Then the same process, in reverse, when we arrive at the restaurant. After the slow walk in the parking lot from the car to the front door, we wait for seating, amble to the table, pull back chairs and guide them in. Ordering was easy, they would always get the same, a tuna melt for dad and macaroni and cheese for mom. They ate slowly, deliberately chewing each morsel. Alice and I would finish our meal and patiently wait for them to finish. Then, getting them back home entailed the whole process in reverse order.

At times I would get frustrated and try to hurry the process. To no avail. I finally realized that this is what it is. You can't push the river to make it go faster. It will take half a day no matter what I say or do. Might as well resign myself. They're old and this is what old people do. And truthfully, even though I sometimes experienced frustration, our trips with them were never a burden. How poignant was our time with them, what an honor it was to serve them in this way. How fortunate we were to still have parents. Looking back, we miss the precious moments of our visits with them.

With the perspective of time, we have greater acceptance of their infirmity. This is especially true now, as we have grown closer to their age. We have left the faster pace of our younger selves behind—moving slower, thinking slower, speaking slower. In not too many years, we might find ourselves in the same condition as our parents were, hastening slowly, bemusedly observing our children's frustration with our plodding ways.

Disappearing Elders

When we traveled to Islamic countries, notably Egypt and Turkey, we had the opportunity to visit the homes of several families. The living situation there was very different than in the West. Many families lived in compounds, where multiple generations resided together. This provided the opportunity for younger and older generations to intermingle. Youngsters could experience the elder generation up close. There was familiarity of the young with the wisdom of their elderly relatives, and they could see how adults in the family honored them. The elders, in turn, could be rejuvenated by being around youngsters.

Very different from here in America, where children leave home and set up residence as soon as they are able. (Though more recently, because of financial constraints, adult children are moving back to parent's homes.) Elder relatives are shunted away to their own "over 55 communities" or placed in facilities for safekeeping, where they're walled off from view. There are occasionally visits, on birthdays or special occasions, but elders are usually not a presence in the household. They are "disappeared."

Not only are elders disappeared from the household, they are disappeared from the culture. Look at magazine racks in the supermarket, turn on the TV. Most of who you'll see are actors or models in their twenties and thirties, a few in their forties. Oh, there will be ads with models with grey hair plugging laxatives and wrinkle cremes and vacation cruises, but they are not really old. They just have youngish faces with grey hair. For the most part, you won't find images of older people. Where are they? An ET visitor from outer space would think that humans only last till forty.

Green Bananas

Alice's grandmother, when she was in her mid-eighties, had slept on the same mattress for thirty years. The bed springs had lost their spring and the bed sagged in the middle something terrible. Every morning she would get up with an aching back. The whole family tried to buy a new bed, but she refused. "It's not worth it to spend the money. I'll only live another year or two," she said. She lived another ten years, still with the same mattress, still with the same backache.

Sorry to say, I have the same "stinkin thinkin." We had the old dishwasher for twenty-five years and it started to make strange noises. Alice wanted to get a new one, but, considering our age, I said, "Let's not. It's still got some life left." We got a new dishwasher. The same issue keeps coming up. Should I get extensive dental work that will improve my bite? Though not perfect, my choppers still work OK. Should we get a pet? It would probably outlast us. Should we purchase the 10-year extended guarantee for the dishwasher?

Sort of like the old joke. A financial advisor is trying to get his elderly client to buy bonds that yield in ten years. The client responds, "Ten years! I'm so old, I don't buy green bananas."

Becoming An Expert

Life as usual. You go along, living your ordinary days, going to work, feeding the dog, taking out the garbage. Then, a pain, a weakness, a cough, a smattering of blood, or something just doesn't feel right in your gut. You're concerned. You make an appointment with the doc, who takes your temperature and your blood pressure, checks

My mother always used to say, "The older you get, the better you get... unless you're a banana.

Actress, Betty White

your reflexes, and writes down your symptoms and then orders some tests. Days later, you're called to the office for results, and the doctor, with serious demeanor, gives you the bad news. "I'm sorry to have to tell you this, you have #@*%<!." Shock! What! How! Why!

However, once you have a diagnosis, there is some sense of relief. At least you know. Knowing doesn't help much. You might find yourself buffering between, "We're gonna defeat this #@*%<!," and abject depression.

Then the research begins. Google #@*%<! and try to discover the prognosis, treatment protocols, medications, side effects from medications, alternative treatments. Read and try to understand the obscure medical terminology in journal articles. Call for a second opinion. Talk to friends and acquaintances who also have had #@*%<!, or who know someone who has.

A short while ago you were just living your life. Now, reluctantly, you know all about #@*%<!. You've become an expert.

I am becoming an expert. About a month after I wrote the above, as part of my yearly check-up, I took a blood sugar test and discovered I have low-grade diabetes. I am doing all the things I've written about—researching, talking to friends, etc. I'm now becoming an expert in diabetes.

Falling

"Pride goeth before a fall" says the Bible. Not quite true. Inattention goes before a fall. My balance is not what it once was. I walk like I've had a glass of wine or two. I've taken a few spills recently. Luckily, no damage. In every case, I was not paying attention. My mind was somewhere else.

The Center For Disease Control reports that falls are the leading cause of injury and death for people over 65. One out of every four people 65 and older has a fall each year. Of those falls, one in five results in serious injury, like a hip fracture or head injury. Thirty-six million older adults will fall in America each year, resulting in 32,000 deaths. So be careful. Pay attention.

Disappearing Words, Disappearing Mind

How many times have I rushed into a room, full of purpose and intent, and found myself without the slightest idea of why I have come there? How many times have I repeated over and over, until I could find a pencil and paper to write it down, "17632, 17632, 17632?" How many times have I misplaced my phone, my file, my book, my pencil and paper? How many times have I said to a friend, "Stop me if I've told you this before." The other day I couldn't remember my social security number. My mind is disappearing. There are online memory tests you can take. I won't. I'm afraid of getting the result.

Writing this book, I'm finding that I must refer to the thesaurus much more often now than with my previous books. Familiar words have become unfamiliar, and at times I can't seem to find the right one. Spelling? Some words I can't spell enough to even look them up in the dictionary, so I select other words. People's

FEAR OF ALZHEIMER'S
A raven pecking thoughts and memories, one at a time from the terrified man's brain

49

names disappear into the black hole. If I meet someone who looks familiar, or who knows me but I don't recognize or remember their name, it's the routine—big smile, look happy to see them, and it's, "Hi, how are you?" Sometimes, when I'm with Alice, and a person with a familiar face but no name comes into view, I'll need to whisper to her, "If I don't introduce you, you know why."

Memory is strange. Though I can remember where and when we got almost every object in our house, and can recall faces in minute detail, remembering names is particularly difficult. This following conversation is not unusual. "The actor, what's his name, tall, heavyset, he was in the movie about the spy, played opposite the actress who was also a singer, you know her, she was famous for the song about…"

There seems to be a pandemic of memory loss. Other people I know who are in my age group complain about the same thing, but the fact that I am not alone in my memory issue doesn't make me feel any better.

Each time a lapse for words happens, my mind churns up fears. At the end of their lives, both of my parents had symptoms of dementia. Am I getting dementia? Is this the beginnings of Alzheimer's? I Google the Alzheimer's Association, check off their list of common symptoms and find a few familiar ones. Will I need to eventually end up in an assisted living memory care facility? I can't think of a worse way to spend a declining old age than to have words, thoughts and memories delete from my memory banks. It would be as if the "me" that I've always known has become a stranger. My sculpture, "Fear of Alzheimer's" graphically depicts my fear. A terrified man with a raven pecking away at his brain, removing memories, one-by-one.

The past has passed, and I tend to remember the good parts and forget the bad anyway. For now, as long as I have access to my pencil and paper, I will be OK. (If I can remember where I left that darn pencil.) I'm covering my fear with humor of course, but my sculpture more accurately depicts my terror.

There's a real upside though. I've noticed that as my mind becomes less dominant, there's more room for my heart to grow stronger. And it has.

Old Time Horror Movie Monsters

I remember the monsters from the old, black and white horror movies of the twenties, thirties, forties and fifties? Boris Karloff, Lon Chaney, Vincent Price, Bela Lugosi. What do the the vampires, ogres, witches, ghouls, zombies and other demonic beings that used to terrify us in horror movies of old remind you of?

Bony, trembling hands, wrinkled, sallow skin, bald pate or sparse, whispy white hair, receding gums and missing teeth, bloodshot eyes, grating voice, shuffling gait.

Who are these monsters? Old people, of course. Interesting that the ugly, frightening images we used to scare ourselves with are of senior citizens. Speaks to the fear we have of getting old.

Fatigue

It's a fact. When you get older, you have less energy. I find it frightening. Year by year, I have less energy than the previous one. I see elders barely older than me who hardly have the energy to sit upright in a chair. Could this be me in a few years? Day by day it's different. Some days I'm jet propelled, as full of vim as a five year old after a nap. Some days I'm awake, but feeling twenty years older than I am, with no wind in my sails—dead in the water.

Fatigue is a real issue for elders. It's no joke when your get up and go gets up and goes. When you're too tired to exercise, do laundry or other tasks, it becomes more difficult because unfinished business grows from a hill to a mountain. After awhile, the mountain starts to look overwhelming. Not only that, procrastinating becomes habitual, and becomes the way you deal with things you don't enjoy doing. It's not just the unpleasant things that we spurn. We're sometimes too tired to go to the party or play, or to meet friends. We could easily become a hermit or the old lady with cats.

When tired, you might find yourself lying around a lot. Alice's mom had that tendency and used to caution us, "Don't fall in love with your bed." Diminishing energy makes the bed or the easy chair

When we are young, we sneak out of bed to go to parties; when we get old, we sneak out of parties to go to bed.

Richard Reeves

seem like an awfully attractive alternative when compared to having to do things that are difficult or uncomfortable.

There's too many tasks I've been putting off lately because I've felt too tired. Simple things like cleaning up the hen house, extending the backyard fence, taking care of correspondence on my desk. These things have been on my "to do" list for a long time and I have been just too tired or uninspired to start them. It feels like I won't have the energy to finish, so why start. Is it because I'm too tired to do these things, or does the thought of doing them make me tired? Whatever the reason, my "to do's" just languish and keep adding up. Every time I pass the chicken coop or fence or look at the piles on my desk, it makes me exhausted and want to go lie down and take a nap. In love with my beautiful bed.

OLD MAN WATCHING TV
Tired old man, lulled to sleep by the television

Growing Up, Growing Down

Life Magazine was a popular weekly photojournalism magazine that eventually became monthly, finally ceasing publication, except for special issues. When I was a kid, the family next door would give us the issues they had finished reading. I loved poring over the magazine, fascinated by photos.

There was one set of photographs that strongly impressed me, so much so that I cut it out of the magazine and saved it. Pictured in a series of black and white photos was a man and his young daughter standing next to him. In the first photo, she appeared to be maybe three years old. The next photo looked to have been taken a few years later and she had grown. The series went on, with snapshots taken at several year intervals. The girl grew to be a beautiful young woman, and the man was aging, with wrinkles and graying hair. The later pictures in the series show the woman in late middle age, standing taller than her father, who was shrunken and bent.

What shocked and fascinated my young mind was that I was seeing the aging process unfolding right before my eyes. It was shocking for me to recognize that this would be me, this would be the fate of my body as I grew to adulthood and beyond.

Superhuman Elders

"You're only as old as you feel." "Age is just a number." That's what they say.

Often I come across a well-meaning article about some superhuman athletic feats of elders, meant to cheer us old folks up, or inspire us to believe that we can go on being young at heart or body almost forever. There are stories about elders who climb Everest, break-dance, or lift hundreds of pounds dead weight. (I even write a bit of things like that in these pages.) Here's an example of what I mean by Jeffrey Somminfeld.

> *At age 100, marathoner Mike Fremont said he does not try to just beat his best time, he defies time. After 60 marathons, he holds four world records. When people suggest to him that older people should slow down, he laughs, saying, "I think they ought to speed up."*

What's your response to this? I'll tell you mine. While on one hand I admire Mr. Fremont for his accomplishments, on the other hand, what he's doing feels foreign to me. He's a rare, rare bird I don't identity with, nor do I care to. I'm not inspired to train to take up marathoning, or mountain climbing, or cross-country skiing, nor do I wish to parachute out of an airplane. I wouldn't want to do that to my body. I'm satisfied with the way I'm aging. I take my vitamins, do my moderate exercise, and watch with a mixture of horror and curiosity as my body slouches toward my grave. My primary exercise in my elder years is my mind and soul. The marathon I want to run is wisdom. I want to be a champion of aging with acceptance, meaning and serenity. That's what I want to have accomplished when I get to the finish line.

Transitions

We've been going to a lot of ceremonies lately—births, graduations, weddings, funerals. (There's usually not much about retirement.) Transitions—transiting from one state to another—beginnings, endings combined with new beginnings, and new endings. Every new beginning has an ending attached. These transitions have offered opportunities for contemplation for me. The births—new life, the open future. Graduation—ending of childhood and entry into the adult world. The weddings—end of "singleness" and the beginning of a shared life. The retirements—finishing with work life and entry into open possibilities. The funerals—celebration of the conclusion of a life.

Being old has given me the perspective of viewing the succession of generations. Children of family and friends have children, and now those children are beginning to have children. We sat at a restaurant the other day, enjoying a meal with Janet, eight months pregnant. How her life will completely transform in a month or two. A party last week, celebration of Shayna's graduation from college. She was so excited to be at the starting line, ready to enter the world with her new degree and her dreams. Yesterday, Sunday, a wedding. My heart was full as I watched both James and Piper weeping with joy during the ceremony. We were long time friends of the bride's grandparents. My thoughts drifted to Alice and my joyful tears, at our wedding forty years ago. On Saturday, we attended the celebration of the life of our friend, Riley, who had died at eighty-five. We had been friends for four decades. There were people attending who had known him for seventy years. We greeted friends and acquaintances we hadn't seen in a long time. They had gotten so old. We smiled and told them, "You look great" (for an old fogey). How old must we look to them as they repeat to us, "You look great."

Bittersweet Wisdom

Old and wise fit together like hand in glove. We tend to ascribe wisdom, the "Golden Gift" of age, to a person with grey hair and wrinkles. But it doesn't always work that way. Wisdom is a special quality not gained simply by adding up the years. There are more than a few young people who are wise and old people who are stupid. Wisdom comes from encountering life's difficulties, showing up with your full self, and as best as you can, muddling through with as much awareness, dignity and care as you can muster, then making sense of your experiences and retaining memory of what you've learned. Wisdom is not being satisfied just staying on the surface and nibbling around the edges, but diving deep, looking within for meaning and purpose. And it's not keeping what you've gained to yourself, it's being willing to share what you've gained with others.

We should not be so quick to ascribe to elders, even genuinely wise elders, the dignified quality of "wise." Wise elders are as capable of acting just as reckless, petty, difficult, scared as we "normal" people are. These human qualities are an essential part of growing up and growing wise. Wisdom comes from learning from our weakness and stupidity.

The Winter of our life is a pivotal time. It is a time of great contrasts. As elders, there is no moment in our lifetime, other than the age we are now, when we have the potential for more wisdom and vision into the future as we look forward, and more experience and perspective of our past as we look backward. And yet, it is also true that there is no time in our life when we have more potential to experience greater pain, heartache and suffering.

Bittersweet, the contrasts make aging bittersweet. Opening to the bitterness of the sorrows of our old age might allow us to taste the delicious sweetness that being old and alive can offer. True wisdom resides here, in the openness to be present to taste and savor both bitter and sweet.

Men And Aging

Loss of physical strength, not being in charge anymore, increasing fatigue, needing help, being seen as "less than," fat replacing lean muscle, lessening libido and onset of impotence, these are some things about getting older that affect men more than women.

Male cultural stereotypes that demand men be protectors, powerful, productive, competent and competitive are challenged as a man ages. Men are supposed to be the strong ones, the doers, the supporters, yet, as they get older and their abilities deteriorate, they find themselves standing on the sidelines as younger men take over. This hit to the male ego takes its toll on a man's sense of his own value.

An aged man is but a paltry thing,
A tattered coat upon a stick.

William Butler Yeats

As he gets older, he can become uncertain of his identity. If he is not "The Man" anymore, who is he? This challenge to male identity can be positive. The male stereotype is, in many ways, confining, unreal, lacking in true masculine aliveness. By relinquishing these stereotypes, a man can grow more into his full masculine self, genuinely strong and powerful. Instead of being just a man, he can expand to become more of a human. At any age.

Women And Aging

Being a man, I can only guess what women feel as they get older. It must not be easy to become a crone in the eyes of the world. As your youthful beauty fades, no longer are you lusted after, no longer are

56

you even noticed. As you pass childbearing age, you are barren, no longer are you able to perform the function of motherhood. With these losses, who are you?

There is the mythic concept of the Triple Goddess—the Maiden, the Mother and the Crone. The Maiden represents youth, new beginnings, purity, innocence. The Mother represents fertility, ripeness, giving, fulfillment. The Crone represents the culmination of a lifetime of experience, wisdom and compassion. She is a healer, seer, mystic and guide. Released from the constricting roles of just being an object of desire or a birther and caretaker of children, an elder woman can become free to be herself. She can be a font of wisdom, a source of guidance, a person of power and grace. This is a potential she might be able to realize if she is able to let go of Maiden and Mother roles, and fully embraces Crone.

Young People And Aging

Ageism allows those of us who are younger to see older people as "different." We subtly cease to identify with them as human beings, which enables us to feel more comfortable about our neglect and dislike of them… Ageism is a thinly disguised attempt to avoid the personal reality of human aging and death.

Robert N. Butler, gerontologist who coined the word, "ageism."

Some young people see old people as a threat. When they look at an old person, they fear that they are looking at their future. And the future is not pretty. Aging is a disease, they think, a disease that disfigures face and body, saps energy and erases the mind. And the disease is terminal. So young people might tend to avoid old people. They don't want to become contaminated.

Old People And Aging

We've been to life school and gotten an education that could only be obtained by living long. We've seen loved ones sicken and die, been threatened ourself numerous times by illnesses, suffered through some which were severe, maybe even life-threatening. We've gained and lost, succeeded beyond our wildest dreams and failed miserably, made foolish, foolish mistakes. We've shed tears and had our heart broken, and possibly broke other's hearts. All life's lessons we have digested and assimilated, and this has given us a wide perspective. All our experiences have gone into making us the unique old person we've grown to become. Year by year, we have been sculpted by time.

"Fresh"

In our youth obsessed culture, the ideal for us elders is to look young, feel young, act young, think young. Youthfulness is the goal we set for ourselves and society sets for us. But youthfulness is for the young, and we are not young.

Let me suggest another term that might be more appropriate for people in our station of life. That term is "freshness." Being fresh is the opposite of being stale. Stale is bored, dull, tired, stagnant, drab. At any age, a person who is fresh, sees the world and lives with an attitude of openness, curiosity, vitality and joy. To have a fresh attitude is to be in touch with the newness and spontaneity of each succeeding moment.

The quality of freshness is independent of number of years lived. I have known old people who are fresh, and I am sure you have too. When you meet them, you are inspired in their presence. You cannot forget them.

"Golden Years"

A term that was popular in the past when referring to "Senior Citizens," (another infrequently used term), is "Golden Years." It mostly referred to the Autumn of life, fifties and sixties, maybe seventies, when, ideally, a person's life is settled, they've gained perspective, they have health and energy, and still have plenty of things to look forward to. (Imagine glowing images of sunny days, fishing, golf courses, cruse ships, smiling grandchildren and rocking chairs.)

For many people, late seventies and beyond are not golden years. For them, this time might be termed, the "Leaden Years." Reversing alchemist's search for the Philosopher's Stone, lead is gradually replacing the gold. Energy is winding down, sickness, losses and death are what's coming up for those of us past the golden years.

I believe that it is possible to maintain the gold and delay or even diminish the lead. In order for that to happen, it takes a decision. The decision is that you'll make the effort to turn whatever experiences that come to you into gold. You'll need to use hardship as an opportunity to learn acceptance and grow in compassion, to reach out for that which brings you joy and aliveness and vitality. Whatever your capacity, to be curious, maintain a sense of humor, and to accept, with gratitude, that you are still alive, still kicking. The fact that there are elders who have done that and are doing it should serve as an inspiration for you.

Strangers

Alice has always been the grounded one, while I have been somewhat of an absent-minded professor. She's sharp and enjoys handling the finances, making appointments, arrangements for trips, being in charge of the house, things like that. This is good. If I was in charge, I'm so disorganized, I'd probably make a mess of things. (But I can lift heavy boxes and mow the lawn.)

In the back of my mind I assumed that if one of us got dementia, I'd be the one. But lately, I've been worried. Alice has been uncharacteristically forgetful. She's left the stove on, the refrigerator door open, water running in the bathroom sink. She's missed appointments, increasingly lost or misplaced things. I'm worried. Is this the start? Will I be the caretaker? I would gladly serve her. But what if we were both mentally incapacitated? What if we both needed to be in a facility. What if we were there and I didn't recognize her, or she didn't recognize me, or we didn't recognize each other? Strangers to each other. That would be tragic!

Near the end of their lives, my parents both got ill at the same time and needed hospitalization for a few days. Since they were a married couple, medical staff placed them in the same room. The strange thing is that they didn't recognize each other, probably because of the novel environment. When we visited, my mother motioned for me to come over to her bed. She whispered to me, "Who is that strange man in the room?" I told her, but she still didn't quite get it. When they returned back home, they were fine.

A High School Reunion

Several years ago, I accompanied Alice to her 60th high school reunion. Though I didn't know anyone, I had a great time. Alice whispered in my ear and kept me informed of the gossip from over half a century ago. Old acquaintances, some Alice had known since grammar school, were there. Everyone was wearing name tags with pictures from the senior yearbook, or else they surely would not have recognized each other.

As the dishes were cleared and dessert being served, the Master Of Ceremonies, the former Student Body President, banged on a glass with a spoon, calling for everyone's attention. The room quieted down. Harold was a handsome

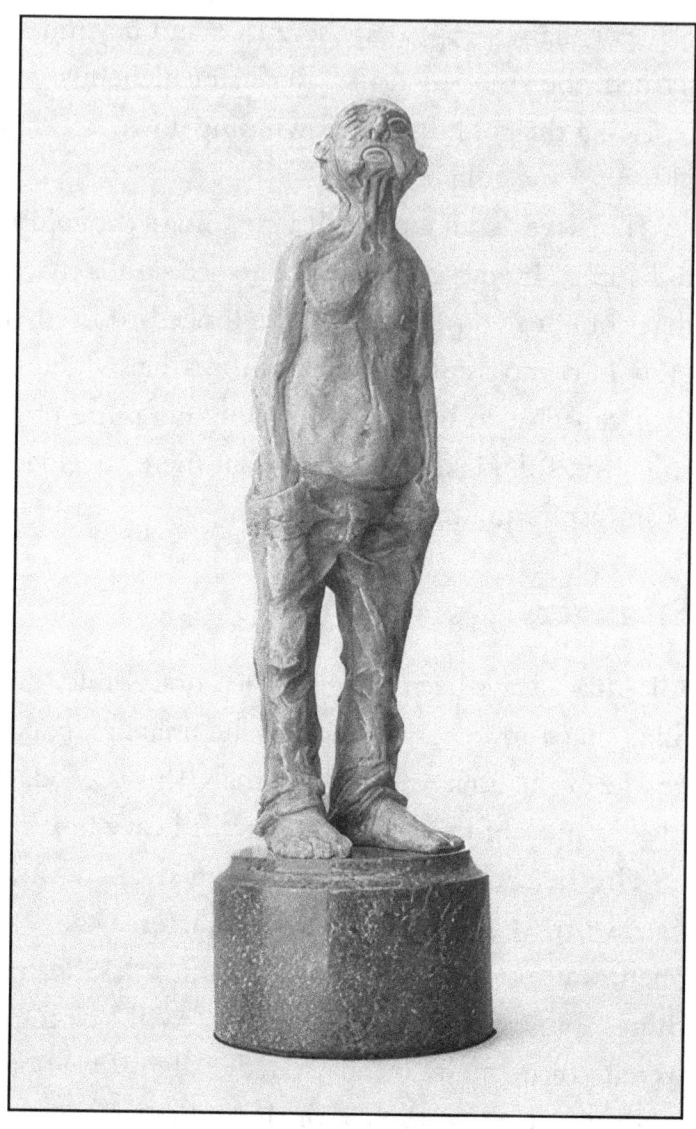

ALZHEIMER'S MAN
A disheveled old man with dementia stands confused not knowing who or where he is

dude in his day, popular with the girls, but now bent and grey, unrecognizable. He started off speaking a few words about high school life in the fifties, then launched into a detailed account of his recent eye operation. I'm sure that evening there were many more conversations about operations, medications and illness, in addition to boasting of accomplishments and pictures of grandchildren shown.

Most of us go to high school reunions for a taste of the past—old friendships, old jokes, old crushes. Or maybe a chance to boast. For a few hours, we enter a time warp and travel back in time. And then, as you leave the gym or the banquet hall, time travel slowly ceases. You begin to enter present time as you walk to your car in the parking lot. Start engine, pull out of lot, and you've come back to now.

We're all grownups now. Thankfully, our adolescent high school drama is behind us. What does it matter who was most popular, most athletic, most beautiful or handsome. We've put in our time, created our lives, and now our lifetime is running out. There was a feeling in the air, among this group of elders who are on the cusp of entering their eighth decade, that there would not be too many more reunions.

It was a lively evening, lots of laughter, lots of catching up, lots of reminiscing. But as the reunion was drawing to a close, and people were beginning to file out of the hall, there was a glum moment for all. On the wall, to the right of the door that lead to the outside, there were several posters with column after column of the names of those classmates who had died.

Just A Few Years Ago

Change. I've been scrolling through our photos on the computer, going back year by year. How different our life is now compared to just five years ago. Now, my hearing worsening, I've cut back playing drums. I rarely sculpt, just not moved to. A devastating fire destroyed 30 years of Alice's artwork and turned it to ash in minutes. Her work has completely changed. No more portraits. Her paintings are now abstract. We used to travel a lot, all over the world. Now it's rare that we leave our little town. I spend more hours writing on my iPad. And our faces—while it's not impossible to make out the facial features of our younger self hiding in our present countenance—it's getting harder to recognize that guy or gal from the past as time goes on.

Alice spends time in front of the bathroom mirror putting on makeup, as she says, tongue-in-cheek, "Repairing the damage." Sometimes, when she catches a passing glimpse of herself in the bedroom mirror, she'll jokingly exclaim, "Kill it with a stick." She describes the changes in her appearance as, "From girldom to ghouldom." Alice and her mom used to sometimes sing a song together, based on an old rock and roll tune. They changed the lyrics. Instead of "Rock Around The Clock," it's now, "Rot around the clock." Its good she can maintain a sense of humor about her aging.

Five years ago I was curious as to how my face had changed over the years, so I impulsively shaved off my beard that I had for more than two decades. Instant regret! I didn't recognize the face of the old man staring back at me in the mirror. When Alice saw me, she asked, "Did you get a head transplant?" Needless to say, I began growing my beard back immediately. Though men don't use makeup, a beard can cover a multitude of sags, splotches and wrinkles.

I've taken to wearing suspenders. Suspenders! Old men wear suspenders. My grandfather wore suspenders. Alice used to call me, "The Buttless Wonder." What little butt was left dissolved and my pants kept slipping down. Suspenders work fine, but every time I pass a mirror, I'm reminded of my grandfather.

Accelerating Decline

Look at how rapidly our bodies change when we are young. After birth, our growth rate is phenomenal. We seem to grow day by day. When we reach adolescence and adulthood, it seems as if our rate of physical change slows and becomes almost imperceptible. We look similar at 40 as we did at 30. Then, as we reach middle age and beyond, the changes in our face and body speed up again. Sags and wrinkles appear everywhere as if overnight. Aches and pains too. In our later years, we "grow down" as rapidly as when we were young children growing up. It's all relative. For a ninety-year-old, eighty-five is young.

Generally, as we age, we might go through a series of milestones. These can be defining moments—becoming grandparents, retiring, loss of a partner, moving to a more protective environment like independent living, then to assisted living, then to hospice care. Compared to midlife, these changes tend to occur more rapidly as time goes on.

Alice exhibited a series of portraits she painted of my old aunt, titled, *Aunt Kitty, 89 to 97*. The exhibit documented my aunt's progressive physical decline in late old age. The rate of decline year to year was striking. In just eight short years, Aunt kitty went from riding a horse to riding a wheel chair. The last few paintings were where the changes were most striking, as she was confined to her bed. The final portrait was shortly before her death.

Matchbooks

It's going to be a cold night. I'm lighting the kindling in the wood stove in the bedroom. The matches I'm using came from a box I found while cleaning up my parent's place, getting ready for sale. There are scores of match boxes and matchbooks, each bearing the names of restaurants, bars and nightclubs my parents visited so many years ago. This was a form of advertising popular back then when nearly everyone smoked cigarettes. *Fox And Hounds, Juniors, I'll Fornaio, Little Joes, Ah Fongs, Ye Olde Kings Head.* Italian restaurant, Jewish delicatessen, Chinese, British pub, burger joint. These were places my parents visited when they were younger, probably an evening out with friends, maybe in the 1960s or 70s or 80s. I can see them in my mind's eye, young and full of life, talking, laughing, enjoying themselves. Memorable moments in time. My mom must have picked up the matches at the cash register while dad paid. None of these places exist now. I looked them up. They went out of business decades ago. Remnants of happy memories of long ago, memories that vanished with my parent's deaths. But the matches still work well.

Generations

It's a family gathering at cousin Pamela's. A lively crowd. The adults are gathered, most of the older ones are sitting together, the middle generation is mostly standing or moving about or tending to the children. Snippets of conversations can be heard—clothes, politics, kids, business, gossip. The children are running, yelling, wrestling, chasing the dogs, who are sniffing the floor, hoping for a morsel of food to "accidentally" drop from someone's plate.

I'm sitting alone to the side, watching. I'm looking at the children, James, Wish, Sage, William and all the rest, thinking about their future, and my future. This batch is young, five, six or seven. I'm thinking, what kind of people will they turn out to be? What will their life be like? What would their world be like. What newfangled creations await them. Music, art, science, society. What will they do when they grow up? Will they get a college education? Will they marry? Will they have children? Will their children have children? These young ones are from another generation, another world, just as I will be from another world to them when they grow up and look back. Hippies, Beatles, protests, Women's Lib, wide lapels and bell bottom pants. My world to them will be as antique as my parent's world was to me as I looked back—old movies, black and white photos, padded shoulders on blouses, men's slouch hats, wide ties, big band music, jitterbug, Frank Sinatra, Rita Hayworth, Humphrey Bogart. This was my parent's generation. Theirs is passed. Mine is passing. The children's world is coming.

Their world is not for me to know. Already I feel as a stranger in a strange land. I look at the magazine rack in the supermarket. Popular actors, singers, politicians and sports figures have names and faces that are unfamiliar to me. I watch the news on TV. New trends, new gadgets, new technologies leave me baffled. Many of the persons and events the newscasters are reporting on seem from another world. I'm a stranger in a strange land.

Right Relationship—My Place Among Generations

Each generation, as it's members grow out of adolescence and arrive on the world stage, makes the announcement, "We're here, and we intend to fix the mistakes of the previous generations and do things right." We in the Boomer generation did this in spades. The fervor waned some when we faced the complexities of the real world.

Every generation, those that came before me and those that come after, has its own experience, its own events, its own spirit of the time that informs it. I can only know of those generations through stories and old photos and films. But without living through their times, I can never really know what it is like to be a member. Every generation is unique. Every generation has its truth. Every generation has it's story. Every generation has it's wisdom. The truth and the story and the wisdom should be listened to and respected. It's easy to judge and dismiss, but there is much to be learned if we keep an open mind.

As an old man, having gained greater perspective, I'm coming to see more clearly my place among the generations. It came to me almost as a poem or a mantra;

Men are my brothers
Women are my sisters
Older men are my fathers,
Older women are my mothers
Younger men are my sons,
Younger women are my daughters.

This understanding has altered the way I view people and has influenced how I try to treat them. I'm seeing people, whatever age and generation, more as my family constellation.

I relate most closely to the men and women in my own age group. It feels right and good to take my place among "the brothers and sisters" who are my contemporaries. We have lived together through times of change in art, music, armed conflict and social and political upheaval that characterized our generation. With our shared history, we are uniquely suited to understand each other in ways that older and younger generations cannot. In that sense we are like siblings.

At my age, I find fewer older men and women with whom I can hold as parental models, as so many are not alive. However, I consider many admirable elders from preceding generations who have passed on, as "fathers and mothers" who I have learned from and respect as honorary parents. I count Mother Theresa, Ram Dass, Muktananda, Justice Ruth Bader Ginsberg and Nelson Mandela among them.

Seeing younger men and women as my children has really altered my outlook. I'm more aware now of my responsibility to the younger generations. This "fatherly" parental view has informed my desire to make the world a better place for ensuing generations. It is giving me the juice to write and speak as a mentor. I am now more able and willing to step up to assume a space as an elder wisdom keeper, and make an offering of my time and energy and resources.

I am honored to take my place among those who walked before me, those I walk with, and those who walk behind me.

My Disappearing World

I visited my old neighborhood. There used to be a drug store on the corner. It is no longer there, replaced by a cleaners. The playground of my grammar school, where we used to chase rabbits, is now a parking lot that serves a strip mall. A three story building stands where there was once a gas station. A few days ago, on a trip to Los Angeles, I drove by the house I grew up in. Torn down, the empty lot surrounded by a construction fence. I can picture each of the rooms in my mind in exquisite detail. Now ghosts.

The physical world of my youth is changing. Little by little, the world I grew up with, the world that shaped my life, is fading away. The people I've known, places I've been... gone. Replaced by new places, new people.

I used to frequent the nearby store my parents had shopped at. I knew the old proprietor when I was a kid. His son, who many years ago took over the business when his father died, has recently retired. Now his middle-aged son runs the business.

This was my world. Now it belongs to others. Changes.

Some Day

In the late sixties, my band played at a "Human Be-In," a large hippie event in Hollywood. The club was filled with people milling around, long hair, love beads, colorful clothes, smell of incense. Every once in a while, a deep male voice kept booming over the loudspeaker, ramping up everyone's expectations by saying things like, "It's about to happen. Soon it will be happening." Well, after hours of announcements, hours of waiting, nothing happened!

Sometimes, when you do nothing but wait for something to happen rather than take action, nothing will. Except that you'll grow older.

"Some day" usually never comes. "I've always wanted to travel, to see the world. Some day, I will." "I've spent years getting my education, but I hate my work. Some day I'd like to open a restaurant." "My wife and I are having marital problems. Some day we should see a therapist." Tomorrow and tomorrow and tomorrow. But tomorrow never comes. Instead, we take care of immediate needs. We live with limitations. We pay the bills, do the laundry and take the dog for a walk. We put off till tomorrow. When tomorrow does come, we're old and it's too late. Nothing is sadder than to get old, come to the end of your life, realize you had put off living, and regret all you didn't do what you wanted to. Some day.

A Dream

I've just awoken from a dream, a nightmare. In the dream, I'm part of a movie crew, working on a film. I'm in an old, deteriorating wooden cabin. (My aging body?) The cabin is in the path of a thundering herd of buffalo. (The destructive force of time, old age, illness, death?) I'm tasked with protecting the cabin. (Keeping the body safe, healthy?) The sound of hooves is getting closer. (Impending debilities?) I'm rushing around, making sure the cabin is secure and no buffalo can enter. (Protection? Preservation?) A door has opened. As I shut the door, I notice a door at the other side of the room is wide open. (Vulnerability? Helplessness?) I rush to close it. (Effort to safeguard from harm?) This happens several times. Each time, I hear the sound of thundering hooves getting louder and louder, and feel vibrations through the floor. (Impending death?) I awake in panic.

Lemonade

Zen master Shunryu Suzuki Roshi has described life as an ocean voyage.

Life is like
stepping onto a boat
which is about to sail
out to sea
and sink.

OK. You die, but let's delve deeper into this somewhat humorous take on life and death.

You embark on a shiny new cruise ship. Everything's ship-shape. Plenty of fuel and supplies. Well trained, helpful crew. Lots of things to do on board. Eventually, you leave the harbor and you're out on your own in open waters. The smooth seas begin to get rough. The ship begins running low on fuel, low on supplies. Waves are getting big, tossing the ship around, making you seasick. The ship springs a leak, then another, and begins to take on water. You know this, you see it as it's happening. You know that soon you will be sinking, but you are helpless, there is nothing you can do to prevent it.

This is our life dilemma. This sad fate of the increasing deterioration of our body and mind and eventual death is the reality every human is faced with as they grow old. Knowing that this will be the downward trajectory of our life, how shall we live, how shall we face our fate? Is it possible for us to use this sad reality at the end portion of our life to, instead of becoming immobilized and depressed, instead of rearranging deck chairs on the sinking ship, to take on the challenge the passing years presents us and become enlivened by it? Maybe even use it to add great meaning to our life? Can we turn sour lemons into lemonade? I hope so. This is what I am trying to do in my life and in this book.

Lemons are bitter. Lemonade is made palatable by the addition of the sweetness of sugar. I write in this book about the sugar of old age—sweet wisdom, sweet understanding, perspective, inner peace. But lemons are bitter. Old age is tough. There is no escaping the bitter taste. Honestly, I don't like it. But here I am, here we are. Lemons or lemonade? We have a choice. I choose lemonade.

The Achievement Of Admirable Elderhood

Most of this chapter on getting old is out of balance. It focused on the bitter lemons of aging—the losses, the sadness, the negativities of growing old. That's lemons, not the lemonade. The sweetness comes from becoming an elder who lives their life in a wholesome and loving way. Such an elder is one who is deserving of being admired. That is a worthy accomplishment. It's a goal to be achieved through intention and effort...and luck. Unfortunately, admirable elderhood is an achievement that not all aging people are capable of. Sometimes, physical infirmities and mental debilities create insurmountable barriers. And many elders, though they may be physically and emotionally capable, are unwilling to aspire to live their lives in a commendable way. But those who are willing and able to take on the challenge of becoming an admirable elder are deserving of our appreciation and respect.

An admirable elder is not invariably tied to the culture they were born in. They have embraced the freedom to travel their own path. In a sense, they *must* be a rebel. Their rebellion takes the form of defying values of the existing culture, a culture that promotes superficiality, acquisitiveness, entertainment, ease and comfort. No matter what their limitations, these mature elders continue to question, choose to go deep, and are willing to buck the system. They have chosen to live their lives in service to the values of truth, kindness, harmony, and integrity. By and large, these are qualities that our society might admire, but they are not necessarily qualities that our society rewards.

An older person, through living their life in an admirable way, becomes a model, a mentor, a wise benefactor, a bridger of generations, an agent for positive change, and a beacon of strength and righteousness for all those they come in contact with. The person who they have grown to become, because of their wisdom and experience, can enlighten and inspire coming generations.

However, if we as individuals fail to do the necessary work to realize our potential as admirable elders, besides failing ourselves, we also fail the culture we live in. We become negative role models. By our example, we are confirming society's shared misperceptions and counterproductive beliefs about aging. By our example, we reinforce the destructive stereotypes that our youth-oriented culture holds about being old—frail, ugly, obsolete, helpless, useless and irrelevant.

Just think, if each of us were to meet the challenges of aging by working, at whatever level we are able, toward becoming the most vital, loving, creative, wise, generous, authentic elder that we can possibly be, consider the effect this will have on a personal, interpersonal and societal level. If we elders did this with the force of numbers, society could not help but respond by becoming a joyful playground where peoples of the Earth can thrive. And elders, far from being marginalized and demeaned, would be honored and celebrated as valuable sources of wisdom, as guides, and as models for the emulation of succeeding generations. Such a revolution will not happen on its own. It has to start somewhere. May it start with you.

A Positive View Of Aging

In spite of the lemons, what you'll find in this book is, overwhelmingly, a positive view of getting old. Aging, even with all its considerable challenges, is not the time when everything is running down and the best of our life is past. Our later years are the *culmination* of our lives. Our earlier years are *preparation* for this powerful and deeply meaningful stage.

LETTING GO

TIME IS A THIEF. It usually leaves us alone when we're young, but steals more and more from us as we grow older. There is very little we can do to stem the tide of loss. It's part of being old. We can try, but we will be asking for a load of frustration if we expect to turn back the clock. And though we might be able to delay a minute or two, eventually, the thief of time takes its toll.

Losses will happen. They are easier to deal with when we incorporate an attitude of "letting go." The more we are able to practice letting go when we are young, the easier letting go will be when we are old.

Caterpillar To Butterfly

A caterpillar is a glorified worm. How does this drab insect metamorphize into a beautiful multicolored butterfly? *It lets go of what it was.*

When it becomes ready, the caterpillar finds a safe place, hangs upside down and turns into a chrysalis. Within the chrysalis, what was the caterpillar, over a week or so, undergoes a complete transformation. Only when all traces of its original form dissolves, can the future butterfly be born. Death of the caterpillar gives life to the butterfly. Breaking out of its cocoon, the butterfly spreads it's colorful wings and soars in the wind.

To become who you are, you sometimes need to let go of who you were.

Letting Go Of "Childish Things"

In the Bible, the Apostle Paul wrote, "When I was a child, I spoke as a child, I understood as a child, I thought as a child: but when I became a man, I put away childish things." What might be some of the childish things and understandings that Paul felt must be left behind when we grow up?

On a superficial level, Paul might be referring to growing up and taking on the responsibility of an adult. But let's go deeper and also add one word, "when I became an **old** man." So, what are some things elders would be wise to let go of as they grow past middle age?

"Childish things" to let go of as we grow to become an old person might be the objects and understandings that served us when we were younger, but are no longer useful for us now.

The "toys" we are holding on to may not be beneficial to keep. Toys could be the attachment to objects we have used to impress others and bolster our ego—expensive cars, jewelry and other objects of conspicuous consumption. This doesn't mean we should get rid of these things. "Putting away" might be coming to understand our true worth and not needing "props" to show others and ourselves how worthy we are.

Thoughts and emotions which are harmful to self and others might also be considered childish things. Jealousy, greed, inflated pride, vengeance, conceit and the like, do not serve us or others and would best be worked with in order for us to "put them away." As we grow more mature, we might work to put away striving to be admired by all, the need to be better than others, need to be right, to be perfect, to be important. These kinds of ambitions are better left to youth.

When Paul wrote of childish speech he might have been referring to communication in a larger sense. That might include the way we behave with other people. A wise elder would consider others and value kindness of speech and action in their dealings with the people in their lives.

It would be beneficial as we grow older, to let go of the belief that the source of our happiness and peace of mind resides outside ourself, in the objects we possess, in the relationships we form, in the sense pleasures we obtain. We know from experience that whatever comfort and satisfaction we receive from these things is only temporary. The blast of happiness and enjoyment soon fades and we find ourselves seeking for other objects, other relationships, other sense pleasures.

What we really want for ourselves is a source of lasting peace and contentment, and that can only come from inside us. So an understanding that aging teaches us is to look within. Looking within involves quieting our mind so we can hear the still, small voice inside that speaks truth and wisdom. And following that voice. It will lead us to acceptance and grace.

What aging also teaches us is that we must not only look within. In order to find the peace we seek, we might also look upward, toward the spiritual realm or toward concordance with a divine being or a power greater than ourselves. For many of us, peace resides in finding a spiritual base. Practices such as prayer, meditation, contemplation, etc., will help us to form that base.

One could say that the process of growing to be a wise elder is analogous in many ways to the process of putting away childish things.

Two Approaches To Letting Go

Holding on to old ideas or feelings or objects or people that no longer serve you is an unneeded weight on your shoulders. Letting go will lighten the load you carry.

Say you have a psychological issue, maybe you are feeling anger toward an important person in your life and that anger is eating you up inside. You might go to a psychotherapist and seek to work through your anger. Together, you would examine the source of the anger, what that person did, what you did, what they can do, what you can do. You might explore your family history and look at incidents that might have been significant in predisposing your angry responses. This psychological work could, over time, help you understand the causes of your anger and let go of it's hold over your psyche.

Another approach might be to feel into the anger and to experience its painful effect. What effect is it having on your body, mind and spirit? How is it influencing your relationship? How is it affecting your peace of mind? Feeling the negative effects may lead you to an understanding of the nature of anger. That understanding, and the uncomfortable feelings in your gut of that come from holding on to the anger, could fuel a willingness to let go of the angry feelings you are holding. That letting go could be a natural outcome, and the letting go may happen on its own.

I cannot recommend one approach to letting go over another. Whatever it is that you are carrying that no longer serves you, the process of letting go is specific to each situation, as is the approach you use. The important thing is to let go of holding on.

Letting Go Of "Objects"

We spend the first part of our life acquiring, and the second part, letting go. Of course, that's a gross generalization, but it holds some truth.

As children, we go to school to acquire a basic education. As young adults, we learn skills that will serve to help us get a job or acquire a career. We earn money so we can acquire a partner, create a household, purchase furnishings, afford children, save for the future. And then, after their education, the kids leave the nest to go on to their own life. We retire. With the children gone, and with no need for so much space, we get rid of excess furnishings, part with treasured mementos, sell the house and move to an apartment. After awhile, we are separated from our partner by divorce or death and we find that it's becoming difficult to live alone without help. So we opt to downsize even more, move from our apartment to much smaller accommodations in a senior living community, or we take up an offer by our children to move into a room in their house. Then, with need for more help with daily living, we are moved with a few belongings to share a room with another person in an assisted living facility. Lots of letting go.

Alice and I live surrounded by "stuff." Wherever we have gone, we picked up some oddity that caught our eye that we could hang up on a wall or place somewhere in the garden. Our property is interesting to visit. A person can spend hours wandering around, looking at tribal sculptures from

New Guinea, or antique rugs from Turkey on our floor, Art Deco lamps or old soft drink signs advertising soda for 5 cents. Thankfully, we are beginning to outgrow the need for more. No longer do we give in to the impulse to shop on eBay, nor are we drawn to stop at every garage sale or thrift shop we pass. It's time to start getting rid of stuff instead of trying to acquire more. We're starting to do that, and there are times when there are bags waiting to be taken to the thrift shop and our garbage cans are overflowing with stuff we've outgrown. Our kids will thank us for not leaving a mess for them to clean up after we're gone. We are taking seriously, the core of the old, wise statement, "What you own, owns you."

Letting go of things is not simply getting rid of clutter or making life easier for our kids. It's much more. Letting go of objects we don't need is a practice for learning to let go…of everything. And the truth is, at some point, everything we own will be gone. Everything. The more tightly we cling to anything, the more painful it will be when, one by one, things are ripped from our grasp. So it is important to realize this, and practice letting go, letting go.

There may well be a time in Alice and my life, when one or both of us will need to move from our spacious property to smaller quarters, maybe even one room in an assisted care facility. You never know what changes the next moment will bring. Hopefully, by that time, we will have learned to be able to let go lightly.

Letting Go Of My Family History

I was the recipient of the remnants of my family history—albums of old black and white photos, letters, memorabilia from fifty, sixty, a hundred and more years ago that my mother and Aunt Kitty had collected. Some of these were passed down from their mother. I inherited this treasure trove after they all died, almost two decades ago. I kept the stuff in plastic boxes in the barn, safe from rats and mice. For all this time I didn't have the heart to go though it. I needed to allow time for sadness and undigested feelings to gradually recede before I could look at it again.

The passage of time had done it's work and I had been feeling ready for awhile to go through the stuff so our kids wouldn't have to. I made the decision, called my brother, Steve, and together we sat outside on the patio and went through the boxes. Steve and I are the last of immediate family, so there was no one who would find these things of interest. Photos of family long gone, birthday cards, old school report cards and homework assignments, letters, high school yearbooks from the twenties, tickets to plays and sports events, drawings done in grammar school. My mother, hoarder that she was, kept everything. These were the last remains of my parent's life and their parent's lives and Steve and my early life. We dove in and were relentless. The garbage can next to us was full to the brim.

It felt to me that I was not just getting rid of things, I was, in a way, letting go of my parents, letting go of my younger self. For these two decades, I had avoided saying goodby to a past that was dead and gone. I felt it was important for me now to view these things for one last time for a sense of completion before throwing them away. Somehow, the act of letting go of these objects was a way I could clear space to move forward with my life, freer and less encumbered by the past.

I set the full can out to be picked up by the garbage truck the next day. Then, just as I turned away to leave, my eyes caught a glimpse of a packet of letters I had written my parents during my travels in my early twenties. The bus trip to the East Coast, visit to the 1964 New York World's Fair, my new job as an epidemiologist in San Francisco, the trip meeting my brother in Europe and then going on alone to Morocco. After a moments hesitation, I grabbed the letters, knowing that, for one more time, at some later date, I would re-experience that wide-eyed young boy/man, scared and excited, and about to enter the big, wide world for the first time. I put the letters back in the barn, awaiting a time when I'll again revisit a piece of my distant past.

Letting Go Of People

I keep people's phone numbers in a card file on my desk. (I admit it, I'm a dinosaur.) I hadn't updated the numbers for awhile, so I sat down recently and started to go through the file. There were lots of changes. People had moved or changed their phone number. What struck me most was how many cards of friends and family I had to remove because they had died. I shuffled through the whole stack of numbers and addresses. Each card I threw away was a life and a shared relationship. I felt sadness. My circle of loved ones is shrinking and my file is getting thinner.

I think about my Aunt Kitty, who died at 97, our friend's dad, Jim, 101, or our neighbor, potter Beatrice Wood, who died at 105. What must their card files have looked like. Probably very slim. Many cards dis-carded. No cards of childhood friends in their file. How sad and lonely might it feel to be "the last."

Yesterday I was sitting in our car in the supermarket parking lot, waiting for Alice to finish making last minute purchases. I watched scores of people moving to and fro, busily pushing carts, dragging kids, loading groceries into the trunk of their car, going about, purposefully living their lives. I was thinking, "Most likely, every one of these folks, including their kids, will be dead and buried a century from now." Lots of letting go to be done by family and friends.

Letting Go Of Being Your Parent's Child And Your Children's Parent

Even as an adult, when I would visit my parents in the home they lived in for fifty years, it was uncanny. I would automatically slip into feeling like a kid. So many familiar sights and smells, timeworn roles and old stimuli would catapult me back to the time I was a child when in my parent's presence.

There was a point where that changed, never to change back again. A role reversal began. My parents, in their seventies, were still independent, still able to negotiate life by themselves. Then, as they approached their eighties, they required more help from us. We found ourselves going with them to medical appointments, doing the shopping, helping with taxes and financial record keeping, and finally making the majority of important decisions regarding their welfare. We had become our parent's parents.

And now, with both of us in our eighties, we're seeing the need beginning for us to allow our kids to take on more responsibilities for our welfare. What comes around, goes around, and we may eventually become our children's children.

Letting Go Of Physical Abilities

This is a hard one. No one escapes "body rot." As we get older, we watch as our body weakens year by year, month by month.

We took our hike on Sulphur Mountain this morning. It was just a couple of months previously that we had hiked the same route, yet we both wanted to turn back a bit earlier than the last time. And that last time, we had wanted to turn back earlier than the time before. The way back is mostly uphill. Our legs hurt, we were out of breath, had to stop and rest frequently. Is this me, the guy who, in the past would bound up mountain trails, move boulders, climb trees? Body rot.

I can't carry the 50-pound sacks of chicken feed like I used to, and have to use a dolly. I find it harder to open jars. I'm more mindful when bending down. I've become—I hate to use the word—more *fragile*. If I'm not careful, I can hurt myself by overdoing physical activities. No doubt, deterioration will continue. No matter what we do to slow it down, our bodies will continue to weaken as it has. Sadly, we have to let go of the sense that we will remain the same. Entropy. Body rot.

Now, we've hired Ruben to do much of the outdoor work I used to enjoy in past years. He's a lot younger. Truth is, I feel relieved. For years, I hadn't enjoyed lots of the maintenance.

Letting Go Of Dreams

Our friend Troy spent many years, hours of grueling daily workouts and classes, training as a ballet dancer. We watched him perform as a lead dancer with dance companies. He was good, very good. Then he married Brook, and soon daughter Jaiden arrived. His dream of dancing in major international companies receded. Needing to make a living for his family, he took a job working for a computer company. All that remained of the dream he had spent years of his youth working towards was some videos of his performances, old newspaper reviews and tattered flyers. He let go of a treasured dream in order to take on another dream—being a father.

Some of the musicians I played with when I was younger went on to have illustrious careers. Reading about them and watching their performances on stage and screen, I have become wistful. It could have been me on the stage, doing what I loved doing while receiving accolades from an admiring crowd. This was not to be. I had to let go in order to follow another dream.

We have limited time in this life, limited energy. We can realistically accomplish only what we can, given our limitations. Every path we choose to travel down means that other paths will be foreclosed. Some dreams will have to be let go. It may be too late for some. Maybe our interests have changed. Maybe we are finding fulfillment in our current life. And maybe it may seem that it would be too arduous a trek to begin at this late stage of life.

If we are able to let go lightly, without a great deal of regret for what might have been, we can move on with our life, living fully into the dream we are living in now. Sometimes a dream is just a dream.

Letting Go Of The Need For Other's Approval

When we were young, we hungered for mommy and daddy's approval and would show off for them every chance we could get. We grew older and sought to be popular and well-liked in school and appreciated by the teachers. We pursued our boss's approval, our partner's approval, our mentor's approval when we became adults. Now, when we've become older, hopefully, the cloying need for other's approval drops away. We're left with the one need for approval that is of any consequence— appreciation of our own self.

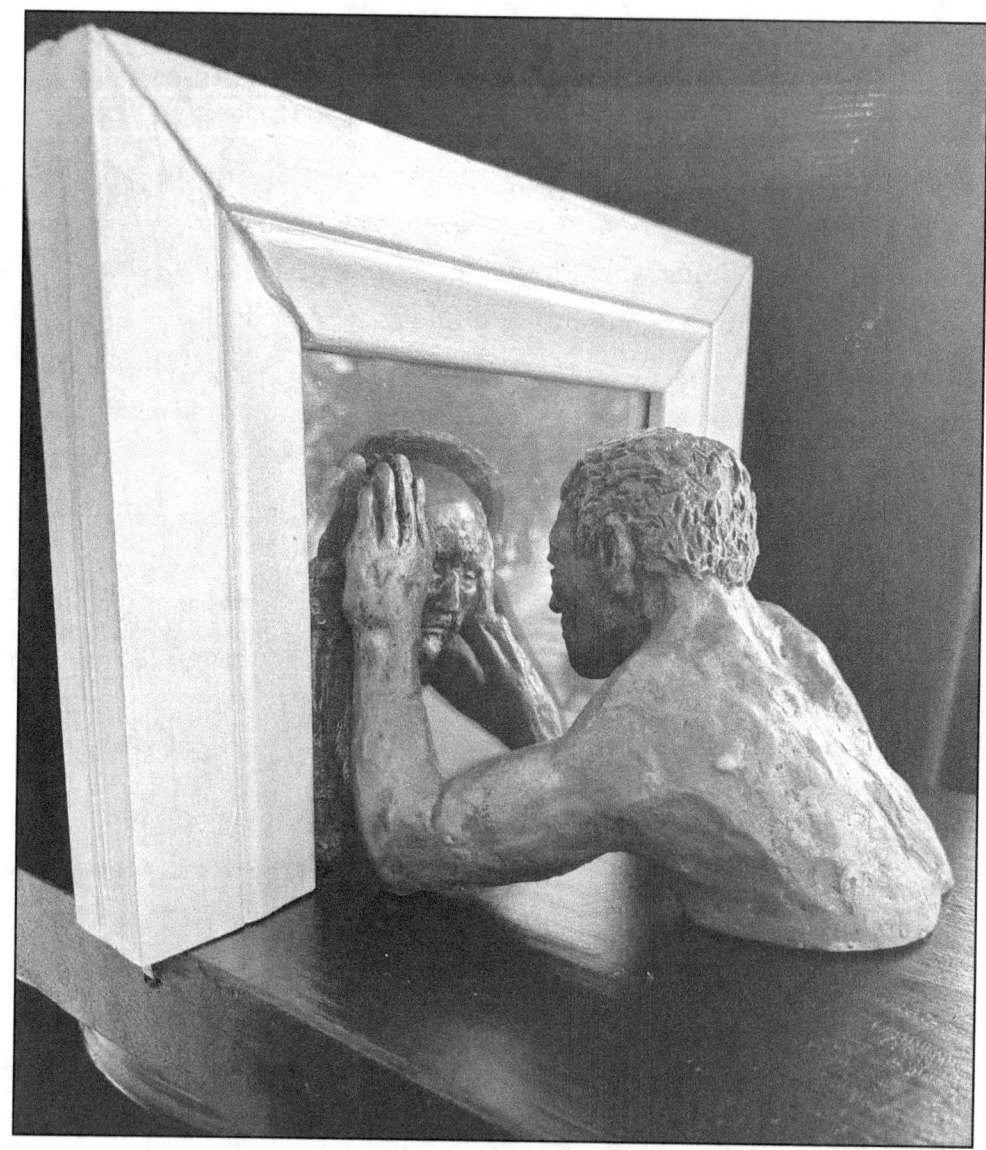

MIRROR OF TIME

Two figures: A young man, looking in the mirror, and trying to touch the reflected image of his future , while an old man, seeing himself in the past, tries to make contact with his younger self

Letting Go Of Our Younger Self-Image

I had an interesting encounter with my bathroom mirror the other day. Usually, it's a quick glance—hair combed? Beard need a trim? Remnant of breakfast clinging to lip? This time I took some minutes and really looked at the old face staring back at me. I grabbed my reading glasses for an up-close view. Without a lot of judgement, I noted how my face had changed as I aged. Wrinkles, sags, blotches. Still me, but the young face I wore as a youth had dissolved, never to be seen again.

Letting go of things is the easy part. They are only just things. It's much harder for most of us to relinquish the outdated view we have of ourselves as we grow older. We're no longer that young person anymore.

Especially in our youth-oriented culture, to be old is to be invisible. For women who have defined their value by their physical beauty, the pain of watching time slowly strip away the main characteristic by which they valued themselves is excruciating. Each wrinkle, unwanted pound, each grey hair and age spot, is a painful razor slice that reminds her, "You're getting old." What is she to do? Get rid of the evidence? Women spend billions of dollars every year on facelifts, tummy tucks, medications, exercise programs and skin creams and elixirs that promise to turn back the clock. But the hands of the clock refuse to run backwards.

I am not at all saying that looking younger is a bad thing. Do what pleases you and have fun and enjoy it. But know that you can only cover up the effects of age with a layer of paint. Underneath the paint is still the old face and body. That is who you are, and if you don't accept who you are, you are in for a painful ride.

Same goes for a man who, when younger, had defined himself by his chiseled good looks, his physical prowess, his muscled physique or his position of authority. He suffers when he believes he has lost strength or become a "nobody" as he aged or entered retirement.

Letting go of your younger self-image, whether physical appearance or sense of importance, is a humbling experience. But it is an essential step on your way to maturity. You are who you are now. The younger image you have of yourself is just that—the image of a person who no longer exists.

Letting Go When Necessary

We had a great party for my eightieth birthday. Over fifty friends and family came. It was a beautiful sunny day. Alice spent days preparing everything and cooked a delicious meal for all. The high point for me was when I and Jimmy and Tom, consummate keyboard and bass player, gave a concert for the crowd. These were musicians I had played with for many years. We sounded great, had a ball playing all the old tunes, and everyone enjoyed our music. I was in bliss.

My musician friends didn't know, nor did anyone else, including Alice, and maybe even myself, that I would be making the decision to never play drums again. The end of that evening, after going back-and-forth in my mind, I made that difficult decision. No more. The next morning I photographed my drum set, my beloved, longtime friend, so I could post it for sale. Then I disassembled the drums for the last time. Alice came out when I was doing this and started weeping. She said, "It's like a funeral." And it was. I wiped away a tear.

I had played drums since I was fifteen years old. For sixty-five years, being a musician was part of my history, part of my identity. A lifetime of memories came flooding back. Joyful moments communicating with friends in a language that was beyond words. But it was right to let go. My ears were ringing from the loud sound of the drums, and I didn't want to compromise my hearing any further. Feeling raw. Feeling sadness. In and out of mourning. But I ended right. I went out with a bang!

Letting Go Of "Your Story"

When we've lived long, and encountered our share of suffering, there comes a time when it's possible to become bored with our "story." We've told it many times, to our friends, our lovers, our therapists, ourselves. How, growing up, we didn't get enough love from our parents, how our lover betrayed us, how a business partner cheated us, how we don't feel worthy enough or beautiful enough or appreciated enough.

Your story is of the past—not now. These things might have affected you, but you are not your diagnoses, you are not your history and your history is not your destiny. You are not just a manic-depressive. You are not just a victim of domestic violence. You are not just the child of an alcoholic. You are a resilient spirit that, though influenced by the past, resides separate from these past experiences.

One of my former clients is a survivor of sexual abuse. He goes to support meetings twice a week, most of his friendships are with other survivors, much of his identity revolves around being a "survivor." Not to denigrate the powerful, life-changing impact of sexual abuse, but there is more to life than the wound you carry, and you limit yourself if you dwell on your pathology.

In order to heal, it is sometimes necessary to look back into your history and open up and work through old wounds. But there is also a time to let them be and move on with your life. You don't need to be victim any more than you need to be villain. And sometimes, by letting go of our stories, we can open to include other's stories, to see from their point of view. This can be the beginning of the healing balm of forgiveness, of others and of self.

There's a problem with letting go of our story though. What will we have left to feel bad about? What will fill up our hour of therapy? What will we complain about when we have lunch with a friend?

Old Dog Consciousness

Spiritual teacher Ram Dass talked about what he called, "Old Dog Consciousness." Picture a senior hound, laying on the front porch, lazily watching life go by. He'd been around for awhile, seen a lot, has a few scars from dogfights when he was younger. He opens one eye when the mailman comes in the yard to drop off a packet of letters. Goes back to snoozing. A cat walks by the front gate. The old hound lifts his head and looks. No big deal. Just a cat. Seen one, seen them all. The German Shepard from down the block, comes and pees on the gatepost. No need to prove who's boss, no need to establish territory. Been there, done that.

Some elders are fortunate to have old dog consciousness, ODC for short. They have nothing to prove, no one to prove it to, including themselves. They've fought their battles, competed, won or lost. Did their best. Loved, loathed. Followed their path. Enjoyed what life offered them. Received and survived life's blows. Now, like the old dog, it doesn't matter much what happened in the past. They've let go. No ambition except to relax and enjoy the warm sun on their flank, the occasional pat on the head, and sit in front of the blazing fire in the fireplace. Contented.

Letting Go Of Worry

There are many things that we can worry about when we get older. However, worry accomplishes nothing more than creating anxiety, agitation and endless overthinking. Worrying is mental masturbation. It is taking a fear, working it over and over in your mind til a molehill becomes a mountain.

The Serenity Prayer of Alcoholics Anonymous provides a prescription that can help reduce worry. It goes, *"God grant me the serenity to accept the things I cannot change, courage to change the things I can, and the wisdom to know the difference."* The prayer asks us to discriminate between things we have control over, and things we don't. When we are clear about what we have no control over, there's nothing we can do about it and it's easier to let those things go. (In a very different vein, activist Angela Davis has another take on the Serenity Prayer that's worthy of consideration. *"I am no longer accepting the things I cannot change. I am changing the things I cannot accept."*)

Worry is difficult to change, but I think that if people would contemplate about and recognize how useless and

> *If you can't do anything about it, don't worry about it.*
>
> Advice by Jeanne Calment, age 122, documented world's oldest person.

86

painful worry is, they would do what they can to try to let it go. But then, they might start worrying about worrying too much.

Poet Mary Oliver wrote a poem that seems especially appropriate. It is titled, "I Worried."

The poem begins,

"I worried a lot. Will the garden grow, will the rivers
flow in the right direction, will the Earth turn
as it was taught and if not, how shall
I correct it?"

The poem ends,

"Finally I saw that it came to nothing.
And I gave it up. And I took my old body
and went out into the morning,
and sang."

Letting Go Of Negative Judgements About Aging

Years ago I visited the home of friends, the late human potential workshop leader Jinendra Jain and his wife, Katherine. As we were having dinner, an elderly man would come into and out of the dining room. I asked Jinendra, "Who is this old guy?" He answered, "In India, it is considered an honor and a blessing to have an old person living in your house. We didn't have any elder relatives who lived close to us, so we found this old man who needed a place to stay, and now he lives with us. We are honored to have him around."

Spiritual teacher Ram Dass wrote that he became insulted at first when an Indian friend who he hadn't seen for a long time exclaimed upon meeting him, "Ram Dass, you look so old." He didn't realize that this friend meant it as a compliment. In India, being old is considered an accomplishment.

What a different view of honoring old people from Western culture. Here, we tend to look down on old people and are content when they are stowed away in their own 55 and older communities. We dread getting older. Many of us find it difficult to be around the aged because their presence reminds us of our future fate. Many of us elders have taken to believing our society's judgements about aging. And we apply those negative judgments to ourselves.

Books like the one you're reading now can be helpful to assist you to break the negative judgments you've accumulated about aging. The more you read and contemplate about the positive aspects of aging, the easier it will be to let go of those negative views.

Let Go Lightly

In the movie, "Croupier," Jack, the protagonist, describes the way gamblers should approach their gaming. "Hold on tightly. Let go lightly." It might also be a way we should approach the game of life.

As I have written earlier, "Time steals our strength, our energy, our health, our beauty, our independence, our memory, our friends and family, our relevance." This is a real robbery. When age causes the circumstances in our life to change, it becomes appropriate to relinquish obsolete objects, thoughts and self-images. If we do not, it is increasingly painful to continue to hold on.

I am slowly learning the hard way. The sense I hold of myself as a man is still tied to my physical strength, my ability to fix things and my not needing to ask for help. My strength is not what it once was. Time and again, even though I think I know my limits, I still hurt my back lifting objects that are too heavy for me. In recent years, mechanical devices have evolved into electronics. I have less knowledge about these "new fangled" devices and less interest in trying to repair them. Let someone else do it. I need to be realistic about my limitations and ask for help when I need it. I need to let go lightly.

In unfamiliar surroundings, or circumstances that are beyond my ability to help, I am still ashamed to admit that I am confused or cannot solve a problem. I need to lay aside my shame about not being a "fixer," and the one who knows everything. I need to discard my false masculine ego with its debilitating pride, and ask for help if I can't do for myself. I need to let go lightly.

As long as I don't let go lightly, I will continue to cause myself injury and pain. I will continue to feel frustrated, exhausted and isolated.

Shortly, you will read about my friend Riley who was dying. As the dying process stole more of his former self from him and he was confined to his bed, a shadow of his prior self, he didn't wail about losing the robust self that was. Riley watched with interest as he lost strength and energy, moving toward the inevitable conclusion of his life. With each loss he would let go lightly, without resistance. The term he would often use was, "Allow." To allow is to accept what is, as is. It is to let go lightly. Riley allowed the changes that came with his illness. His passing was not difficult because he let go lightly.

"Letting Go" Mind

The cat who has lived with us for the last four years, Roameo, is an indoor/outdoor cat. He likes a soft bed, and he also likes to roam in the fields any time of the day or night. He lets us know when he wants out by going to the door, or mewing loudly, or, if all else fails, biting our feet. We open the door, he looks around for a moment, and then scoots out, off to adventure in the wilds. We live in the country, and there are animals lurking, mainly coyotes, who would love to have him for dinner. Several times he has returned bloody and freaked out.

Roameo is a free being, and he would be miserable if contained in a room or a house, so he has his freedom to roam. We love him and want him to be safe and happy. But each time we open the door to let him out, we have to "let go." We must realize that this may be the last time we see him.

There is the Zen story of a wise man who coveted a beautiful glass goblet that he kept locked away in a cabinet when not in use. An acquaintance suggested that he was emotionally attached to this mere object. "No," he replied, "This is a beautiful glass and I enjoy it's exquisite design and it's usefulness.

But for me, the glass is already broken, as it will be some day. While it is here, and I am here, I can take pleasure in its beauty and its usefulness. And when it breaks, I will know that I have enjoyed it fully."

And so it is with each other. No one knows what the next moment will bring for Alice and me. Somewhere in both our minds is the understanding, especially at our age, that we will not be together forever. At some point, our time together will end and we will have to let go. Occasionally, when Alice or I are about to leave home on a separate errand, we'll say to each other in half-jest, "If I don't see you again, it's been a good run." *Half*-jest.

Holding On

Why is it so hard to let go sometimes? There are lots reasons we hold on to old ways of doing and being, even if those ways no longer serve us.

We're locked in by habit is probably the main reason it's difficult for us to let go. Habits are strengthened by repetition. Similar to the way ruts in a road are deepened every time a vehicle passes, each repetition of a habit strengthens the habit and makes it more difficult to "get out of the rut." Usually, it takes effort to make a change. The more deeply engrained the habit, the more effort is required to make the necessary changes.

We're afraid of the unknown is another reason we hold on to unproductive ways of being. We are comfortable with the world we know. The uncertainty of that which is unknown makes us nervous. Fear of the unknown keeps us polishing the bars of our cage rather than walking out the unlocked door. Fear also blinds us to other possibilities that are right before our eyes. It keeps us on the straight and narrow path, but limits our ability to envision new ways of doing and being.

We fear failure. When we attempt to make a change, we often don't take into consideration that failure is part of the process. It's an important and necessary part of the process in that it reveals what doesn't work and indicates the things we need to improve on.

We don't know what to do. Often, the decision to let go requires that, rather than free fall, we need a plan of action. We need to research and devise an effective plan in advance that can serve as a map that will deal with potential problems and can help us get through a rocky period. We need to eliminate, as best we can, things that would foil that plan. We need to line up support with people who can help us if necessary.

We lack motivation. I think the major reason we keep holding on to old, unbeneficial ways is that we're just not motivated enough. Letting go of old habits and acquiring new ones takes effort and time. Nothing will happen if motivation is not there. Either our situation is not dire enough, and we are not in great pain, or the positive reward promised by change is not great enough to get us moving. So we keep holding on to our barely satisfactory situation, rather than letting go into the possibility of freedom and greater joy.

Practice Letting Go

Most people's tendency is to hold on. If something bothers them, they chew on it, fret over it, don't allow it to be. To let go takes practice. Life provides you endless opportunities to practice. You're driving along and a car cuts you off—breathe, and consciously let go of the rising anger. You're waiting in a line for a cashier and the person in front of you has a complicated transaction that is taking an inordinate amount of time—breathe and consciously let go of the frustration. You're harmed by someone's foolish mistake—breathe and let go of blame and judgment.

I suggest that you'll benefit if you take on the task of consciously practicing letting go. See the minor losses and frustrations that occur in everyday life as opportunities to work with loss. Then, when the big losses occur, a shocking medical diagnosis or the death of a loved one, you will have had at least some preparation in dealing with and integrating loss into mind and gut and heart.

It's an important part of my spiritual practice to try to let go whenever the opportunity arises. A half hour ago, I was deeply engrossed in my writing when Alice came into the room with a non-emergency request for help that could have easily been delayed. I immediately stopped writing and, without a second thought, went to help her. I purposely let go of my need to finish the sentence I was working on. Because I had spent years practicing letting go, letting go of my writing was easy.

Letting go is a conscious choice. The more you practice letting go, the better you get. The better you get, the easier your life will be. Keep practicing so you'll become a champion at letting go.

Letting Go Of Trying To Change Things Or Make Them Better

One key to letting go, of things, of the past, of your former self, of your life, is to not resist "what is." It's to allow the thing you want out of your life to be just as it is for now, without trying to change it, ignore it, push it away. Resistance makes it more solid. Let it be.

There is a distinction that can be made between "letting go" and "letting be." Letting go implies action, an active attempt to release things. Oftentimes, however, things will come and go by themselves. No need to speed things up or slow them down. What if the only action that is needed is no action at all, just patience?

Be quiet, allow yourself to settle. Breathe. Out of the silence, what needs to be done, what needs to be known will emerge. Listen. Be curious. Explore simply by being aware. Listen to your fears, listen to what draws you, what repels you. Listen to your resistance. Allow these experiences into your consciousness, into your gut. If it is right for letting go to happen, letting go will happen. It may not happen on your time schedule, but it will happen. Trying to push change brings on resistance. Allowing brings on a softening. Softening allows change to happen on its own. As soon as we try for change or pursue a fixed idea of outcome, we are out of the present, away from what is actually happening.

Patience. When the apples on our backyard apple tree are not ripe, they are difficult to pull from the branches. And if we bite into them, they are hard and taste sour. However, if we have the patience to let be and wait until they become ripe, they are easily plucked from the branch, and the flavor is perfection.

All Is Borrowed

Letting go would be easier if you truly understood this...there is nothing to let go of, because there is nothing you have. Nothing is actually yours—the things, the people, the pets, even your body, even your experiences—you don't own them. They share their moments with you for a period of time, long or short, then they disappear...or you do. Either way, all is borrowed, nothing is owned. Understanding this makes letting go easier. Then, when you let go, you let go of the wind.

Letting Go Of Expectations

Very rarely do things turn out as planned. We can have a great vision, do our research, make all our preparations, execute perfectly, yet that will only increase the probability that we will get the result that we had hoped for. There always exists some factor that is out of our control, an event, an illness, traffic jam, flat tire, or change in weather which comes out of left field, that can muck up the outcome. Sometimes the only thing you can do when your expectations are dashed, is to let go and laugh alongside God.

It's common for us to have the illusion that we are in control, that if we do the right things, our expectations will be fulfilled. While it's important to take the right steps and cover the bases in order to get the results we want, it's also important to let go of expectations. Expectations are of the future, life is in the now. The more our mind dwells in the future, the less we are able to be in the present. The more effective we are in this present moment, the better our next moment will be. So, do the right things and trust that all will turn out the way God ordains.

Sometimes, when things don't work out the way we planned, it turns out even better than we expected. Years ago, a friend and I had been looking forward to sitting together at my roommate's birthday party at an Italian

If you want to make God laugh, tell Him about your plans.

Woody Allen

restaurant. As we were filing into the seats at the long table, I hesitated a moment. Just then, someone darted ahead of me and sat next to her. She and I shrugged our shoulders in disappointment as I was forced to turn right instead of left. I ended up seated at the end of the table beside an attractive woman I had seen before but didn't know. We began a wonderful conversation and were so engaged that, for the whole night, we were completely unaware of anyone else at the table. Two months later we were married. The woman was Alice. That moment of hesitation that forced me to turn right instead of left, transformed both our lives.

Letting Go Of The Belief That We Cannot Make A Difference

"We're old, we're out of date, nobody is interested in what we have to say or what we do." This type of thinking is not uncommon with elders. But to believe this is to fall into a sense of uselessness. We may not be in a position to change the world, but we can certainly change the experiences of those around us.

On vacation awhile ago, Alice was busy for a few hours and I found myself walking around the tourist section of town. I entered the storefronts of several businesses. In the first one, I commented to the proprietress of the spiritual bookstore how beautiful and serene was the atmosphere she created and how peaceful I felt being there. She couldn't stop smiling. Next door was a skate board shop. I was taken with the young, heavily tattooed proprietor's gigantic collection of plastic super heroes on shelves that lined the walls. I asked permission to photograph it. His chest swelled with pride. Down the block was an artist's gallery/studio. I complemented the artist on her current work that rested on an easel. I had the nerve to make a suggestion for a small change that would greatly improve her painting. She did make the change, and later sent a copy of the altered painting along with her thanks. Next door was an art workshop for mentally and emotionally challenged adults. When I purchased one of Cody's small clay sculptures, the teacher glowed with the knowledge that he would feel so proud when he received the money, knowing that someone appreciated his work.

Small interactions, maybe not earth shaking, but they probably made a difference in these people's day, or week, or maybe even influenced their positive sense of self. These short connections certainly made an impact on me, so much so that I'm writing about it now.

Letting Go Of Safety And Certainty

Our friend Michael is in his late seventies. He loves to travel and has done so all his life. He left home at seventeen with a backpack and a few dollars in his wallet and he traveled the world. Now, unless he has a firm destination, he will only purchase a one-way ticket. If he can, he leaves things open because he never knows what unplanned adventure lies ahead.

Many of us elders, as we've grown older, have gotten allergic to uncertainty. We want to be comfortable and safe. Spontaneity is uncertain, so we leave nothing to chance. We plan in detail what the next week, or day, or hour will be. Because of our planning we're rarely surprised.

Life is an adventure. Part of the excitement of adventure is that there is a touch of fear. Adventure requires us to let go of the known and step out when we don't have everything locked down and our safety net is not securely in place. That can be fearful, but it can be exciting as hell.

Letting Go Of Yesterday

Evening. The sun sets. The day ends. We fall in bed and sleep. All that was, the joys, the traumas, the sorrows, the triumphs, all that is over. No matter if the day was incredibly beautiful, or incredibly disappointing, the beauty is gone, the disappointment is gone. Whatever was that came – allow it to go. Yes, the beauty of yesterday is part of us, the disappointment too. But our job now is not to be caught up in savoring the beauty of past, or grieving our disappointing losses. Our job is to let go of the old, make space to welcome in the new.

Dawn. As the sun rises in the East, a new day has arrived and is awaiting for us to live it. So, throw off the covers, pee, wash your face, brush your teeth, get dressed and show up. Show up as a newborn. Open yourself to take in the new day's experiences as if never experienced before. You've just been given a gift of 24 hours. Receive it.

Go forth into this fragile, blessed world we share, with laughter and tears at the ready. Love, work, enjoy. Hold on for dear life. And then, when the time comes, let go. Let go for dear life.

ENDINGS

The day we are born is the day we begin to die. It's only a matter of time.

Grandpa Semu Huate, Native American Chumash elder

In each life there are two lives, and the second one begins
when we realize we only have one.

Attributed to Confucius

Letting Go Of Life

OF ALL THAT IS DIFFICULT to let go of, letting go of our life is probably the most inconceivable to think about. One moment, to be breathing, alive, and awake, and the next, to be a stone cold slab of dead meat. It's mind-boggling to think about the ending of our life. One breath away. All the experiences we've had, all the feelings we've felt, the love, the hate, the jealousy, the gratitude, it all evaporates at the moment of death. As the proverb says, "When an old person dies, a library burns."

The "Long Sleep" is fearsome, especially from the perspective of a person in the prime of life. When you're young, you have so much more life ahead of you, so much more to see and experience. The loss of that potential life is sad. However, my experience of many of the elder people I've known at the end of their lives is different. They're old, they lived their life. They've been there, done that,

THE EMBRACE

An old man, as he is being held helpless in the clutches of the GRIM REAPER

and there's not a lot of things they are raring to do. They're tired. And often, very often, the accumulation of aches and pains and debilities of body and mind have added up over time, making for overwhelming physical and mental challenges, challenges they don't have the interest or energy to take on. In that case, they told me it can actually be a relief to pack it up and move on. They welcome the Grim Reaper with open arms.

For many, it's not the fear of death that scares them, it's the prospect of a long, drawn out, painful dying that they fear. Uncertainty, helplessness, expense and indignity might be in store. I questioned myself, and I've asked other people this question, "Would you rather die suddenly, unexpectedly, painlessly in your sleep, taken by a heart attack or stroke. Or would you, at the same age, rather die over a period of two months, with increasing degrees of pain, growing from mild to moderate?" According to my unofficial survey, most people would choose a sudden death in sleep. No pain, no anguish. But I would choose a protracted, moderately painful death. For me, the added time is precious. The pain is worth the chance to bid farewell to those I love and have the opportunity to contemplate my life and prepare for my death. I feel there are important things that need to be said to my loved ones, things that, if not said, would make my passing incomplete.

I love you.
Thank you.
I forgive you.
Please forgive me.
Goodbye.

Beginners

We are all beginners when it comes to death. Each death is a first time, a unique, one of a kind, never previously occurring experience. You can't practice it. When your parent dies, it's your first and last time for you to experience their death. When your best friend dies, it's your first and last time for their death. And when the time comes for you to cease to exist, it will be your first time. You're a beginner.

Longevity

A friend, Anna says, "My mother is 93 years old," and we say, "How wonderful, 93." But is it wonderful? Longevity is overrated, especially if accompanied by infirmity. Who wants to live a long life, with final years full of pain, confusion and loneliness. Not I. Quality of a life is more important than quantity of years. I'd prefer a short life full of excitement and meaning, over a long, boring life. Actually, I'd prefer a long life full of excitement and meaning. I think one of the reasons longevity is valued is that many people are so afraid of dying they want to put it off for as long as possible.

I Watched Many Deaths

When I was a kid, I was witness to hundreds of deaths. There were numerous murders by pistol, or less frequently, by rifle. I watched people die by explosion, or occasionally, by knife or shot by arrow. A few were poisoned. I watched these, in black and white, on the TV or movie screen. At the time, eschewing gore, these were often bloodless deaths. A cowboy, shot off his horse, laying in the arms of his loyal sidekick, breathing a dramatic last breath, a soldier falling back dramatically after being hit by a bullet, a bad guy, justice served, shot by the cops. Very different than the bloody deaths in today's cinema.

These deaths we watched were more like games to us kids, and we played shoot-em-up with our toy six-shooter cap guns. Our back yards and in empty lots in the neighborhood were scenes of murder and mayhem. Death was the centerpiece of our play. We would compete for the most athletic death throes and trade off who would be the killer and who would be killed. After a few seconds of laying still, the dead would immediately rise, and then take their place as the killer. It was all great fun.

I must have been around five or six when I went with my mom and dad to the local movie theater to see the 1948 movie, *I Remember Mamma*, "a heartwarming family drama." It was heart warming until there came an extended death scene of old Uncle Chris, played by Oscar Homolka. My young mind couldn't comprehend what was going on, but I knew it was significant, and I knew it was sad. I replayed that scene in my imagination for years. That movie scene was my first conceptualization of death until a few years later, when my grandfather died, and I experienced the deep sense of sadness and loss from a real death.

An image we have of death, The Grim Reaper, the harvester of souls, is a tall, gaunt, silent figure, black cloak, skeletal hands holding a scythe. He waits for us at the end of our life, when he will usher us from this world into the next. But we should remember that we don't meet him only at the end of our days. He is a fellow traveler who accompanies us silently every day of our lives.

We can't know if our days will be many or few, but we should bear in mind that this visage of death is with us every step. If we remember his imminent presence, we will more easily celebrate being alive and be grateful we haven't met him on this day. That remembrance, and the celebration and gratitude for another day, will prompt us to make our tomorrow richer and more full.

They say that age kills the fire inside of a man, and when he hears death coming, he opens the door and says, "Come in, give me rest." That is a bunch of lies. I've got enough life in me to devour the world, so I fight.

Zorba, in Nikos Kazantzki's Zorba the Greek.

Sadness

The digital clock in the bedroom shows 4:32 am and I can't sleep. I've been feeling the weight of sadness for the past week, which is not like me. The world news is getting me down, but I think my sadness is more personal. My thoughts are about endings.

The cat is up and wants out. He and I enjoy a minute of petting and neck scratching before I open the door to let Roameo out into the brisk early morning air. There's been lots of coyote activity this week, howling and feathers from the neighbors unlucky chickens. I hope he'll be OK. I go to the kitchen to heat some water for tea. Beautiful, inviting country kitchen we created. I return with the cup to the bedroom and see Alice's peaceful, slumbering form in the darkened room, hear her breathing. The sound of her breath and the rise and fall of the covers is reassuring. My heart fills with love. Such sweet moments.

The sadness comes when I realize that these moments are transitory. There will be a time when the cat will not be. Our kitchen, our house will not be. Alice and I will not be. Endings, especially when our life has been so comfortable and sweet, are not easy.

We have been blessed with good health so far, but there are signs of inevitable breakdown. Alice's shoulder and hand. My hearing, cataracts and neuropathy. Both our failing memories. It's possible that one or both of us can sail through to a very old age healthy and hardy, but it's not probable. Chances are that, sooner or later, we will be entering the most difficult period of our lives. I'm feeling the weight of potential challenges that may make our coming years painful. Not the least challenge is our inevitable separation by death. The price of love. Thinking on these things, I'm sad. I'm afraid.

Alice has awakened and made her way to the bathroom to pee. She returns to bed and snuggles in under the covers while I run my fingers through her hair, kiss her on the forehead and whisper, "I love you." Death is far away. There is only this moment and it is so, so beautiful.

Arrivals/Departures

Envision in your mind's eye a gigantic airport terminal, with many gates for passengers arriving and departing. The arrival gates are for travelers coming in from different countries, China, Tonga, Uruguay, etc. The departures all exit from one enormous gate. No matter from where they arrive, they depart to the same destination.

This airport is for those arriving by being born, and for those departing by dying. And it's very busy. The arrival gates are full of noise and activity. Passengers of every ethnicity are arriving and are met with joyful greetings. Every day there are 401,300 babies born in the world. The gate for departure is busy too, but quiet and somber. Every day there are 158,685 deaths. That's 6,611 per hour, 110 per minute, almost 2 per second.

Imagine that you are in the cavernous departure terminal. Imagine yourself surrounded by the milling hoard of the one-hundred and fifty-eight plus thousand dead. Mostly they're old, but some are young, some newborn. You are merely one of those many thousands. You had said your goodbyes to loved ones. Stripped of name, lost, confused, overwhelmed, no identity. No longer rich, credentialed, honored, loved. Nobody special. How humbling.

The fact that you have at one time come to the arrival terminal means that, at some point in the future, you must inevitably book your departure. You never know the date and time you will be leaving. You have an open ticket.

How Do I Want My Last Days To Be Like? Or How To Die Well

Alice and I used to belong to an entertainment troupe that would go around to assisted-living facilities where we sang and danced and played music for those of our parent's generation in order to brighten the resident's day. We weren't very good, but that didn't matter much. Their eyesight and hearing wasn't very good either. We felt some of them really appreciated us.

In many of the facilities, the resident's days were beyond boring, spent lying in bed or sitting around staring apathetically at the TV set. No interest, no feeling, no hope. They were fed, washed, diapers changed, but most of them were the living dead, just biding their time, waiting to die, many hoping it would happen soon. The 45 minutes we spent singing and playing the old songs

Do not go gentle into the good night,
Old age should burn and rage
at close of day;
Rage, rage against the dying of the light.

Dylan Thomas,
20th Century Welsh poet

from their past and dancing the Charleston and Lindy Hop, was at least 45 minutes of momentary respite from endless monotony. For me it was depressing, part of the depression being that I saw the possibility of me living like this some time in the future. I couldn't wait to get away to the fresh air.

This is not the way I want to spend my last days. Neither would I want to "burn and rage against the close of day." To fight against death doesn't appeal to me.

If I had my choice, and to a degree, I believe I do, I would want to "die well." I would want to be engaged, in my last days, curious, heart-full, spiritually uplifted, loving. I would want to feel that I had lived the life I was meant to live and that I had done it with integrity and soul, and that I had no regrets or incompleteness. With that, I could welcome death.

Of course, there are no guarantees that I would be able to pull this off. At my end, I might be dealing with great physical pain, panic, sorrow, emotional upheaval, confusion, and these might be what would occupy my consciousness in my final days. But I know that if I don't do the work of growing emotionally and spiritually now, there is little chance it will happen spontaneously at the ebbing days of my life or on my deathbed.

The end of life is not an easy time. But it is not totally out of my control. I believe the way I am choosing to live my life now will greatly influence the way I experience my last days. If I make it my mission to be engaged, curious, heart-full, spiritually uplifted and loving, right now, there's a chance I will retain at least some of these qualities at the end portion of my life, maybe even at my last breath. Then I wouldn't have to burn and rage at the close of day, but could slip away contentedly.

Truth is, we cannot design how our death will be. It will happen when, where and how it will happen. There is a good chance it won't go according to plan. Death can be messy, undignified. The only latitude we have is how we face what happens. And the way we live our life now can help influence the way we face our final day. Or maybe not. It's well worth a try.

Surrendering To Death

Dennis, Alice's ex-husband, knew that death was closing in on him. It came time for him to fill out an Advance Directive, a form that tells others your end of life choices. There is a provision about decisions to withdraw treatment in case you would not regain consciousness. Dennis chose to have medical services keep him alive, even if he was in a persistent vegetative state, with no chance of survival if life support was withdrawn. His son and daughter tried to get him to change his mind, to no avail, so fearful was he of dying.

In our culture, death is the enemy. It's war. Physicians are soldiers, with medications and surgery and complicated electronic instruments as their weapons. Survival is winning the war. Death is defeat. It's a costly battle. Costs for care in the last few months of life eat up the lion's share of health care expenses for elders in the US, many billions of dollars to fight the losing war with death.

Yet, there is a time to surrender, there is a time to die. In some cultures, when a person got old and felt they would be a burden on their family, they would wander off

To everything there is a season, and a time to every purpose under the heaven: A time to be born, and a time to die; the time to plant, and a time to pluck up that which is planted.

Ecclesiastes 3, King James Version

104

into the wilds to die or commit suicide with medical supervision. In America, with our death aversion, physician assisted suicide is legal in only a handful of states.

I was very touched, as were many Baby Boomers, when, in the sixties, I read the influential, back-to-the-land book by Helen and Scott Nearing, titled, *Living The Good Life.* Helen and Scott, in their later years, moved to the country, built their stone house by hand and advocated a simple existence on the land. Approaching his one hundredth birthday, still relatively healthy, Scott decided he had lived enough of life. He decided to stop eating and died eighteen days after his birthday. He surrendered his life and chose a conscious death.

Surrendering to death is not giving up on life. It is not fleeing in terror if you see death approaching. Not, out of fear, fighting and grabbing at every straw in order to preserve another minute, another breath. Surrendering is opening to the Reaper of Souls as you see his unavoidable approach.

Musical Chairs

You've probably played the children's game, musical chairs. A group of chairs are set up in a line, back to back, say 10 chairs. Eleven kids are chosen to circle around the chairs while music is playing. No one knows when, but the music stops suddenly and there is a mad rush to sit in the chairs. Ten chairs will be occupied. There is one person who will be left without a seat. That person is "out." Next round, a chair will be taken away and there will be nine chairs and ten kids. And another one "out."

Our life is a game of musical chairs. We don't know when the music will stop and we will be "out" and the game will be over for us. We've all had friends and family who were "out." It's a blessing to be able to enjoy the game of life while you're still "in."

In the long term, waking up every day and expecting to live is a demonstrable error...sooner or later.

Stephen Jenkinson

A Macabre Reminder

When we were in Rome, we visited the chapel in Cimitero dei Cappuccini, the cemetery of the Capuchin monks. It was an amazing place. Gallery after gallery, placed in artful, symmetrical patterns all over the ceilings and walls, were the skulls and bones of monks who had died over a period of five centuries. What a reminder it must have been for the monks who lived, worked and prayed in the monastery, to know that, in time, their bones would be part of the decor.

As we left the chapel, we spied a small sign on a table by the door. A stark reminder for the visitors. In several languages, it read, "As you are now, we once were. As we are now, so will you be."

Bones

In one of Shakespeare's most quoted (and misquoted) lines, Hamlet holds the skull of his father's jester in his hand and says, "Alas, poor Yorick! I knew him well."

There's something very powerful about being in the presence of human bones—seeing them, touching them, contemplating them. My brother, a chiropractor, has a human skull with connected spinal column on a stand in his office, ostensibly to illustrate to his patients where back problems can arise. I have been drawn to it every time I visited. Steve knew a little bit about her origin…yes, the bones were from a female. She was a small woman, from China, probably late middle-aged when she died. Once, she was someone's baby, a teenager, possibly a wife, a mother, and finally, an old woman. She had probably lived and loved, hoped, worked, despaired, enjoyed her body, and then sickened and died…her life path not too different from what mine has been and what my future will be.

And there she is now, gathering dust in the corner of an office in Southern California. Bet she never expected that.

A Joyful/Sad Wedding

Our friend David was a famous stage and screen director. He had been married and divorced numerous times, as often happens to those in "The Business." And now that he was old, in his early eighties, he gave up on love and resigned himself to live alone in his beautiful house at the end of a country lane in our village of Ojai. Our dear friend Kelly, too, even though much younger, had despaired of ever finding true love. Yet they met, and their love grew. Surprising themselves, us, and everyone around them, their love blossomed into the love that they had both hoped for.

They lived together in joy and harmony for almost two years, and then, not unexpectedly given the disparity in their ages, David was handed a death sentence. Cancer of the pancreas. David rapidly declined and in weakened condition, was taken by ambulance to the local hospital and given just days to live. It was from the hospital bed that David expressed his dying wish. He wanted Kelly to be his wife.

It was Saturday afternoon. Where could we find a rare official who possessed proper certification and could draw up and issue a marriage license and legally perform the ceremony? After many, many phone calls, most unanswered, a few "sorry, can't help" responses, we finally located an official, at a party with his wife, who was able to come and issue the license and conduct the marriage ceremony. Late in the evening they arrived in their party clothes and filled out the papers that would make David and Kelly man and wife.

It was there in the hospital, surrounded by a few friends and hospital staff, that David and Kelly were married. Kelly held a bouquet of flowers picked from the hospital grounds. David beamed an ear-to-ear smile with elation he hadn't felt for months. Tears of joy mixed with tears of sadness.

Their time together as a married couple was brief. A few days later, David lapsed into a coma and died, husband to the woman who had revived his heart.

Obituaries

When we had the local newspaper delivered, I would often read the obituary section. Often the obit was accompanied by a picture, usually one taken decades previously. I found it fascinating to learn about the deceased person's life, encapsulated in a few paragraphs. Of course, it would be just the barest details—things like their age or birth date, parents names, spouse, children, hobbies, religious affiliation, occupation, where they lived, details of the time and location of the celebration of life and where to send donations. In those scant few sentences was a flesh and blood life lived. What was left out of the column were their dreams, their hopes, their failures, their adventures? Who did they love? How did they love them? What about themselves were they hiding that they didn't want others to know?

What usually caught my eye was how old those people were when they died. Some were children, some had made it alive for over a century. I compared their age to mine. How old will I be when I pass away? What will my obituary say? Will there be someone reading my obituary and wondering about my life?

Making Out Our Wills, Buying Cremation Plans

What a strange but rewarding experience, to sit together with our lawyer in his office and fill out our wills. A couple of hours of deciding what goes to who, tax strategies, DNRs, HIPPAA Forms, Advance Directives, financial and health Powers of Attorney. All businesslike, rational, intellectual discussion, yet these very papers we have affixed our signatures to will one day be held and read by our heirs in this very office and will guide how our estate will be divided after we're dead. Weird to think about, isn't it?

Similar feelings arose when purchasing plans for our cremation. Yes, we're going to be burnt. A neatly dressed, soft talking, very considerate salesman helped us. His

> Always go to other people's funerals, otherwise they won't come to yours.
>
> Yogi Berra

company offered convenient pickup of the bodies (our bodies), and various plans, various styles of urns that hold the ashes (our ashes), various ceremonies, various legal considerations. Actually, it doesn't matter. Once our living spirit leaves, we believe that we're just a dead carcass. At least we won't be subject to embalming chemicals, lipstick and pink makeup to hide the blue tinge of dead skin, perfume to cover the stench, and the hassle and expense of being placed inside a casket and planted six feet underground.

It's rewarding to take care of business that will ease the minds of our children during a difficult time. It's also a valuable experience for us to digest the reality of the eventual ending of our lives. And for us to work through such an emotionally taxing procedure with equanimity is a win for us.

A Good Day To Die

As the Indian braves are about to attack the wagon train, they were reputed to shout, (in translation), "Today is a good day to die," meaning, prepare yourself to fight to the death, and if death comes, welcome it. Another interpretation to the expression was given by a woman of the Ottawa tribe, which carries a different meaning. "It means we should be ready to die on any given day. We should always be prepared to die, and have no regrets. That's why it's important to begin each day fresh, and not let past problems and present distractions cloud how God wants us to live." (Michael Steltenkamp, Black Elk: Holy Man of the Oglala.)

If we have lived and are living our lives with integrity and kindness, if our conscience is clear, if we have shared what's in our heart with our loved ones, and what's on our mind with those who need to know, if we have settled scores and repaid what was owed, if we have not left important goals undone, or if undone, accepted that it's OK for them to remain undone, then we can be able to leave lightly. Then, today, tomorrow or any day is a good day to die.

Ask yourself the question, "Are you ready to die today?" Don't answer quickly. Think about it. It's a good question.

Riley is dying

My dear friend Riley will be dead in a few days and he is OK with it. He says, "I'm looking forward to the adventure," and he means it. Fortunately, the morphine is managing pain, and he is alert, mind keen as ever, and he has retained his wry sense of humor. But he is fading away. He sleeps a lot, is losing weight and is confined to his bed now. No matter. Riley accepts it all. With each loss his body sustains, his mantra is, "Allow, Allow."

Is it possible for someone facing imminent death to be at peace rather than in panic? I didn't think so. Riley had always said that he wasn't afraid of dying, but I never believed him. I told him scornfully, "You'll see when your time comes." Well, his time has come, and he is truly not afraid.

Riley's fearlessness didn't arrive out of the blue. For many years he was engaged in spiritual work, contemplation and meditation. He played with past life regression and this gave him an unshakable "knowing" (rather than just a belief), that there is an afterlife. But more than his prescient experience of future lives, I believe Riley's acceptance of his end of life comes from the way he has lived it. He feels complete. For the most part, he has done in this life what he wanted and needed to do. He's lived an honorable life, enjoyed good friends and family, helped many people who were in need. There is really nothing left for him to accomplish. Very few regrets trouble his sleep. Of course, he is beyond sad about having to leave his beloved wife, Rhoda, his son, Jud, and his grandkids. And of course he is concerned about the heartbreak his passing will create for them. Sadness is part of separation.

Riley is harvesting the fruits of his life now. There are streams of friends, relatives and former clients coming to be with him, say goodbye and wish him well on his journey. The love he sowed he is now reaping. He is basking in the love that is surrounding him, holding court in his bedroom like the King he is. Walking into that room, you can feel the sweet love…from Riley to others, from others back to him. It is palpable. Eastern spiritual traditions say that the end of life is a most auspicious time. Hindus and Buddhists believe that the moments before death determine the next incarnation you take on. If this is so, Riley will have earned a great future.

Riley and I have been close friends for almost four decades. We worked together as co-therapists, collaborated on a book, went on vacations together and enjoyed spirited conversations over delicious meals. But these last few weeks have been the most intimate times we have spent with each other. In this time we've taken hours and shared our lives and dreams, our disappointments and triumphs, our wisdom and foolishness. Barriers down. Hearts open. What a blessing to be able to spend this precious time with Riley. And what a lost opportunity that we were so busy, or so afraid, that we didn't make the space in our schedule, and in our heart, to be wide open the way we are now with each other.

Time becomes more precious when we know it's running out. Now, more than ever, with Riley's imminent passing, that remembrance sticks with me. It reminds me to cherish love. It reminds me to not put off the phone call to the people I care about, to tell them I love them. It reminds me to share my heart with them as if there will be no tomorrow for us.

And for all anyone knows…tomorrow may not be.

A few days after this writing, Riley fell into a final coma and passed on. Fly free Riley.

A Dream

It's been nearly a year since Riley died. I had a dream last night. I was sitting around a table with five or six guys. Riley was there. I reached out and grabbed his hand and told him I loved him. We both cried. I awoke and my eyes were wet with tears.

This body is a vehicle of consciousness, and if you can identify with the consciousness, you can watch this body go like an old car. There goes the fender, there goes the tire, one thing after another—but it's predictable. And then, gradually, the whole thing drops off, and consciousness rejoins consciousness.

Joseph Campbell

Still Here?

I wake up early this morning. I glance over at Alice laying in bed asleep beside me. Asleep? A moment of panic. I don't see her breathing, hear her breath. My eyes frantically search for any movement in the blanket covering her. None. Is she still here? Then, the tiniest of movement, a slow, gentle rise and fall. Relief!

A Funny Death

Death is usually a sad affair. It's not often that, at the moment of death, a person's family surrounding his deathbed bursts into uncontrollable laughter. It happened with Alice's Uncle Mel.

Mel had a good life. Feisty, affable and well-liked, he was an artist, a man of the sea, an inveterate raconteur. Always with a pipe planted in his mouth, Mel was confident and composed, and he lived life on his own terms. He did life his way.

Mel also had a good death, the kind of death everyone wants. Healthy, vibrant and pain free at nearly 90, he started feeling pains in his heart no more than a week before his death. Not willing to go through complicated medical procedures that had the chance of prolonging his life but a few months or more, he rapidly declined. In his last moments, he lay in coma on his deathbed, surrounded by close family. Breathing the jagged, arrhythmic breath that dying people do, Mel was obviously close to death. Music was playing on the CD player, opera, Mel's favorite. The powerful voice of Pavarotti, singing the iconic Frank Sinatra song, "My Way," was reaching the dramatic finale. Mel's breath weakened, and at the moment, the very moment Pavarotti intoned the final words of the song with a powerful crescendo, "I DID IT MY WAY," Mel drew his last breath.

How dramatic. How appropriate. There was a moment of shocked silence, then we all burst into hysterical laughter. Standing hand-in-hand in a circle around the bed with Mel's body, we all shared our appreciation how Mel had truly done it his way.

First and last stanzas to the song, "My Way," by Claude Francois, et al.

And now the end is near
And so I face the final curtain
My friend, I'll make it clear
I'll state my case, of which I am certain
I've lived a life that's full
I traveled each and every highway
And more, much more
I did it my way
For what is a man, what has he got
If not himself, then he has naught
Not to say the things he truly feels
And not the words of someone who kneels
The record shows I took all the blows
And I did it my way

Saying Goodbye To Dad

The day before my father died I sat at his bedside, holding his hand. His eyes were closed as I leaned forward and slowly spoke into his ear. "You were such a good father to me. Your kindness and generosity made my life so sweet. I watched you and learned to be a good man by following your example. I admire you and I can never repay you. Thank you." Dad let out a breath and his body relaxed. A faint smile played on his lips as he lapsed into a quiet sleep. I felt a powerful sense of completion, as if a very important transmission had just taken place for both of us.

Who's First

We've talked about it. Who will die first? Who will survive? Neither is a good option. And neither is a choice it is up to us to make.

To die first is sad. To miss out on the sweetness of life, the joys of the beauty of sunsets, the mystery of a starry night, meals with friends, snuggling in bed at night. But to be the survivor, to experience these things alone, without the beloved, that too is sad, beyond sad. So much of the enjoyment of life has to do with sharing with each other. But to live alone and wander aimlessly within the emptiness of all the familiar places, a constant reminder of the gigantic part of our life that is missing, is like, again and again, ripping a scab off a wound that is trying to heal. And never will.

So the survivor, the one who outlives the other, is providing a great sacrifice, a great gift to the other. The tears they shed and the emptiness they feel will have spared the other unbearable grief. Spared them from watching the hearse carrying the body away. Spared them from sitting in the front row at the funeral. Spared them from coming home and opening the door to silence. Spared them from going to sleep in an empty bed.

Given a choice, both of us would choose to be the survivor. We choose this not because we are hungry for life, but because, out of love for the other, we would be willing to take on the burden of grieving so the other won't have to.

How We Die

Emmanuel, a disembodied spirit who is reputed to speak through a human person, was asked about dying. He replied that people should not fear dying, because, "It's absolutely SAFE. It's like taking off a tight shoe."

It almost doesn't matter what is the cause of death, all dying tends to follow a general pattern. The process can take forms that vary with each individual. Here's a general outline of how humans die.

114

Weeks before death

Most people who are dying feel tired and want to sleep more. Heart beats with less force and organs receive less oxygen. Less desire for food as stomach and digestive system weakens.

Days before death

Control over breathing starts to fail and become erratic. Many want to sleep more and for longer periods of time. Skin color may change and skin may become paler and more mottled as blood circulation declines. Some may have hallucinations and some may become unconscious.

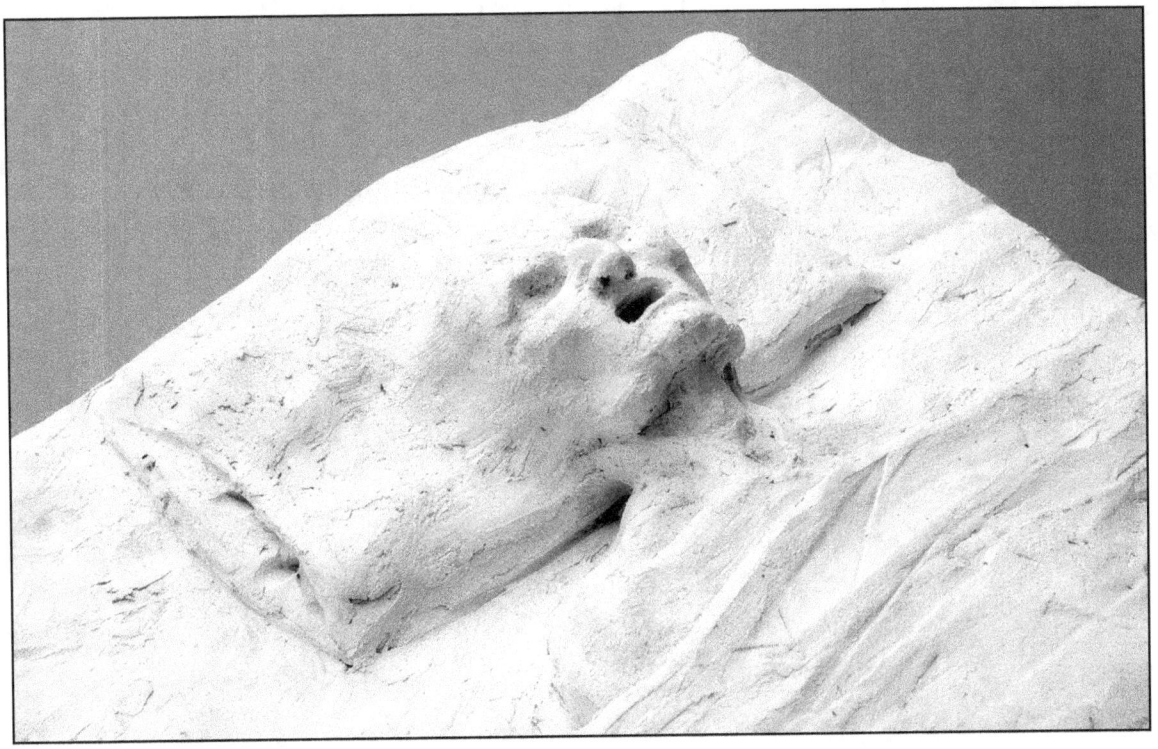

DEATH BED
Dying man in process of dissolving and disappearing into the bed

24 hours before death

Often, a dying person will spend most of their time asleep or unconscious. Blood pressure decreases, difficulty swallowing, less urine output, some loss of bladder and bowel control. Possible restlessness and confusion. Possible short periods of alertness.

Hours

Blood supply declines further, skin cool to the touch. Breathing weak and may stop completely for short periods of time. Gasping, "rattling" breath sound may ensue, due to mucus at back of the throat. Often unconscious. A final out-breath, no in-breath. The moment is often so gentle that those present are unaware that the person has died.

At death

No breath or heartbeat register. Reflexes don't respond to testing. Eyelids may be half-open, pupils fixed. Mouth may fall open. Skin starts to cool, eventually matching surroundings. Body stiffens, starting at face and neck, moving down to the extremities. *Finis.*

You can know all there is to know about death—the physiology, the psychology, the theology—but you can never know what death is like until it is happening to you.

When the Indian saint, Ramana Maharishi was dying, his devotees entreated him, "Please don't go, don't leave us!" He told them, "Don't be silly. Where could I possibly go?"

Advice To Keep In Mind If You Are In The Presence Of Someone You Love Who Has Just Died

"When someone dies, the first thing to do is nothing. Don't run out and call the nurse. Don't pick up the phone. Take a deep breath and be present to the magnitude of the moment.

There is a grace to being at the bedside of someone you love as they make their transition out of this world. At the moment they take their last breath, there's an incredible sacredness in the space. The veil between the world opens.

We know they were going to die, so their being dead is no surprise. It's not a problem to be solved. It's very sad, but it's not cause to panic. Sit at the bedside and just be present to the experience in the room. What's happening for you? What might be happening for them? What other presences might be here that might be supporting them on their way? Tune in to the beauty and magic.

Being present in the moments after death is an incredible gift to yourself. And it's a gift to the person who just died. They're just a hairs-breath away. They are just starting on their journey in the world without a body. If you keep a calm space around their body, and in the room, they're launched in a more beautiful way. It's a service to both sides of the veil."

Sarah Kerr, Death Doula

Alice and I were laying on the bed with Beulah, her mother, as she was dying. Her son, Robbie, was on the floor. We watched, listened, as Beulah's breath became weaker, more irregular. Finally, in a suspended moment, there was no more breath. The spark that animated the Beulah we knew, who laughed and hungered and loved, was forever extinguished.

We were enveloped in silence, deep silence. We had just witnessed a miracle, a sacred moment. No tears. No words. Just silence. We watched in awe as Beulah's face changed. Before our eyes, every wrinkle disappeared. Her skin became like alabaster, smooth, white. Her body gradually cooling.

Here we were. The three of us. Together. Sitting, watching, thinking, feeling. Thoughts, memories coming, thoughts, memories going. Quiet conversation.

A timeless hour or two passed. We washed the body that had been Beulah, and then began the phone calls and noise and busyness that happens after a death.

Goodbye To Life

Part of the sadness of dying is that we must say goodbye, to our body, to our friends and beloveds, to our history, to our life. No physical body will we inhabit. No more seeing beautiful sunsets, no more delicious sensation as we first bite into an apple, no more bliss as the steam rises and hot water pelts our skin in the shower. No love. No looking into the eyes of our beloved, no lively conversations with dear friends, no holding our child in our arms. Our lifetime of memories evaporate. Our face covered in cake frosting at the raucous fifth birthday party, our first kiss, the enchanting vacation in Spain. No emotions. No joy, no sadness, no excitement no hurt, no awe. Gone. Thinking about these precious moments makes me sad for their loss, but also makes me deeply appreciate having had these wonderful experiences and living this wonderful life I've lived so far.

Assume that you are fully awake and of clear awareness at the end of your life, about to take your last breath, "What would you want to feel and say as you are about to enter into the unknown?" Think about it.

My answer to this question came to me immediately, without thought. It was, "Thank you."

Afterlife

Is there life after death? Is there a heaven? Do ghosts exist? Do we meet our loved ones after we die? Are we greeted by angelic beings?

Beulah saw her husband, Sumner, several times after

On October 5th, 2011, computer guru Steve Jobs died. His last words he uttered were, "Oh Wow, Oh Wow, OH WOW!"

he passed. As real as could be, there he was, standing at the top of the staircase. My dad was mentally present before he died, and yet we watched as he had several conversations with mom, who had died nine months before. We have spoken to several people who have had classic near-death experiences of lights, tunnels, angelic beings and visions of "heaven," meetings with loved ones who had previously died. Researcher Robert Monroe has cataloged thousands of near-death experiences, many with those same phenomenon. Gary Spivey, our psychic friend, speaks to dead people all the time. His clients say that what he hears is often only known by the client and the dead person. He is told by the deceased that heaven is heavenly. That would be nice.

Do people see these phenomena because they desperately want to, or is there some other scientific explanation? Or is there really an afterlife? I don't know. It sure would be neat to meet

THE IMPENETRABLE VEIL
A couple, separated by death, trying, to contact each other.
She is listening, he is trying to peer through the veil

up with Alice after we both pass, or my parents, or any number of people I've loved. We'll have to die to find out.

Parent's Grave Sites. Two Visits

Alice's father, Jack, died at 42, of a sudden heart attack. She was 12 and her brother Robbie was 5. In those days, grieving wasn't as understood or valued, and it was as if Jack disappeared from the family and his absence wasn't mentioned. Parents didn't want to upset their children with talk of death. And Alice didn't want to upset her mother. So there was silence, and a hole in Alice and Robbie's heart that endured, but was ignored.

When Alice was in her late thirties, thoughts of their father began to well up in both she and Robbie's hearts. Their silence broke and they began talking together and remembering Jack. Then, on a whim, as she was driving on an errand and passing the cemetery where Jack was buried, Alice decided to visit his gravesite for the first time since the funeral so many years before. Standing next to Jack's grave on that winter's day, reading the inscription on the headstone, the weight of all those years of silence began to lift, and Alice was able to release her father.

My parents died within months of each other. After their funerals, we never visited their graves. Too raw. Then, ten years after their deaths, Alice and I felt ready to pay our respects. We drove the 70 miles to L.A., entered the cemetery grounds and were given directions by the attendant. The cemetery is immense, sited on rolling hills, with many thousands of graves covering over 35 acres.

We arrived at the area where we had been instructed, and picked our way toward my parent's burial plots. This was not the old style cemetery, with upright grave stones. In-ground plaques marked each grave. At the time, maybe one or two funerals were being held in that whole vast cemetery, and, of course, one of those was taking place right next to my parent's graves. A large carpet had been spread over the area and mourners from the adjacent funeral were sitting in folding chairs over and around mom and dad's final resting place, covering their markers.

We stayed a little while, disappointed, but touched by the sheer irony. We said our goodbyes to my parents from a distance, and headed back to our car.

A Dream

Alice was awakened this morning by the sound of her own whimpering. She was having a dream, a nightmare. In her dream, we were together, having fun in a crowded bar at night. We somehow became separated. She went outside to look for me, but became lost in an unfamiliar urban environment. Entering a dark alley, she was disoriented. Then she heard an ominous low growl. At that point she awakened in a panic. I held her, stroked her hair and told her, "It's alright, I'm here, you're OK now." Dreams like this have been interrupting our sleep lately. Their meaning is not difficult to interpret. We are afraid of being lost to each other by death.

Separation

Alice had been painting a portrait of me. It's a large canvas, 3x5 ft, and my image is larger than life. I'm seated, staring straight into the viewer's

PAINTING OF RICHARD
With unfinished hands

eyes, with a sweet, somewhat goofy smile on my face. There is a lot of love in that painting. Alice had been working on it for a long time. She was hung up on the hands and has resized, reconfigured and repositioned them over and over.

I walked into the studio while Alice was painting. She was standing before the canvas, tears running down her cheeks. I went over to her, put my hand on her shoulder and asked what was wrong. She said, "I'm thinking about if you die before me and I'm looking at this painting, how devastated I will be. Our life is so beautiful now. How painful it will be without you. We are so much a part of each other's lives. To not sleep with you, to not have you open jars. I love these hands I am painting. When I reach out for your hand, it is always there for me. I can't bear a time when your hand won't be there when I reach for it."

Then she told me her irrational fear. "I'm afraid that if I finish the hands in the painting, you'll die. That's why I can't seem to get them right." My portrait still sits in the corner of the studio. Hands unfinished.

I embraced her. I was in my own sad reverie. What if she dies before me? How devastated I will be. Will I be looking at this painting and thinking about this moment, missing the touch of her hand, her sweet smile, the sound of her voice?

Separation will happen. It will be inevitable unless, by some twist of fate, we die together. Meanwhile, here we are in this moment, embracing each other with overflowing love and sadness. Bittersweet. The price of love.

Bittersweet. The bitter taste of sadness of endings, the sweetness of love made sweeter by the reality of an end. I never believed our love could grow stronger. How can there be more than 100%? Yet it has. As Alice and I have grown older and death has drawn closer, that reality of our end has fused our hearts and made our love even more sweet, our relationship even more strong. The price of love is worth paying.

Little Births. Little Deaths

Death is not something that only happens at the end of life. Death is continuously happening. Our life is full of little deaths. In the morning we wake up from sleep—birth, renewal. At night we fall asleep—death ending. The year of the seasons is a little birth and death. The circuit of the hands of the clock, a little birth and death. Begin a project, a birth. The project ends, a death. Each breath we take in, is a little birth, each out-breath, a little death.

Good End

It's 2:53 AM. I'm sitting up in bed, can't sleep, sipping a cup of herbal tea, thinking about endings… mine, Alice's. Dissolution and endings are not fun, not easy. Shiva calls out the best from us. I'm thinking, how shall I approach this dilemma of our impending endings without falling into a depressive funk?

I'm reminded of a talk I listened to recently by a nurse who was a hospice worker. She said that the most frequent complaint of those who were dying was, "I wish I had had the courage to live the life I was meant to live." That's sad. I don't want those words on my lips when I am on my deathbed.

So what shall I do, what shall we all do, so that we live our lives in a way that we'll be satisfied with the time we've spent here on earth? Important question to ask ourselves. The answer that comes to me is simple—do the best you can. Try to be a good person. Be kind. Be helpful. Do your work, whatever it is, with diligence. Find pleasure where you can without hurting others. Be grateful for what comes to you. Nurture your loving heart. Take care of your beautiful body. Don't neglect your spirit. Don't let fear rule your life. And try not to be hard on yourself.

Our life is a gift. The gift of life is time. The time we have is empty. That emptiness gives us the opportunity to fill it with whatever we can. Part of the gift of life is potential for joy, part is the certainty of pain. That's what makes things interesting. Celebrate the joy, don't dwell too much on the pain. If we do this, we'll be OK and not have too many regrets on the day our life comes to an end.

9 Questions About Your Death

*If you knew you had only an hour to live, what would you do, who would you call, what would you tell them?

*If you knew you had only one year to live, how would you spend it?

*If you died today, what would be your greatest regret?

*Looking back at your life, what about yourself would you be most proud?

*Looking back, what changes would you make?

*What actions would you need to be forgiven for? By who?

*Who would you want to forgive? For what?

*What would you want to be remembered for after you died? How would your obituary read?

*What would you like your funeral ceremony to be like?

This chapter and preceding chapters contain sadness. Alice read the writings so far and said, "Too much about loss and death. I'm reading and I got sad and started crying. You've overdone negativity. You're fomenting fear."

She might be right. I might have overdone the painful aspects of aging. But I realized, I'm not just writing for the reader, I'm also writing for myself. The contemplations of these chapters are contemplations I needed for my own deepening.

Awareness of impermanence, passage of time and death is so powerful because it can grab our attention as nothing else can. We get a grave medical diagnosis, suddenly, our world changes. Future is shortened. An immediate reordering of what we consider important takes place. We begin to think about the Big Questions—Who am I? Where am I going? Is there a part of me that survives? How shall I live now? We are able to let go more easily of that which is nonessential. This is all very good. Probably it would have been beneficial if this had occurred before the diagnosis. But…

The point of contemplating impermanence is not to be immersed in sadness, but to feel more alive by grasping how precious every moment of our life is. Reminding ourselves of our impermanence and of our own death can actually be life-affirming. It can open our consciousness to the preciousness of the present moment. It can wake us up to the preciousness of our life. It can deepen our experience of love as nothing else can. This is what I want for myself, and also what I want for you, the reader.

So now, after considering Time, we'll change directions. We'll leave the darker contemplations about the passage of time, and breathing more easily, turn our gaze toward the lightness of love and relationships. Not just "garden variety" loving. We'll be exploring mature love, love and relationships that can stand the test of time.

OLD LOVERS EMBRACING IN BED (BAS RELIEF)

She gently embraces her beloved

126

PART 2.

AGED LOVING

On January 27, 2013, the New York Times printed a wedding announcement between Ada Bryant and Robert Haire, in Hockessen, Delaware. The announcement immediately went viral. The bride was 97, the groom was 86. They met at their retirement community and their relationship developed from friendship to romance over a series of lunch dates in the community dining room. At first, she turned down his proposal of marriage because of the difference in their ages. She later consented after he wrote a series of love sonnets and slipped them under her door. The Times reported that the bride will not be changing her last name.

LOVE IS ESSENTIAL

We are made for loving. If we don't love, we will be like plants without water.

Desmond Tutu

The philosopher's "first principal," according to French philosopher,
Rene Descartes, is, *I Think, Therefore I Am.*

The lover's "first principle," according to me, is, *I Care, Therefore I Am.*

WHAT DO YOU THINK OF when you consider the word "love?"

It's probably one of three things. Most likely, your first thought is of interpersonal love, the strong feelings of affection and acts of generosity toward intimate partners, close family and friends.

You might also think of objects, ideas or activities you are passionate about, things that hold excitement, desire and interest for you. You might have a passion for peanut butter sandwiches, or golf, or feel passion in your work for charities that help find homes for abused animals. Passion is the second form of love.

The third kind of love is sensual, erotic love. Sexual pleasure.

Simplifying, the source of interpersonal love comes mainly from the heart, passionate feelings are sourced predominantly from the mind and gut, and sensual love, though encompassing heart and mind, is chiefly experienced in the body.

There are many other types of love, but these are the three kinds we will be concerned with here. We'll start in this section, laying the groundwork with a general discussion of love, from my perspective, emphasizing how essential love is to the life of a person of any age. We will go on to explore the nature of sensuality and sexuality in old lovers, and finally we'll look at expressions of passion in the elder years. We'll view these three varieties of love through the lens of time, through the lens of the life experiences of men and women who have lived some, been tested, endured the ups and downs of life and relationships, and have ripened through those experiences. Their love has matured through time.

At Heaven's Gate

When you've died and are standing at the entrance to the Pearly Gates of Heaven, questioned about your life by Saint Peter, you probably won't boast to him about all the money you made, or the stuff you owned, or the acclaim you received through all your talent and hard work. You would instead count as your life's greatest accomplishment that you loved well and were well loved in return. That's what will get you past the gates. So love, love the best you can, love everyone you can. Do your work, accomplish your goals, play and enjoy yourself, but make love the center of your life. Embrace the real purpose of your existence. There is nothing more important you can do in your life than to love. This will get you into heaven, and it will make of your life, a heaven on earth.

What Makes Life Worthwhile?

What makes life worthwhile? What gives life meaning and joy? Is it wealth? Does having lots of money make you happy? There are many rich people who are miserable. Is it fame, awards and the admiration of multitudes? Many famous people are miserable. Is it possessions? Exotic cars, mansions, art collections, a trophy wife or husband? Many people who are surrounded by possessions are miserable. Is it sense pleasures? Is it having delicious food, physical comfort, entertainment, lots of sex? Sense pleasure is temporary, and after it ends in satiation, one is left empty, craving more and more.

These things that people pursue in life, though enticing, are ultimately unsatisfying. So, what is it that can bring you lasting joy and fulfillment?

Love. Love makes life worthwhile. Giving love and receiving love. Love is the magic ingredient. Without love, even living in the most comfortable circumstances can be dry and lifeless. But with love, you can endure discomfort and thrive. With love your life will be worthwhile.

> *Basically, when you get to be my age, you'll really measure success in life by how many of the people you want to have love you actually do love you.*
>
> Warren Buffett,
> multibillionaire financial
> investor and philanthropist

Making A Change In The World

The world is in a bad way. There is so much unhappiness. So much conflict. So much greed. So much distrust. So much hate, anger and ill will. People are walled off, separate from each other. They don't care about others, only themselves, and maybe immediate family and friends.

Is there anything each of us can do to relieve some of the suffering in the world? There's a simple answer to this question, so simple that I'm almost embarrassed to state it. But I will, because it's a true answer—the cure for the ills of the world is love.

Burt Bacharach and Hal David knew it when they wrote—

What the world needs now, is love sweet love,
It's the only thing that there's too little of.
What the world needs now, is love sweet love,
No, not just for some, but for everyone.

John Lennon knew it when he wrote—
All you need is love
All you need is love
All you need is love, love
Love is all you need

Simple, but true. Think about this. If, one by one, starting with those close to us, each of us would open our heart a bit more to the other people we connect with, see them with a bit more compassion and understanding, treat them with a bit more kindness and generosity, the effects of that love would spread from person-to-person. Each person would share their single flame of love with those in their circle, and each of the members of the circle would share with their circle. Soon, the one candle flame would grow to become a conflagration. How different our world would be.

Two Ways Of Defining Love

I've written about love. Maybe it's time to define this most elusive concept.

Most people believe love is primarily a feeling, a yearning to be in the presence of those we love, feeling happy and excited when they are with us, missing them when they are not. The dictionary definition of love reflects this feeling aspect, defining love as "an intense feeling of deep affection."

A word that I think can capture this feeling aspect of love is "Cherish." Other similar words— revere, honor, venerate, treasure. The idea here is that the lover holds the ones they care about in their heart as precious. This feeling of the preciousness of those you love is powerful. While it doesn't include action, the feeling can motivate a person to action. The loving feelings you have toward your beloveds are like gas for an engine. The engine is your behavior, the actions you take to express your feelings of love.

While this kind of emotional aspect is a sweet, essential part of love, it is by no means the most important part. I believe the most important part of love is action. It is how you behave toward those you love. You can speak loving words, think loving thoughts, feel loving feelings, but if you do not act in loving ways toward your beloved, your love is not real.

Love is a verb. Love is what you do. For example, love is speaking to your beloveds with respect, being truthful with them, listening attentively to them when they speak, being dependable with them and doing what you say you'll do, refraining from manipulating them, trying to act unselfishly with them. These are all loving acts. Loving acts are love.

Of course, one could perform all sorts of duties for a person, and like a hired helper, have no feelings for them, and it would not be love. For a relationship to be truly loving, the feelings of love must be connected to the loving actions.

Taking into consideration that the dominant aspect of love is behavior, I offer this as a definition of love.

Love is my desire for the well-being of the object of my love and my willingness to commit my time, energy and resources to their safety and happiness.

While this definition leaves out the hearts and flowers, it gets down to the real nitty-gritty of love. If we add the feeling aspect, the *cherishing*, we have a more complete definition and a more expansive experience of love.

Love Resides In The Person Who Is Loving

When we were young, we searched high and low for Mr. Right and Ms. Right, and we felt that when we found them, our life would be perfect. In the past, we thought that we had found them, but after awhile, it turned out that they weren't really "the one," so we continued our search.

The truth is that love doesn't reside in the person we love, no matter if they are the finest human being ever to walk the Earth. Love resides within each of us. The person we love is the target of our love. We are the one who releases the arrow. Their beautiful qualities, their humor, wisdom, physical appeal are what attracts our love, it is the bait, but it is our ability to love that bestows love on that person.

We are the *source* of love. They are the *focus*. Once we truly understand this, we will put less effort in looking to receive love through another person, and more effort in trying to become more love-able, incorporating noble qualities like integrity, generosity, kindness. These are the qualities that will attract love into our life. And these are qualities that makes love want to stay.

Expand What You Consider Love

Feelings of love can come from many quarters—

- I see two baby sparrows peeking over the edge of the nest high in the rafters of our front porch, watch the parents feed them, and feel the warm glow of love.
- I watch an old video of Ricky, my old band mate, playing music with such unbridled joy, I feel love for him. Ricky died five years ago.
- On the bed, Roameo, the cat, is sleeping on his back, so peacefully, so innocently. I look at him and I feel love arising.
- I ease myself down into the hot water of the bathtub, the steam rising. I feel the warm sensation of love blessing my skin.
- I taste the first bite of the peanut butter and jelly sandwich I just expertly prepared. Mmm! I feel love on my tongue.
- I listen, and my spirit soars to the strains of Bach's Brandenburg Concerto. I feel love in the dance of the music.
- I pass by the bathroom door and catch a glimpse of Alice, looking in the mirror, carefully putting on makeup. She turns and smiles at me. I feel love welling up in my heart.

Love is so much wider than the feelings between two people. Actually, it's wider than the feelings between family, friends and all the other usual objects of love. Potential targets for your love occur abundantly in the world and wait for your eyes and tongue and ears and nose and skin to savor. With an open heart and mind, relish what the world offers so generously.

"Relishing" doesn't always happen on its own. Sometimes we have to use our volition to attend to objects of love that appear before us and the feelings of love that are arising. When we focus our attention on the fledgling sparrows, taste of the peanut butter, the sound of the music, the sensation of the hot water, we amplify those experiences and thus have greater access to these diverse, delicious feelings of love.

Such a privilege to be in this body, and, no matter how old and wrinkled it is, to feel love in the many experiences that come to it.

Love Is Always Inclusive

"I want to be loved by you, just you, and nobody else but you." Those were the lyrics of the song Marilyn Monroe sang in the old movie, *Some Like It Hot.* That used to be considered a test of love, if a person was obsessed by you, focused all their attention on you, didn't allow for any other relationships, that was considered true love. But love doesn't work that way. A person cannot love only one person and not care about anyone else. Remember, love resides in the person loving.

I love that Alice's love is inclusive. She spreads her love wide. Alice has an open heart, a big heart that has plenty of room to include her family and friends. She loves our "grand dogs," Bella and Finny. She has a loving orientation, a readiness to feel love for anyone entering her life. And, best of all, she loves me.

Paths To Spiritual Realization

There are many paths to attain spiritual realization that are typically recommended by religious and spiritual traditions. One could study scripture, contemplating the words of wisdom written by wise sages of old. One could dedicate themselves to selfless service, work without ego toward healing mind and body of those in need. One could purify one's body and mind by correct diet, yogic breathing, and physical exercises. One could turn within and meditate to discover their inner source. I've sampled all of these.

The path I find myself on is the path of love, called Bhakti in Sanskrit. I was initiated on that path by my love for my Indian teacher, then by my love for Alice. It's such an easy and sweet and simple path. Just love. Just be kind. Just do what I can to make those I love feel safe and happy. Just expand the warm heart and loving concern I feel for those close to me so that my love touches everyone I meet, friend or stranger. Just open myself to feel other's love for me. Just open my heart.

A simple, but very powerful practice that can help you open your heart is recommended by Ram Dass. It is an affirmation of your true state of being. Simply wordlessly repeat over and over to yourself, "I am loving awareness, I am loving awareness." Do this on the meditation seat. Do this as you are looking into your child's eyes. Do this in the line waiting for the cashier. Do this while watering the houseplant. It will alter the way you experience your world. It will help you to redefine who you really are.

It's an ongoing process with me. I'm not sure of the way it works, but I think it has something to do with letting go of judgements about people and about myself. As I am able to let go of my internal voice of criticism, I am more able to see, with eyes of compassion, the innate goodness, the child innocence of even those I disagree with or who are causing harm. And of course, letting go of harsh judgments toward myself allows me to see, with loving awareness, my own innate goodness, my own innocence.

Heart Over Mind

I came across a poem/song/prayer in the Bhakti tradition that was translated from the original Hindi. It blew my mind. Completely! It asks to throw away so much of what I, and the culture I was raised in, consider valuable and essential. It didn't make sense to me when I first read it. Yet, when I read it again, and then, again, I realized, this is what I truly want. Here it is.

Make Me a Person Without Intellect
Oh Lord, make me a person without intellect, devoid of intellect.
Take away all my power of reasoning, cleverness, knowledge and wisdom.
Take away all traces of education, culture, and the pomp of the modern world.
Take away my learning, wealth and arrogance.
Oh God, take away all my pride. Make me get rid of false morality and petty rules.
Bestow on me the gift of simplicity.
I don't want worldly enjoyment or yoga. Nor honor and prestige.
Make me as simple as a village dog. As humble as a blade of grass.
Fill up my heart instead with love and faith; Give me the gift of love.
Drown my individuality in the ocean of love,
And destroy my name and identity.

Think about it. What do you consider most valuable? Would you trade the intellectual power of your mind in order to have the indescribable joy of a heart filled with love?

We Become What We Worship

There are no atheists. We all worship something. Some of us worship money. Some worship our and other's physical beauty. Some of us worship our possessions. Some of us worship our intellect. Some worship gaining power and control over others.

I submit that we become what we worship, that day-by-day, we become more deeply embroiled in those things that we consider all-important. Our life eventually centers about those things, to the exclusion of others. Therefore, I suggest you place great care and importance in what you choose to worship. Be acutely aware of where your devotion will lead you. The unrestrained reverence for money, physical beauty and the other things I've listed above can lead to unhappiness, feeling lost, deadness. Worshipping these can lead to greed, and fear, and loss of soul.

So, let me suggest that, at least as part of your supplication, you worship love. If you hold reverence for love, valuing the importance of love in your everyday life and giving your loving generosity to others and receiving other's love in return, your life will be full with happiness.

Love Is A Magnet

When Alice and I met and fell in love, I was involved in my career, working in a psychiatric hospital. I had played drums professionally for awhile, but those days were long behind me. I had always been artistic, but hadn't touched art materials for decades. Alice had also enjoyed drawing and painting in the past, but hadn't drawn or painted for many years.

Our love immediately created a tremendous infusion of energy. Alice began helping me with the community college courses I was teaching and soon we were teaching weekend workshops together. We created new programs for the psychiatric hospital. Alice started taking art classes, and shortly was producing beautiful portraits. She enrolled me, without my knowledge, in a sculpture class. I took to clay and started crafting figure after figure. Jason, my stepson, expressed interest in playing drums, so I bought him a used drum set from a thrift store. He soon lost interest, but I started playing again, and got in touch with my old musician buddies and began gigging around town. Our love was the spark of energy behind all this creative activity.

Our love also had a strong effect on the whole of our lives. I had been somewhat withdrawn from my family, but soon we were visiting parents and brothers, aunts and uncles and various other relatives on both sides. Alice's family became my family. Our coming together brought our two groups of friends together, and we soon developed a wonderful social life, cross-pollinating our various friendships.

The love we share has infiltrated our life and affected our ideals, our health, our home. This energy of love acts like a magnet...it attracts and pulls in joy and creativity and healing. Love attracts love.

"Businessmen's" Love

We live in a society that operates out of reciprocation: you do something for me, I'll do something for you. You scratch my back, I'll scratch yours. That's how most of us do love—like a business deal. We give in proportion to what we expect to receive. We aim for equality. If we are giving too much, we feel we have been cheated. If we have given too little, we feel like we have cheated, or have taken advantage of the other person. Our eyes are always on the balance sheet. Our focus is on creating a deal so everyone is satisfied.

I propose that this businessman's love, with its focus on the balance sheet, is not real love. Real love is about wanting the other persons in your life to be happy. It's about filling their need. It's about enjoying their delight when they receive your gift. With love like this, your reward is feeling their happiness. And when you love this way, other people automatically want to make you happy. Their gift is giving back to you.

Several birthdays ago, as a birthday gift to herself, Alice went out and bought me a beautiful musical instrument she had known I had been lusting after for a long time. She enjoyed surprising me with this gift for her birthday far more than anything she could have received from me. That is an example of real love.

Creating Love

Years ago, Roameo the cat came to us as a kitten from the neighbor's property. The neighbors had left for an extended vacation and the person caring for their property would simply fill up his food and water bowls and leave. Roameo was an affable kitten and liked company. Even though we didn't feed him, he would come and hang around us. When the neighbors returned, they couldn't get him to stay at their property, so they finally told us, "he's your cat."

Roameo became ours, and we became his. We poured love into him, gave him the best, healthiest cat food we could find, constantly gave him gentle, loving belly rubs, made sure to let him out of the house at first indication that he was ready for his morning constitutional. There wasn't a moment that Roameo didn't feel safe and cared for. He absorbed the love we gave him, and he returned it with loving appreciation.

This is the way, the only way love is created—by expressing love. Each of us, by the way we treat others, are the creators of love, or the creators of distance. It's up to us.

ROAMEO THE CAT

Our Engagement

Less than two months after we met and fell in love, Alice and I took a car trip to San Francisco. We stopped on the way, and Alice admired the ring I was wearing. This gold ring with a yellow sapphire held tremendous sentimental value for me, more precious than any possession I owned. Without a thought, I asked her if she would like to have it. Alice excitedly said, "YES," and put out both her hands for me to place the ring on any finger I chose. After a moment's hesitation, I slipped it on the third finger of her left hand, her marriage finger. That was our engagement.

When you feel love so deep in your bones, you KNOW. There are no questions in your mind, no hesitation. Your heart knows.

Attention

When we care about people, we are interested in them. We want to make sure they are OK, that they are safe, comfortable, that their feelings are seen, their needs being met. Many times, people, even our intimate partners, are not "open books." So we must pay attention to them. We must use our senses, our eyes to watch them for subtle cues, like posture and facial expression, our ears to listen for unexpressed feelings beneath their words, cues like pauses and changes in tone. We attend to our "gut feelings," look inside ourself and rely on our intuition to sense what is going on with them. This is all part of love. To love a person is to know them. To know them, we must attend to them.

Human beings are sensitive to each other in ways far beyond what we can understand with our mind. Alice and I were in a rural village in Turkey, standing on the street, watching a man with his dancing bear. Yes! A dancing bear! A group of young women were watching us from their second-story window and invited us to their apartment. As we were sitting, conversing with them in broken English, two of the women took out fans and started furiously fanning Alice. She was confused, until, half a minute later, Alice felt a hot flash coming on. (She was beginning menopause at the time.) The

141

women were attentive to Alice and must have noticed changes in her skin and her face. They were aware of her coming hot flash even before Alice was. They paid attention.

Protection

Those we care about are precious to us. Naturally, we desire to protect those we love. As part of our traditional Hindu wedding ceremony, I placed a *mongalsutra* around Alice's neck. This was a necklace that indicates her marital status. It is a sacred thread with beads and a topaz stone. By wearing this necklace, Alice protects me from all harm. She never takes it off.

In another part of the ceremony, *Saptapadi*, I held her hand and supported Alice as she put her toe in seven small piles of rice that were placed in a circle. This was my vow to support her throughout all the stages of her life, and to protect her from all future obstacles.

These vows to support and protect each other remain alive within us. The vows are an expression of our love for each other.

Self Love, And Lack Thereof

We cannot love and appreciate others without loving and appreciating ourselves. I had a conversation with a friend this morning. She's a beautiful woman, vital, intelligent, creative, in her mid-fifties, deeply involved in international work she developed that has the potential for changing thousands of lives. We were waxing philosophical and were discussing the purpose of human life. She felt that each of us were put on Earth to expand our consciousness. That felt a bit too cerebral to me. I gave her my spiel about love being the reason for living. She realized the truth in that, and started feeling sad. Tears began running down her cheeks. Reflecting on her life, she was feeling lonely. There was no one in her life at this time who loved her and who she could love.

Looking at her work, even though it would be of great benefit, she realized that some of why she was working to create her programs was that she needed to be loved, accepted, appreciated. It could not happen for her because, no matter how much she was loved and celebrated by others, (and she was) she could never get enough love to overcome her deep seated self-rejection. She wanted love in her life and was trying desperately to earn it through her work. But she was unable to give love to herself because she didn't feel she deserved it. In her mind, she was unlovable.

I didn't know what to say. There was nothing I could tell her. I looked down at my hands, remaining silent, feeling her sadness. And I was also feeling myself in her. This book I am writing, some of my motivation is about my wanting to be of service, but, like her, how much is about wanting to be appreciated, to be recognized for how smart I am, how wise? And how much of that approval seeking is due to a sense that I am not worthy of being loved because I am lacking love for myself?

Rapper Snoop Dogg had none of that. In his Hollywood Walk Of Fame speech, upon receiving his star, he said, in part, "I want to thank me. I want to thank me for believing in me. I want to thank me for doing all this hard work. I want to thank me for having no days off. I want to thank me for never quitting...I want to thank me for just being me at all times." Now there's a man who loves and appreciates himself, a man who knows his worth.

HELPMATES, BLIND AND CRIPPLED
This sculpture represents how couples can help each other—he is blind but can walk—she is crippled, but can see

143

Listening Is Loving

Charley was my psychology professor in college. We stayed friends for many years until he died. Everybody loved Charley. He was affable, good natured, and had a great sense of humor. But the thing about Charley that made him so loved by so many people was that he was curious, and he listened. When you talked to Charley, and he asked you how you were, he would not be satisfied by the response, "fine." He had to know everything, in detail. And as you were speaking, he listened, and listened, and asked questions. You felt loved around Charley.

Listening, really opening our ears and listening to another person, is an act of love. The love is in the actual listening, not just play acting like you are listening, or impatiently waiting for them to finish, or thinking what brilliant piece of wisdom you are going to impart next. Listening in a loving way is to attempt to absorb as much as you can from the speaker's words and their body language… listening for the truth sometimes hidden behind their words. Put down your book, turn off your computer. Give your full attention to the person who stands before you. A person listened to in this way feels heard, valued, received. They feel loved, because an essential aspect of loving someone is knowing them, and the way we know them is to listen to them. Listening is loving.

Helen Keller, the famous blind and deaf writer from the early part of the last century, was asked, if she could be either deaf or blind, what would she choose? She replied that she would rather be blind, because being deaf cuts one off from human connection.

We have two ears and one mouth so we can listen twice as much as we speak.

Epictetus, Greek Stoic philosopher

Wasted Time?

I think about myself, in middle age before being able to taste real love. Had I wasted those years? I don't think so. I believe I

144

had to take the time to ripen. It could not have happened any other way. Like a piece of fruit on the branch of a tree, still green, unripe, I needed some time and some experiences of imperfect loves, a few of which were uncomfortable, in order for my love to ripen and come to fruition.

There was a catalyst. For me it was Alice. But without the growth that had previously taken place in my heart, Alice, would have been just another woman I met and we would have passed each other by.

Yes, it was unfortunate that I had to wait later in life before tasting the sweetness of pure love. It would have been great if, years earlier, I would have been able to experience that kind of love, but that was not to be. Those years were not wasted. The accumulated experience brought me to a place where I had ripened. I don't regret and feel deep appreciation for the women I loved, however imperfectly. And I am grateful that I have been so blessed as to have all these love-filled years with Alice. Can't complain.

Sharing Love And Power

This quote by Martin Luther King Jr., though focused on social, political and economic change, is perfect for mature relationships, that value compassion, fairness and equality. "One of the greatest problems of history is that the concepts of love and power are usually contrasted as polar opposites. Love is identified with a resignation of power and power with a denial of love. What is needed is a realization that power without love is reckless and abusive and that love without power is sentimental and anaemic."

Lovingkindness And Changing The World

Humans come in many varieties, many colors, many shapes and sizes. We have different skills, different levels of education, different ways of viewing the world. Some of us are rich, some are poor. Some are emotional, some are reserved. Some are kind, some not so kind. No matter how different we are from one another, on some level, we are the same. I may be a peaceful person, but I have within me the seed of a murderer. Given the right circumstances, possibly a credible threat to loved ones, that seed may germinate. I may consider myself intelligent, but there are times when I am capable of extreme stupidity. In this sense, in our potential, we are not so different from one another. If we maintain that understanding of the characteristics we all share, we won't be so quick to judge and condemn another, or feel that we are so much better than them. Nor would we believe that others are so much better than us.

We might, with that understanding, retain a sense of the unity we share with others. We might know, at the deepest level, that we, as fellow humans, are not just bone and meat and gristle, but are composed of soul-stuff. As fellow souls, we deserve to be held in high regard and treated with deepest respect, all of us, even the least of us.

We talk of changing the world through legal means, or through legislation or political action. We are preached to, offered heaven and threatened with eternal damnation. We try to effect change by throwing money at problems. But these alone won't solve the deep seated problems humanity is facing. If we could add an attitude of lovingkindness, this might just be an ingredient that is needed to change minds and hearts. Kindness and respect toward others and toward ourselves is the medicine that is needed to treat the illness of the world.

Kindness and respect toward ourselves? That is key. Without having self-respect and treating ourselves kindly, we won't treat others kindly, nor will we respect them.

The world will not suddenly become a kinder, safer place. It has to begin somewhere. The coming into lovingkindness by one person cannot help but expand from his or her own self, to lovers, family, friends, strangers and eventually, even enemies. Why not have that lovingkindness begin with you?

In Appendix 2, you'll find an ancient Buddhist practice, called Metta, that has been used to help generate lovingkindness. This is a good place to start to put your mature love into action and begin to change the world.

The Advanced Test Of Loving

In the Metta practice I had described in the Appendix, I left out a part that is included in most of the traditional instructions. It is probably the most difficult portion of the practice. That portion includes the intention to wish benefit on strangers and on people who want to do you harm.

Strangers? Does that include the bum on the street corner, stinking drunk and laying in his own urine? Yes, it does. *Enemies?* Does that include the person who is competing for your job and just undercut you with the boss? Yes, it does. To love fully means to extend kindness and goodwill toward everyone, strangers and enemies included.

It's one thing to love friends, family and lovers. But to extend lovingkindness to strangers and enemies is a whole other challenge. Extending lovingkindness, especially to people who wish to do you harm is very different from turning the other cheek when slapped. It's having compassion and understanding and not angrily trying to make them suffer in order to get back at them. It may even entail wishing them peace and happiness. And if you must take actions to protect yourself and others from their bad behavior, do so without malice.

This is a difficult test. I believe that unwillingness to take on the challenge of exhibiting lovingkindness to strangers and enemies may in some way limit the depth of love you will be able to attain with the other people in your life.

All Of Life Is A School For Love

Life is a schoolroom. We're all here as students. Some of us are enrolled in grammar school, some are in high school, some are in college. No matter what grade we're in, whether we know it or not, we are all here to study the same subject. We're here to learn how to love. We're here to learn how to imbue our thoughts, our speech and our actions with loving awareness.

Your training about love isn't limited to romantic relationships. Every person you meet, every experience you have, every triumph, every failure, these are all subjects for study, all part of the curriculum. The people who judge you, who want to hurt you and see you fail, they are your greatest teachers. They are there to teach you strength in the midst of hurt, equilibrium in the midst of blame, compassion in the midst of anger. They are there to offer you the opportunity to deepen and broaden your ability to love. If you could see these infuriating people who want to hurt you and challenging experiences that frustrate you as teachers who have valuable messages for you, you would welcome them with open arms. They are present in your life to teach you love.

Life offers you many tests in the form of relationships. You are tested by the people you hold dear in your life—your parents, your children, your friends. But you are tested most severely by the one who is closest to you—your intimate partner, if you have one. It is they who live with you day by day, who share your bed, and who know you better than anyone. The tests they present to you in everyday interactions allow you to gauge how far you have progressed with learning the course materials— generosity, kindness, empathy, patience and peacefulness. Are you being honest or are you just trying to please? Do you leave a sink full of dirty dishes for your partner, or do you do them yourself? In conflict, do you respond with anger, blame and defensiveness, or with care and understanding? Are you really listening, or is your attention somewhere else? Are you being straightforward, or are you manipulating for your advantage? If you don't pass these tests, you are held back and must repeat the course.

There is no failure in this school. Every test is a learning experience. Even if you are held back and need to repeat the course, it doesn't matter. You still learn, are still moving forward, except in this case, you mostly learn what *not* to do. When you pass, you graduate and obtain your Masters Degree in lovingkindness. You have become a mature, loving adult, and your love-filled life will be the reward for your accomplishment.

It is sobering to remember that your partner is also enrolled in loveschool, also tested. You are the one who administers their tests, and, of course, it is you that presents the most challenging tests for them.

The School For Love isn't only about relationships, it's also about aging, about bringing love and acceptance to yourself and your life as you grow old. Perhaps these are some of the most difficult tests in this school. It is a great challenge to *imbue your thoughts, your speech, and your actions with loving awareness,* all the while dealing with chronic pain, weakness, illness, loneliness and depression in your later years. These are demanding tests that old age asks of you, and they don't get any easier. In fact, the tests from aging become more frequent and more demanding as time goes on.

As difficult as it can be, you can pass the tests of aging. When facing the challenges from growing old, as much as you can, keep your heart open, keep allowing, keep waking up and being present in mind and spirit. Hiding, going unconscious, denying, refusing to address the issues that arise as you age is a sure path to a failing grade. If you look within, embrace your aging, embrace your impermanence and allow the challenges of time to deepen you, you will progress, you will flourish. And you will be accredited with a chance, not a certainty, but a chance, for a fruitful and rewarding old age. Even then, learning never ends. To become a sage is lifelong learning, Your graduation ceremony for the School of Love will be your funeral.

Is it worth it, is it worth the effort to respond with love when it's easier to judge or ignore or retaliate? Is it worth the effort to love and keep your heart open, when inevitable loss is so excruciatingly painful? Is it worth the effort to embrace life even when you are old and ailing? Of course it's worth it. Your life is too important not to show up with your best and highest self at every point while you are still alive and breathing. Even to just have the understanding that you are enrolled in the School For Love is a game-changer. It will allow you to see the tests and challenges that come your way through your aging and your relationships as valuable opportunities. Take these opportunities offered by love and time to practice becoming the wise and loving person you are meant to be.

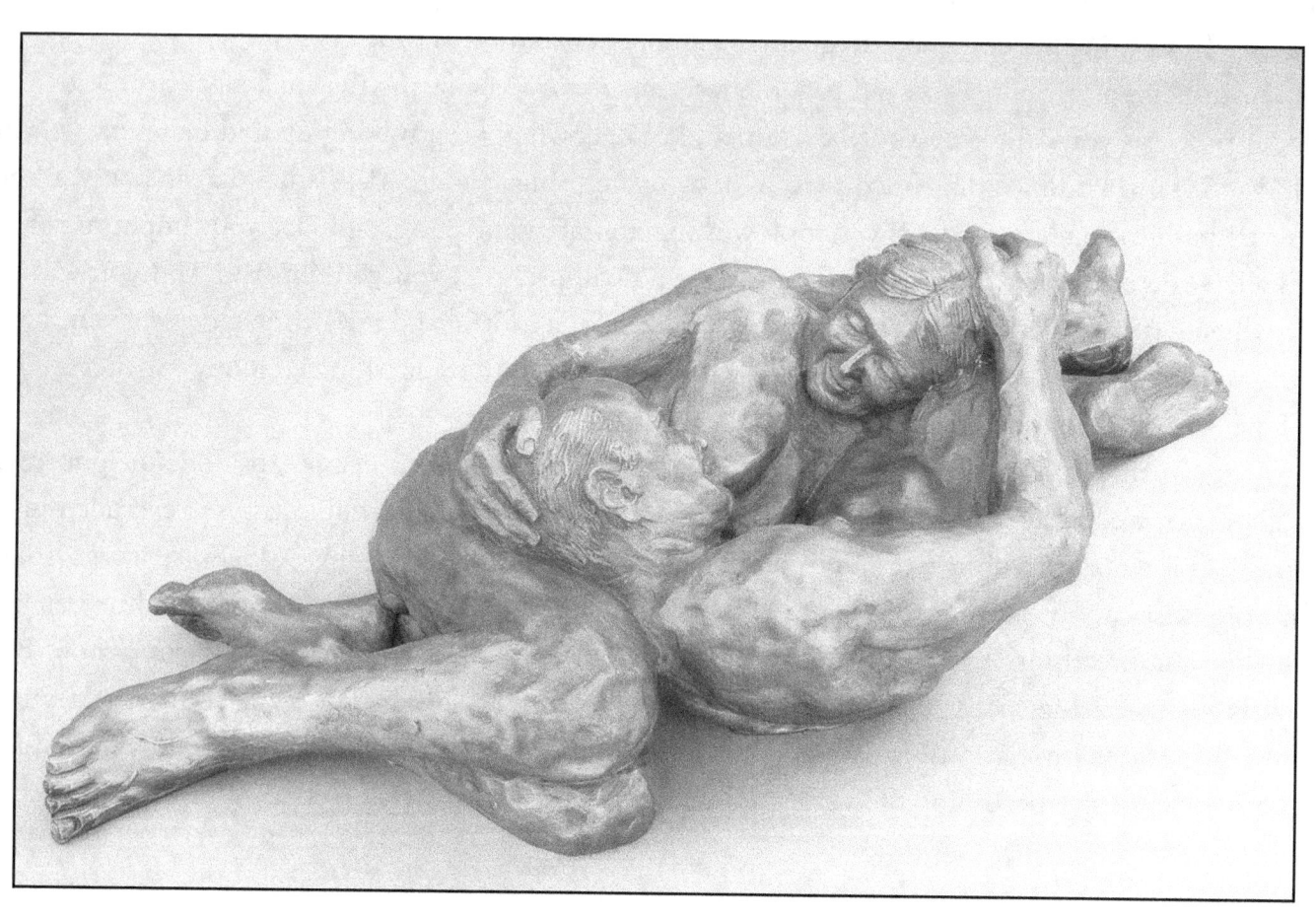

OLD LOVERS RECLINING
Old lovers, laying together and lovingly staring into each other's eyes

SENSUALITY, SEXUALITY AND FADING BEAUTY

SENSUALITY IS ONE of the aspects of love. But we don't usually associate sensuality with elders. When we are young, we see old couples who are holding hands and we think, "how cute." We can't imagine being attracted to a wrinkled old man or woman. We expect grandma and grandpa to sleep in separate beds, maybe separate rooms. The mere thought of old couples "doing it" makes us slightly queasy.

Though the body ages, human beings are still human and still desire to touch and be touched. This section will look at three general topics associated with sensuality; the power of touch, challenges and enrichment of sex and sensuality among elders, and reactions to changing physical attractiveness as one grows older.

TOUCH

The Power of Touch

I was summoned to Chris's room in the psychiatric hospital where I worked. Chris was a big guy, in his mid-thirties. He was moody and prone to dark emotions, known to occasionally become violent and destroy things when a dark mood came upon him.

Chris was sitting on the side of his bed when I knocked and entered the room. He was obviously agitated. The whole room was crackling with the energy of coiled tension emanating from his body. I pulled up a chair facing him. Words would not be appropriate in this situation. I reached out with both hands and asked him to hold my hands. He complied. Almost immediately, as we made contact, I could feel the tension begin to drain from his body. I felt my own tension leaving as well while we both wordlessly sat, staring at the floor in silence. Several minutes passed. No eye contact. Quiet breathing. My only awareness, and I'm sure his too, was the sense of calm and the feel of each other's hands. That touch signified to Chris that, at least for this moment, there was another being who cared, who was willing to be with him and wordlessly share whatever pain he was going through. After a few minutes, the tension broken, I got up to leave. I turned around at the door as Chris, a faint smile on his lips, spoke a quiet, "Thank you."

The Human Need For Touch

Sculptures in the "Old Lovers" series depict couples in intimate embrace. What's incongruous is that those couples are old. Some people report being shocked, even disgusted by the sculptures. They are expecting to see young, beautiful bodies, rather than the old, ragged ones.

I didn't want to depict old men and women in explicit sexual poses, although that would have been interesting. Rather, I wanted to convey the tenderness that couples who have been together for many years display with each other. That is aged love, love that has the beautiful patina of a fine piece of antique furniture, or the complex tastes and aromas of aged wine.

Some might believe that when people get older, they outgrow the need for physical contact. But that isn't true. Human beings are never too old to crave and enjoy physical touch. Alice's grandmother, in her mid-nineties, was in a skilled nursing facility for old people. She became "an item" when she hooked up with a man, also in his nineties. They would often be seen around the facility cuddling and holding hands.

Beyond the simple enjoyment of skin-to-skin contact, touch can signify many things—an offer of consolidation, a call for playfulness, an invitation for intimacy, a confirmation of belonging, etc. The universal significance of touch is the expression of caring. Holding hands, a touch to the cheek, a hug, an arm around the shoulder, these gestures can speak a clear, "I care about you" without the use of words. Words are unnecessary. No one, at any age, needs a translator to interpret a loving touch.

Holding Hands

OLD LOVER KISSING HAND

Old man gently kisses his beloved's hand.

Whenever I reach for Alice's hand, or she reaches for mine, I'll know her familiar old hand will be there for me, and she'll know mine will be there for her. Every time we squeeze our palms together, entwine our thumbs, interlace our fingers, we feel each other's presence in the warmth of that touch.

153

We're reassured by that presence, and in that presence is a thousand unspoken words. Words are not necessary, but if one word were to be uttered that expresses our experience of holding hands, that word would be "love."

It's such a childlike thing to do. We feel like a couple of children when we walk together holding hands. And our hearts are gladdened by the simple innocence of that sweet touch.

Also, I love to kiss Alice's old, wrinkled, creative hand. It's such a beautiful gesture. Humble. Loving.

Hands-On Pleasure

Holding, patting, kneading, caressing, massaging. My palm resting on her shoulder, arm around her waist, my hand brushing hair back from her forehead. Touching the skin of Alice's body is MY joy. It's like when you pet the soft fur of a dog or cat. Half the enjoyment comes to you from the pure pleasure of your own touch. It may seem like you are engaged in the act of giving pleasure, but actually, you are also receiving pleasure. Of course, I enjoy Alice's enjoyment, but I get so much pleasure touching her.

"Owning" Each Other's Body

There is only one person who has free access to my body—Alice. Other people can kiss me on the cheek, put their arm around my shoulder, hug me, but Alice is the only one who has tacit permission to touch me as she wishes. And I am the only one who has her permission. We trust each other with our bodies. We've earned that trust. We honor each other's precious body and respect each other's boundaries. It's so sweet to be owned in this way. We take full advantage. We're constantly touching each other—holding hands, massaging shoulders, foot rubs, not to mention erotic touch. I place myself in Alice's loving hands and she is in mine. I am owned.

Massage

While Alice and I often spend time massaging each other, we will occasionally treat ourselves to a professional massage. What a luxury, to be kneaded, squeezed and manipulated by an experienced body worker for an hour or an hour and a half, and to relax and be slathered with slippery, sweet smelling oils. Massage therapists know just the right places to release the tension in tight muscles. It's a treat, and also a great way to experience loving touch, especially for people who do not have a partner in their life.

We also find self-massage valuable and healing. The stretch class we take twice a week includes periods of massaging our own feet, legs, neck and shoulders. The advantage of massaging ourselves is that it's our own body and we are aware of the places in our body most in need of touch, and the right pressure, duration and location where touch will do most good. Self-massage is a direct and powerful way that we can show love to ourselves.

Since many elders are not "coupled up," they may be experiencing a kind of "hunger" for being touched. While not a perfect solution, many of our friends schedule regular massage sessions. Massage is beneficial for health as well as mental health.

To Bed

Alice and I spend lots of time in bed, so we searched around to gift ourselves with a supremely comfortable mattress, one that works well for both of us. But the joy of a comfortable mattress is only half of it. The other half is the joy of cuddling with each other's bodies. We sleep together naked, and, through the night, change positions, spooning this way and that, half awake, enjoying the new sensations as we turn, back to belly, belly to back, back to back, belly to belly. It's our nightly dance.

If one or the other of us gets up to pee, we know we'll have the pleasure of getting back into the comfortable, warm bed, with the waiting comfortable warm body. On cold nights, while Alice is getting ready for bed, I'll sometimes stay on her side of the bed till she gets in. I love the sound of her sighs as she slips under the covers I have pre-warmed for her. Ahhhh!

LOVERS IN BED
An old couple in intimate connection in bed

Missing

The thought of living on after one or the other of us is gone is terrifying. Going to bed alone is terrifying. The body is such a solid representation of a soul, so when a body is missing, it is clear that the soul is gone too. And with it, the beloved. Every moment I sculpted "Left," (Pg. 276), I was feeling the sadness of being without Alice. Depicted is an old woman, sleeping alone, her arm reaching out to a spot in the bed where her beloved no longer is. The sheets and pillow are still holding the impression of her partner's missing form. Alice hates this sculpture.

ELDER SEX AND SENSUALITY

The "ick" Factor

There was an article awhile ago in the Los Angeles Times that discussed sexuality among older couples. The author termed the response many people have to the picture in their minds of an elderly couple "doing it," as the "ick" factor. In all probability, our most common mental image of a couple's sexual activity is two people with firm, smooth, muscled physiques, not two old, wrinkled and flabby carcasses, the pale, dimpled flesh shaking and quaking with each weak thrust of the hips. Ick!

Besides the "ick" factor, we just don't think of grandmas and grandpas as sexual beings. It's as if once a person reaches a certain age, the interest or ability to have sex evaporates and is replaced with the overwhelming desire to engage in bingo or shuffleboard or canasta.

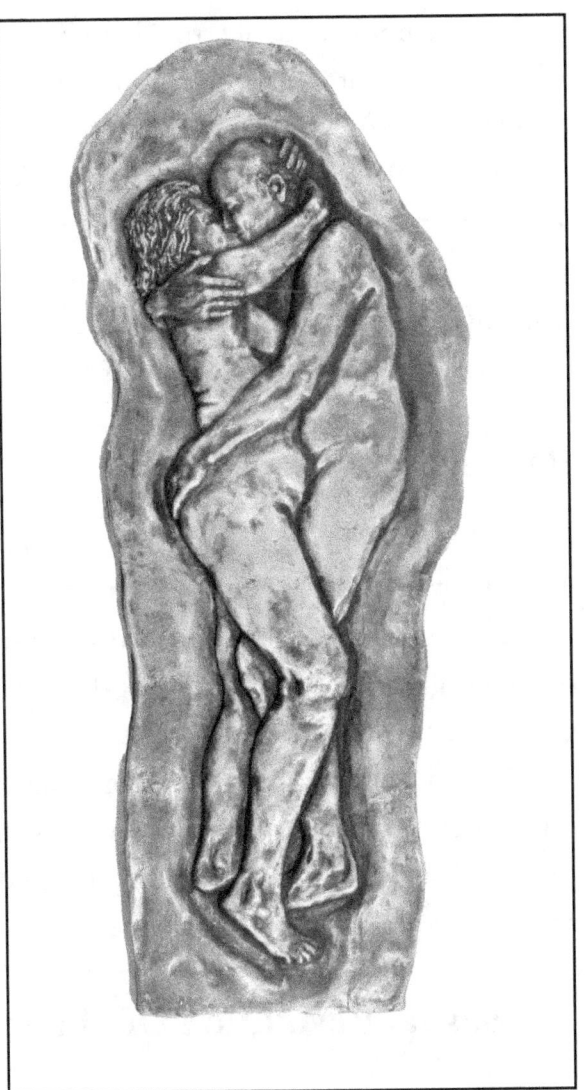

OLD LOVERS STANDING AND KISSING

157

This is not necessarily true. I attended a talk by a woman who works at a senior residential facility, whose job was providing recreation and entertainment. She spoke of leading a discussion group. The topic was "firsts." They talked about first car, first house, first boyfriend or girlfriend. It was a sedate discussion. Then an old guy with a smirk on his face asked, "What about first sex." The room came alive with memories of spicy incidents that made the speaker blush. Apparently, the spice isn't only in the past. She recounted that at night at the facility, there are sounds of doors to rooms opening and shutting and lots of residents quietly creeping around. They were having recreation and entertainment. There's more to granny and gramps than meets the eye.

Raw Eggs

When I was in my late teens, I listened in fascination as an older boy told a group of us of a sexual encounter he had had the previous night with a much older woman. The one thing that stuck in my mind was his description of her breasts. He said that "feeling her up" was like holding the membrane of a raw egg in his hand…without the shell. Ick! Obviously, the only breasts worth touching are firm, perky boobs, not soft droopy ones.

Cut to this morning. Spooning in bed with Alice, I reached around under her t-shirt and cupped one of her breasts in my palm. It was just like a raw egg…without the shell. But this time, there was no "Ick." It was a pure joy for me to hold that 83-year-old body in my arms and caress that silky soft breast.

The Sexual Revolution Of The Sixties

We have a friend, a rocket scientist who worked on many of the early NASA satellites. On the desk in his office is a replica of a metal plaque that was applied to the outside of the satellites so that any extra-terrestrials out there would know what earth beings looked like. It consisted of etched line drawings of the solar system with the planets and an arrow pointing to earth. Also there were drawings of two humans, a naked male and female. The figures lacked genitals. That was the state of the repressive Puritan mindset of many Americans toward sex, prior to the advent of the Hippies and Boomer generation.

In the Sixties, at least on the East and West coasts and some urban population centers, young people rejected the rigid rules of older generations and explored and practiced new forms of sexuality. Premarital sex, homosexuality and multiple sexual partners, were some of the things that shocked their parents. They eventually influenced a whole generation of young people the world over. These Boomers are now the elders who are in their seventies. They bring their pioneering attitude toward sex into their old age.

The New Sexual Revolution

For years now, gerontologist/sexologist, Dr. Pepper Schwartz has been speaking and writing about the New Sexual Revolution. This has been largely brought about by the Boomers, members of that revolutionary generation who, during the '60s and '70s, heralded in so many social and political changes and radical innovations in art, music, fashion, etc. And sex.

Dr. Schwartz sees three Sexual Revolutions. The First Revolution had to do with the introduction of contraception and the decriminalization and popularization of abortion. The freedom that flows from the right of couples to decide when or if to bear a child was emancipating. Also included is the downfall of the previous generation's prudish ideas about sexuality and the increasingly widespread acceptance of premarital sex.

The Second Sexual Revolution saw women rejecting the role of exclusively servicing a man's sexual appetite while denying their own. Women started demanding their own pleasure and fulfillment in sexual relationships. Gay liberation was on the rise, as gays exited the closet to greater acceptance and respect by the straight population. New forms of relationship and sexual expression began emerging; swinging, serial non-monogamy, polyamory.

The Third Sexual Revolution involves the remnants of the Boomer generation, forging new frontiers as usual. The fastest growing age population in the world is 65 and older. In the US, fueled by the Boomers, the 65 and older population grew by over 1/3 in the past decade. Not only are there more oldsters, they are living longer, as much as ten or twenty years longer. And Boomers are expecting their extended age to be full of health and vitality. That includes sex and romance. Surveys indicate more and more couples continue sexual activities into their eighth and ninth decades.

People over fifty in search of partners are being aided by media. There are a plethora of 50+ online dating sites for seniors, with names like Silver Singles, OurTime, Date My Age and Senior Sizzle.

Medicine and technology also provides physical aids, such as Viagra, Cialis, and various pumps and electrical devices for men, and lubricants and libido supplements for women. And there's a wide selection of pleasure enhancing vibrating devices for everyone's enjoyment.

As Dr. Schwartz has said about the Boomers, "It's still sex, drugs and rock and roll. It's just different drugs."

Elder Sex

Elders are having sex. One study of 75 to 85-year olds found that nearly one quarter reported sexual activity once or more times per week, roughly the same as younger groups. And, in spite of physical limitations, they report satisfaction with their sexual experiences. What are the factors that lead to their satisfaction? Elders 65 and older in another study, report that authenticity, deep communication, exploration and risk, transcendence, connection, vulnerability and being fully present, as the most common factors that lead to sexual satisfaction. Elder couples, more than young people, because of their maturity, are more likely to display those characteristics. These are precisely the ingredients that make for a deeply intimate sexual life.

Geriatric sexuality brings with it unique problems beyond physical limitations, especially at facilities for the elderly. What about sex and dementia. Is there consent in that case? Should a woman consider a female partner, in light of the fact of the scarcity of males? What should be the official rules, if any, regarding sexual acting out at elder facilities? No simple answers.

Old Sex, Less Sex, No Sex

Many experts believe that it's healthy, if they are able, for even very old couples to continue to have sex. It's certainly possible that couples can have positive sexual connection into late old age. And Alice and I continue our satisfying sexual lives, albeit drastically reduced frequency and modified performance. The question in my mind lately is, is this appropriate for us at this time in our lives? This has lead me to several diverse opinions.

Sex with Alice is beautiful. The quantity of my earlier years has been drastically reduced and replaced by quality. Even though I rarely ejaculate and usually have a flaccid penis, I really enjoy touching and being touched. It's a wildly satisfying sensual experience, a trip. And I love slowly arousing her and loving her body and bringing her to orgasm. Making love to Alice's body is my way of giving to her unconditionally. It feels so good for me to give so generously. It's not just me. We're partners. Alice feels the same generosity I do when making love to me. We're together, each of us loving and being loved. Sharing our bodies. Feeling oneness within our separate realities. A heartfelt form of communion we can access in no other way.

And then there's biology. Sex was invented for a reason—to have babies, to continue the species. Childbearing years generally begin in the teens and last till the end of the thirties. Once those years are over, the useful biological function of sex is over. Increasingly, the organs don't work so well. Is it time to turn our attention to other

Older adults are doing it, they're having fun doing it, and it's good for their health. So why are we putting an expiration date on their sexual lives just because they're old.

Jane Fleishman, sex researcher and educator specializing in sex among elders.

things? To be obsessed about sex when we are old runs counter to our biology. Obsession is motivated by the mind, not the body. And when the mind is obsessed and the body won't cooperate, it's a recipe for frustration.

Also, there is the issue of diminishing passion with elder couples. With most couples, sexual desire is at its peak early in a relationship. Experts estimate that, in general, frequent passionate lovemaking quickly declines between six months and two years after the inception of the relationship. What does that say about sexuality in a relationship that has lasted twenty, thirty or forty years?

So, should one, as they get older, follow their biological clock, renounce sex and become celibate? Many spiritual traditions advocate celibacy as a noble practice, part of a path for spiritual attainment. However, this is usually reserved for monks, not for those engaged in intimate partnership.

It's so much easier to let go of the sexual drive when we are older. Our bodies have changed, our circumstances have changed and our interests and desires have changed. Physiologically, the sexual drive has let go of its strong hold on us. Lust has cooled. Instead of being driven by hormones, making love can now be a decision to connect with each other through our bodies and enjoy the wonderful sensations these bodies are capable of.

Sexual Generosity

In many ways, my sexual experience now, in my eighth decade, is the best I've ever had. Alice says it's the best she's had too. I don't mean to cast blame on my previous lovers. They were all fine sexual partners. It was not them, it's me. It's because I've become a better sexual lover. I say this in spite of the fact that I am suffering from a host of age-related sexual disabilities, and in spite of the fact that our sexual interludes are much rarer now than before.

I ascribe our greater sex to two causes. I'm more present for Alice and for myself during sex, and I've become a more generous lover.

I'm more present for Alice because I am more present for myself. I am more in the moment when we're making love, not striving to reach orgasm, not trying to be a great lover, just enjoying the sensations that arise, and just enjoying following Alice's enjoyment.

I am also a more generous lover. I spend far more time giving than receiving. I derive great joy from giving Alice pleasure. Lucky Alice! In the past, when I was young, my greatest concern was my own satisfaction. More often than not, that left my partner high and dry. Now, my generosity meets Alice's generosity, and after a lovemaking session, we both experience a sense of closeness and connection unlike any other time.

Sexual generosity is a sharing of intimacy. It's a communion, a union, together. There is no depletion after lovemaking or after orgasm. On the contrary, there is a greater sense of intimacy, a deeper love. The loving feelings last beyond the act. Instead of coming from sexual need, sexual generosity is a desire to share. In that sharing is a genuine expression of the love that a couple has for each other.

Exercourse

Though it's not impossible for people to have active sex lives into their eighties and nineties, aging commonly has effects on people's physical and mental sexual experience. For women—vaginal dryness, thinning of the vaginal wall, painful intercourse, flagging desire, loss of interest. For men—inability to have or maintain an erection, loss of libido, inability to orgasm, lack of energy and more. Some aging individuals and couples, because of these problems, resort to masturbation or renounce sex entirely and become celibate. This is no fun when you still have sexual urges.

So what can individuals, and couples who desire the closeness that sexual intimacy brings, do, when faced with age related disabilities of sexual function?

One solution, which I find useful, is exercourse rather than intercourse. This is only foreplay. I say *only* because, for many people, foreplay is seen as only the precursor to the main event, which is intercourse. Using fingers, hands, mouth and tongue to play over the entire body can be a much more intimate experience for both partners than intercourse.

We tend to believe that our genitals are the exclusive source of sexual pleasure. Actually, any part of our body that has nerve endings can provide us pleasurable sensations. With that in mind, what a wonderful, joyful playground our whole body can be.

Also, exercourse can provide longer lasting pleasure than the few minutes, or seconds, from humping. (Average time after entering the vagina before male orgasm—5.4 minutes. *I wonder how they obtained that statistic?)*

There is no right way to do sex. Whatever gets people off, and is consensual and not physically and emotionally harmful is good sex.

*One study of men over the age of 65 found that 91% experience some degree of erectile dysfunction. ED medication is less effective than advertised and much less effective as men get older.

Men's Performance

As we age, men especially might be subject to "performance" issues. If we can't get it up, we can't "perform" sexual intercourse. The sexual act can be many things. One thing that it is not is a performance. It's especially not an ego performance that intends to prove to ourselves and to our partner how much of a man we still are.

In the bedroom, the proof of our manhood our partner really wants is probably totally different from the one we might try to offer if we have doubts about our masculinity. She wants to feel our loving heart reaching out to her through our gentle, patient hands. She wants to allow her body to be the generous source of our pleasure. And she wants to rest in the oneness of laying together in the afterglow of our loving embrace. This is not a performance.

Variety

Sex manuals are written for young people, not seniors. They often recommend varying your routine in order to experience new sensations and to try to keep sexual interest alive. But I can't imagine old people, Alice and I included, getting into strenuous postures, talking dirty, bondage, role playing, watching porn, or Alice wearing sexy, gauzy outfits, and any other recommended seductive solutions for overcoming sexual boredom. Picturing these things seems silly to me. We don't need *new*, we just want *loving*. There is no greater aphrodisiac than lovers who are generous and receptive, and who deeply love each other and demonstrate their love with their loving touch.

Elder Porn

I was curious. Is there pornography with old couples? So I checked online. Of course there is old people's porn.

There it was. Grandma and gramps going at it. Full on lighting, illuminating every wrinkle, crease, grey hair, wart and varicose vein. Crepey pale flesh, droopy, jiggling breasts,

OLD LOVERS SPOONING
An old couple, comfortably snuggling belly to back, back to belly

belly fat flopping. Some people must enjoy watching this stuff or else it wouldn't be here, but for me, it was a total turn-off. The icchh factor multiplied by ten.

Then I realized that every single one of those couples I had been watching were quite a bit younger than Alice and I. I wonder what I would have felt if I were watching me and Alice in action? Would I be disgusted? I'll never know. Neither will anyone else.

Tea And Sex

One of the women Alice painted for her Women Of Age series was Sosei Matsumoto, master of Japanese Tea Ceremony. When we visited her in her traditional tea room, Mrs. Matsumoto generously treated us to an abbreviated formal ceremony, which could extend to hours. The ritual is conducted in total silence, using slow, graceful movements, each choreographed according to centuries old tradition. It is actually an extended form of meditation in action, focusing on sights, sounds, smells and taste. Everything that occurs during the ceremony is part of the meditation. As the tea was being prepared, we were to bring focus, for example, to the sounds as they were occurring—the quiet clink of a cup gently placed on a saucer, sound of water boiling in the samovar, then the quiet splash of the liquid being poured into the cups. The atmosphere of reverence brought magnification to every sensation of smell, taste, sight and touch as we were able to savor a simple cup of tea as never before.

Imagine if you brought this intent focus into your lovemaking. What a beautiful journey that might be.

Slow Hand (lyrics of the refrain of a popular song, recorded by the Pointer Sisters, written by Bettis and Clark)

I want a man with a slow hand
I want a lover with an easy touch
I want somebody who will spend some time
Not come and go in a heated rush
I want somebody who will understand
When it comes to love, I want a slow hand.

Mismatched Desire

Couples are rarely a perfect match in their sexual preferences. One partner desires sex more frequently than the other or at times when the other is "turned off." One prefers a certain kind of touching that the other finds unappealing. One is a jack rabbit while the other is a turtle.

Studies indicate gender differences regarding interest in sex are maintained throughout lifespan. Despite flagging testosterone levels, even in old age, men tend to display more interest than women. As Billy Crystal's character in the movie, *City Slickers,* says, "Women need a reason to have sex. Men need a place." Sex worker Nicole Emma, in her TedTalk, said, "Men often feel they need to be connected sexually, in order to express themselves emotionally. On the other hand, women often feel they need to be connected emotionally, in order to express themselves sexually." This is a prescription for mismatched desire. And also for hurt feelings.

The factor of age can have a great effect on the mismatch and can lead to a situation where one partner has lost the desire for sexual connection, while the other maintains interest. Where does this leave the partner who desires sex? Frustrated.

Enforced celibacy, masturbation, prostitutes or affairs are probably not good long-term solutions for most committed couples. This leaves the sexually frustrated partner in a bind. They are feeling powerless because the less sexually motivated partner is in control of if and when sex will occur. This can lead to all sorts of conflict, some direct, and some indirect, and resulting anger, blame, guilt and coercion. Mismatched desire calls for all the patience, understanding and loving qualities a couple can muster.

The partner with lower sexual motivation can be a force for healing, both for their mate and for themselves. If they are able to understand touching, caressing and the sexual act as the gift that is, a gift, in addition to sensual pleasure, of letting their partner know that they are desired and desirable, appreciated and loved, then both partners will be healed. This may mean the lower desire partner might occasionally engage in erotic play, even if the desire is not initially there. This does not have to be considered an unpleasant "duty" or a sacrifice.

Common belief about sex is, first comes interest, then stimulation, then intercourse. But it doesn't have to be that way. Stimulation can also often lead to interest, and interest to activity. The gift of generously saying "yes" when not turned on can quickly change and can result in some very pleasant interludes for both. A generous open heart and mind is a turn on.

A Harmless Man

Years ago I attended a training for domestic violence counselors in a large auditorium with over a hundred attendees. The majority were women. The leader asked the women in the audience how many of them had experienced sexual harassment, rape, violence or threats of violence at the hands of men. Virtually every woman's hand shot up. This was a revelation for me. For the first time, I got a sense of universal fear and heightened levels of stress women must feel being in unfamiliar circumstances in the presence of men they are unacquainted with.

Ask any woman how often she felt unsafe around men. How often did she have to ignore an offensive sexual comment, minimize an inappropriate come-on, laugh at a demeaning joke or hide her anger in fear of antagonizing a man? How often did she do a quick risk assessment as soon as she entered an unfamiliar environment? Men will be surprised at how much this cautionary behavior is a part of women's experience. This is the reality in which many women live, especially those who have had a history of traumatic experiences. There's one of the consolations of being an older woman. You're usually not a target for unwanted sexual advances.

As an elder married gentleman, deeply committed to his wife and to monogamy, I'm not seen as a threat or as a sexual predator. I'm completely harmless. Not only am I harmless, but women, even women who have a history of sexual abuse, sense my harmlessness and are comfortable and open with me. I like it that way. It feels good for me to know that women feel safe around me.

On second thought, I kind of miss being thought of as a "stud." It would be nice if, rather than to be seen as an invisible, old, harmless guy, as I am now, to be noticed by attractive young women. It didn't happen much in the past, but it did happen occasionally. And it felt good. Those days are long gone. For now, the only woman who sees me as a stud is Alice.

Dirty Old Men

The vision of an old man leering at a woman's breasts as she walks down the street, or drooling over pictures of women's naked bodies, is noxious. Somehow, his being an old guy, makes it dirty, and that makes him a "dirty old man." We wouldn't have the same reaction if the man were young—a "dirty young man," and certainly not if it was an elder woman. As far as I know, there's no expression for "dirty old lady," in the English language.

I catch myself at times staring at the t&a of a beautiful young woman, watching the bounce as she walks. If I let myself, I could spend time watching porn. Am I a dirty old man? If I am, I'm not alone. I took an informal survey of my buddies in my age group. We're all dirty old men. Actually, a better term might be, "Appreciators of feminine pulchritude." Some things won't change.

Without A Partner

The reality is that many elders are living without a partner. What then? If the desire for sex is still alive, masturbation and paid-for sex are common outlets. "Friends with benefits" might be another alternative for single elders. Formerly, the term usually referred to young people who didn't want a committed relationship, so they formed sexual bonds with those they considered friends. Studies have shown that this is becoming a more common practice among elders. And the studies indicate participants report high levels of satisfaction among "friends." Love and sex do not have to coexist in order for couples to have enjoyable sensual interludes.

FADING BEAUTY, SHAME AND APPRECIATION OF AN OLD BODY

Bodily Shame

My parents had a friend, Beverly, who grew ashamed of her aging face and body as she got older. Even though she was married for many years, she never allowed her husband, Irv, to see her body during her later years. He would never even see her without makeup. Early in the morning, while it was still dark, Beverly would creep quietly out of bed, making sure she didn't awaken Irv, get dressed and put on makeup. She would be ready to greet him in the morning with a cup of coffee. At night, after the lights were out, she removed her clothes and makeup and got into bed. This went on for many years until her death.

After Beverly died, her body was laying in an open casket at the funeral. Luckily for her, she looked great. The mortician did an excellent job of doing her hair and applying makeup.

Kim Kardashian famously said she would eat shit every day if it would make her look younger.

170

Skin

A body is a collection of bones, organs, muscles, ligaments. This is all wrapped up like a gift by our largest organ, our skin. It is only skin that we see when we look at a person. Our skin is how we identify ourselves and each other.

The skin of an old person is much more, shall we say…*interesting,* than a young person's. Wrinkles, warts, sags, varicose veins, unwanted hairs, old scars, various splotches and dark spots from head to toe. Alice says we look like we've just come from a bad tattoo artist. When Alice was once asked why she preferred to paint old people rather than young, she replied, "I find it so much more interesting painting an alligator than painting a smooth bowling ball."

I love our interesting old skins, no matter how they look. I love to touch Alice's, and love when she touches mine. I love the way the hot water feels when I sink down in the bathtub. I love the bracing cold on my face and hands on a windy, chilly day and the feel of my fleece sweater when I first slip it on.

Even though Alice and I may look like a pair of alligators, I love our old skins.

The Friendly Mirror

"I woke up this morning and the mirror was not friendly. There was an old woman staring back at me. So I pulled out every jar, stick and tube… And there she was, an old woman wearing make-up."

Carol Orsborn

Lying

We have an eighty-year-old friend who lost her husband. Janet has an active social and professional life as a therapist, but was missing having an intimate partner, so she signed up for a senior dating site. She is quite an impressive woman—attractive, successful, vivacious, intelligent, interesting, well-traveled, and she described all her qualities well in her written description for the site. Except, she left out one accurate piece of information: her correct age. And she submitted a picture of herself that was years younger. She was afraid that if she revealed her true age, and sent a current picture, few men would be interested in her.

A man responded who had all the right qualifications. However, he was younger than her, 72 years old. They met for a coffee date at a local coffee shop. They immediately hit it off. They laughed, shared stories, had many common interests and a similar philosophy of life. After two hours of lively conversation, the gentleman said he thoroughly enjoyed his time with her, but regretfully, had an appointment and needed to leave. They hugged warmly and bid goodbye. She never heard from him again.

Young And Old Faces—Then And Now

Nothing much to do this afternoon. Turn on the computer. While surfing the net, I came across a site that showed what famous people, actors and singers, looked like back then, and what they look like now, forty or fifty years later. Fascinating. I finally had to tear myself away after a half hour staring at those familiar faces I recognized when they were younger, yet who had transformed into some old coot or crone who bore just the slightest resemblance to their younger self.

Lots of feelings lit up my brain. How devastating the passage of half a century. A long-haired rockstar idol becomes a bald old codger, a beautiful starlet becomes a wrinkled hag. How did their face disappear, only to be replaced by another.

A closer look and I find common indications of aging they all share, (unless modified by surgery and applied hair color). The thin lines surrounding the lips, bags under the eyes, drooping jowls, "turkey neck," wrinkles around eyes and forehead. Aging spares nobody, and steals youthful looks from even the most beautiful and handsome.

I look at the images even closer, focusing now on the eyes, windows of the soul. There, in almost all of the faces, I find a depth that wasn't in the photos taken when they were young. In the ensuing years they have lived their life, possibly became parents, faced loss and disappointment, been humbled, perhaps undergone illness, experienced the death of someone close. The Autumn and Winter years have etched the kind of burnished depth and beauty in their faces that can only be discovered by taking the time to look.

I go to the bathroom and stare at my own old face in the mirror over the sink. I can't stop smiling.

Eyes Of Love

Barbara, an old girlfriend, sent me some old photos recently that were taken back when we were in our mid-twenties. I was a handsome devil in the old days, and didn't realize it. I look in the mirror now and I can't find any evidence of that young face I wore so many years ago. My body too. I've put on some pounds and inches.

Alice looks at her old photos and has the same response. She asks me, "How can you be attracted to such an old woman. Are you blind?" I'm not blind. I see her through eyes of love. I see her through "love-colored glasses." What the glasses allow me to see is her inner beauty, which is the glow from her beautiful soul.

I'm no Adonis. Alice doesn't look like a movie star. Still, we are attracted and turned on to each other. Still, we think each other beautiful. Thanks to eyes of love.

When you're young, you're beautiful. When you get older, you get wiser, but less cute.

Bill Maher

I Love The Way My Old Wife Looks

From the perspective of my youth, the physical appearance of any woman over 35 held no interest for me. As a young man, I was only interested in surface beauty, which is the way that beauty is usually defined. It concerns the outer surface of the body…the skin and it's topography.

Today, at eighty, I judge beauty by a very different standard. Now, my definition of beauty has expanded to include inner beauty, beauty that originates within a person's heart, mind and soul. That beauty encompasses their physical, emotional, mental and spiritual being. By this standard, despite her wrinkles, gray hair and sagging skin, I honestly consider Alice to be a stunning beauty.

Characteristics other than the surface of her body contribute to the way I see her. The warmth of her smile, the sonorous tone of her voice, the way her enthusiasm and vitality plays out through her eyes and facial expression, I consider these an important part of Alice's beauty. What about non-physical factors like personality and character traits…her sparkling sense of humor, the incisiveness of her mind, the emotional depth of her feelings, her courage, compassion and authenticity, her kindness and generosity of spirit. Why shouldn't these inner qualities be thought to contribute to her beauty? Those are certainly reflected in Alice's physical appearance.

While surface beauty is dependent on youth, inner beauty is ageless. In fact, the passage of years has lent fine patina to Alice's appearance. Those years, fully lived, have stamped a soulful, indelible image on her flesh, an image of depth rarely attained by the young.

Beauty is in the eyes of the beholder. The feelings we have about a person, positive or negative, influences the way they appear to us. Because of the love in my heart, Alice has become more beautiful to me. A young person, passing her ambling down the street might see an elderly matron. I see an ageless beauty.

There is a saying, "love is blind," which is usually taken to mean that you tend to be unaware of or ignore your beloved's faults and imperfections. A statement that complements this, but is the reverse, is "love enhances your vision." Seeing with eyes of love has allowed me to view Alice with greater clarity.

When I wake up in the morning and look at Alice lying next to me, no make-up, hair disheveled and sleep still in her eyes, I see a beautiful ageless woman. I really do. I enjoy looking at her wrinkled butt and old naked body when she gets out of bed in the morning. When I run my hands through her gray hair, kiss the loose, wrinkled skin hanging from her arms, and yes, hold her raw egg membrane breast in the palm of my hand, there is truly no one in the world that I consider more beautiful. Looking through the lens of my love for her has given me this vision.

A Beautiful Old Crone

In India, a tiny, withered, bent, old gnome of a woman entered the back of a large auditorium filled with people, and slowly began to shuffle down the aisle, making her way to the stage. As soon as she appeared, a hushed silence came over the room. People were transfixed at first, then many rushed to her, trying to be close, attempting to touch her cloak. I was among them. This was Mother Theresa, near the end of her life, the embodiment of generosity, lovingkindness and holiness. Was she beautiful? I would say so. The beauty of her soul shown through the crooked, old body. That beauty was all we could see.

Naked Truth

When Alice was painting her "Women of Age" series, she realized how judgmental older women were about their bodies, including herself. So, in her late 50s, she began a new series of paintings she named, "Naked Truth." These were large nude portraits of older women, who were willing to overcome any self-judgments about their bodies, as well as, willing to remove their clothes for the world to see.

Finding judgment free models was not easy. Nine out of ten women wouldn't even consider it, and most of those who did consider it refused. Older women are not anxious to expose their naked flesh. We even put ads in the local papers seeking elderly ladies who would be willing to pose nude. Not even one response.

Alice finally found eleven courageous women, age 59 to 87, who were comfortable enough to be willing to be painted in the nude. In the process of painting these women, Alice came to a far greater acceptance of her own aging body. Alice wrote in our book, THE ART OF AGING, "At first glance, a naked, aged body, with its bulges, wrinkles and varicose veins is not a pretty sight, especially compared with the firm, smooth body of a young person. My first impulse was to turn away in disgust. However, I spent months in front of canvas in loving communion with the bodies of my subjects. For hours on end I was able to become familiar with and caress the wrinkled flesh with my paintbrush. This resulted in an indelible change in the way I perceived an old body. I saw through eyes of love and acceptance. Now I recognize that every age has its own beauty. Is summer more beautiful than fall? Is fall more beautiful than winter? No, each season and each age has its own variety of beauty."

Eventually, Alice became the twelfth woman (story below), and we turned the paintings into a calendar. I still chuckle over the thought of that pin-up calendar, like in the old, old days, gracing the walls of men's haunts—the back rooms of an auto repair shop or a men's barbershop.

Along with each picture and page in the calendar, we included a short statement, a positive, non-judgmental take about aged beauty. Here they are, starting from 83-year-old Miss January and ending with Alice, Miss December.

- *Beauty will manifest when you look with eyes of love.*
- *Comparing a young face and body with an older one is like comparing apples and oranges. They are both different, but delicious.*
- *Be thankful that you have lived long enough for your age to show.*
- *When you judge, you will see defects. When you don't judge, you will see beauty.*
- *Zest for life is the most effective beauty potion.*
- *Wrinkles and lines are a reward for longevity and the story of your years. Be proud and celebrate them.*
- *Bulges, lines, wrinkles…these cannot ever affect who you are. Who you really are is beyond age and time.*
- *Other people's appraisal of your appearance is none of your business.*
- *Beauty is not the way you look. It's the way you see.*
- *Your body is a miracle. Appreciate…appreciate…appreciate!*

- *Let the signs of your aging body remind you of the preciousness of time.*
- *There is only one you. Your face, your body, and who you are is a unique expression of the universe.*

We had trouble finding a printer for the calendar. Several shops refused the job because of the nudity. A reminder that even in liberal California, we are a country of Puritans.

Alice's Naked Truth

When she had almost finished the series, Alice came to her own "Naked Truth" realization. Alice had always been modest about her body. Because of her modesty, she never for a moment considered including a nude portrait of herself in the project. Recognizing the courage of her much older subjects, Alice thought, "How can I not include myself." So she painted a small self-portrait, partially hidden, with one breast showing. Not very courageous.

Alice knew in her heart this was not really the same courage that her subjects had shown by agreeing to being painted full body nude. So she carefully arranged a photo shoot in the studio at night, with me as the photographer. She stood demurely, in low light, her naked body partially obscured by a large canvas. When she went to transfer the photos to the computer, they were nowhere to be found. The computer had eaten them. Was she being sent a message?

In a couple of days, realizing that she needed to make a bold statement, Alice pulled out a 3 x 6 ft. canvas and began a life-size, full frontal painting of her then 65-year-old body. It was an honest portrait, against a stark black background. She didn't do plastic surgery with the paintbrush. Undaunted by self-judgments, she left freckles, uneven, saggy breasts, veins and wrinkles for the world to see.

The very day she finished the painting, Alice was to deliver an evening talk about her work to a large audience. She decided to give the portrait its first public viewing by placing it on an easel at the entrance of the auditorium, in full view of the audience as they filed in. That was an audacious act, and testimony to the acceptance of her own body she had gained in the process of painting naked old ladies.

"The Dress"

We were on our way for one of our occasional visits to friends in Northern California when, north of the city of Oakland, traffic came to a sudden halt. As far as we could see ahead of us was a red stream of brake lights. Gradually, we were able to make our way to an exit and ended up in a small village, where we thought we could grab a bite to eat and look around. By the time we would be finished, we hoped the traffic would have calmed down.

Near where we pulled in to park, Alice spied a clothing store, and, never one to pass up a chance for new clothes, we headed to the entrance. Just outside the door was a half-price rack. Alice shuffled through it and then went into the store. I was attracted by the unusual rich red color of a dress hanging on the rack. I took the dress into the store and asked Alice, "How about this one?" "It's beautiful," she said, "but it's a young woman's dress and I'd look silly in it." I insisted she at least try it on, and reluctantly, she did. When she came out of the booth, she looked gorgeous. Aside from the stunning color, the dress was tastefully designed and fit her curves perfectly. Alice was still reluctant to purchase it. "I'm an almost eighty-year-old lady. This dress is way too sexy for me. With my wrinkles and grey hair, I'll look ridiculous." I pressured her and we eventually ended up buying the dress, though Alice insisted she'd probably never wear it.

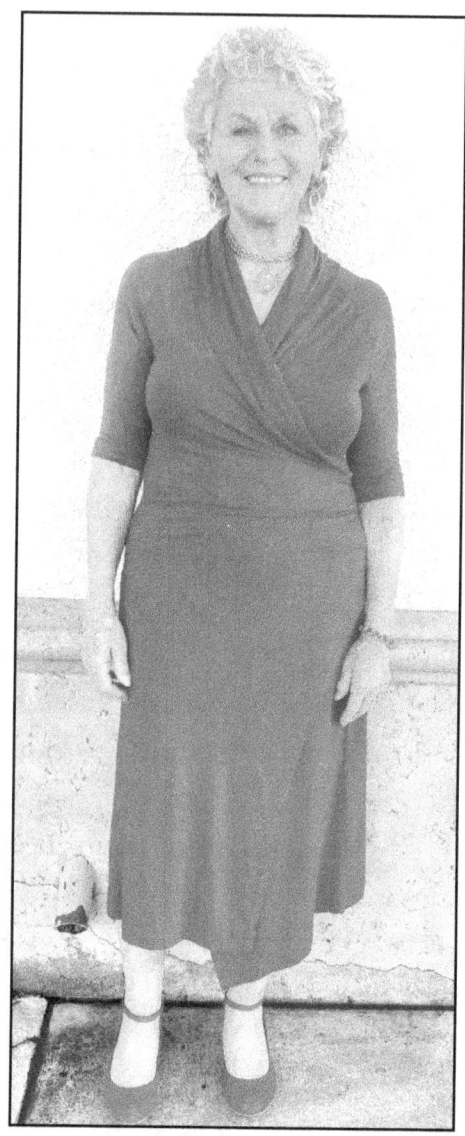

THE RED DRESS
Photo of Alice at her 80th birthday party

Wear it she did; the latest time was at her eighty-third birthday party. Every time Alice wore "The Dress" she attracted stares. Not because of the incongruity of an eighty-something woman wearing sexy clothes, but because this eighty-something woman gave off an alluring, sensual, youthful glow that a beautiful dress served to accentuate even more.

THE DRUMMER

The Drummer. Wildly enveloped in passion.

180

LIVING AND LOVING WITH PASSION

ELDERS LIVING WITH PASSION

Passion burns down every branch of exhaustion:
Passion is the supreme elixir that renews all life.
So don't sigh heavily, your brow bleak with boredom,
Dare to look for passion, passion, passion, passion.

Portion of a poem by Jalal ad-din Rumi, 13th Century Persian poet

When you are inspired by some great purpose, some extraordinary project, all of your thoughts break their bonds. Your mind transcends limitations, your consciousness expands in every direction...Dormant forces, faculties and talents become alive and you discover yourself to be a greater person by far than you ever deemed yourself to be.

Patanjali, ancient Indian sage. Between 2nd and 4th century, CE.

CAN'T WAIT TO TRY OUT the new golf clubs, get started on the recipe you discovered, arrive at your yoga class, pick up the grandkids for the trip to the zoo? You're passionate. Passion is fire. You're feeling the spark of aliveness. You are involved in something that excites your body, stimulates your mind, touches your heart, speaks to your soul and animates your desire. That's passion. Passion is a form of love.

181

Living Their Message

Sitting on our bathroom windowsill is a small rock. On it is painted one word, "Peace," and a small picture of the Earth. Years ago, we bought this from an elderly woman for a few dollars when we visited Washington DC. She was camped in front of the wrought iron fence that enclosed the outer perimeter of the White House. She had been living there year round, sitting on a blanket on the ground with her few possessions, surrounded by hand lettered signs extolling peace and ending war. Enduring severe weather, the jibes of passersby, and frequent confrontations of Capitol Police, she was willing to show up for what was important to her.

There is a group of elderly women originating in Canada, called Raging Grannies. They have chapters all over the world. They attract media attention with satirical actions such as attempting to enlist in the Army at recruitment centers, singing their raucous, satirical songs at anti-nuclear rallies, crashing governmental hearings with "briefs," (baskets of women's panties). This group of grandmotherly matrons use their status as elders in their efforts to undercut the legitimacy of military violence, corporate greed, environmental destruction and governmental insensitivity.

Along the same lines, a little old silver-haired lady, calling herself "Peace Pilgrim," from 1953 to 1981, walked 25,000 miles on a personal peace mission. Beginning at age 45, she gave away all her possessions, donned a bright-colored tunic emblazoned, "Peace Pilgrim" and on January 1, 1953, started walking. Carrying no money and only a few essential possessions, she shared her simple, but profound message of peace in communities throughout the US. She crossed the country seven times, and logged thousands of miles in Canada and Mexico. Her 28-year-walk was cut short when she died in an automobile accident at 74.

These women live their passion for peace.

> *I shall remain a wanderer until mankind has learned the way of peace, walking until I am given shelter, fasting until I am given food.*
>
> Peace Pilgrim

Suffering For A Dream

Years of dreaming about it, many months of preparation, and seven weeks of exhausting climbing and camping in bitter cold. The biography of Edmund Hillary details the extreme suffering he and his Tibetan Sherpa guide endured in order to be the first to reach the summit of Mt Everest, the highest mountain on Earth. They succeeded in late morning, May 29, 1953. After staying for 15 minutes, they began their descent.

Almost exactly sixty years later, in May 2013, a Japanese climber, who had had four heart surgeries, made it to the top. Yuichiro Maura was eighty years old when he summited Everest for the third time.

The Passion Of Creating

There is a flickering black and white newsreel, filmed in 1915, of the famous artist, Auguste Renoir, as he is painting. He sits in his wheelchair in front of the canvas. His hands are so swollen and crippled with painful rheumatoid arthritis that you can hardly see his fingers. A brush is taped to his hand because he is unable to curl his fingers around it. He is in pain, but he is making art. Regarding his arthritis and his art, he is quoted as saying, "The pain passes, but the beauty remains."

My friend, David, was at a performance of the master jazz saxophonist, John Coltrane, in a club in New York City in the late '60s. During the break after the first set, David went to the basement restroom. There was Coltrane, over and over, practicing elementary music scales during the entire break.

I was witness to the noted spiritual teacher, Baba Ram Dass, as he was working on a book with his editor. It was a grueling few hours because Ram Dass could hardly speak. He had recently experienced a crippling stroke that left him paralyzed, in pain and barely able to form words. But here he was, going through sentence-by-sentence, determined to make sure every word of the book was exactly as he wanted it.

Legendary musician, Ray Charles, was dying from painful complications of liver disease. Early one morning, shortly before he died, he put in a call to a friend and fellow pianist to meet him in his studio. For hours that morning they sang and played together. The song they played—"Oh What A Beautiful Morning." The words of the refrain—*Oh what a beautiful morning, Oh what a beautiful day, I got a beautiful feelin,' Ev'erythings goin' my way.*

My dad owned a hall where dancers liked to rehearse because the wood floor had a lot of "give." In 1958, famed dancer Fred Astaire used the hall to rehearse his iconic, *Evening With Fred Astaire* live TV special, which garnered nine Emmy Awards. Fred was just shy of sixty at the time. I was the one who opened the doors for the dancers in the morning and closed up at night. Nearly every morning, for months, Fred was waiting alone at the door. He rehearsed his routines for an hour or more before the other dancers began arriving. He was always the last to leave.

Every day, author Ernest Hemingway would wake up at 7AM, sit down at his writing desk, committed to write between 500 and 1000 words. If no words came, he would continue sitting until the words did come. Sometimes he would be seated at the desk for hours.

And then there's me. It's past 2AM now. I've been writing for hours, trying to sculpt the thoughts just right. Writing this book is my current passion and there are times when I am on fire. I'll turn out the light and try to sleep now, words bouncing around in my head like ping-pong balls.

Experiencing Creative Passion

We don't have to be a Renoir, a Coltrane, a Hemingway or an Astaire. We don't have to create with passion to experience passion. We just have to be open to allow creative passion to move us. We have to open our ears and let the music of Coltrane, or Beethoven, or Stevie Wonder touch us. We have to open our eyes and let the art of Renoir, or Leonardo, or Picasso touch us. We have to open our mind and let the words of Hemingway, or Dante, or Steven King touch us.

In a sense, it doesn't matter if we are the creator or experiencer of a passionate work. If we open to the experience, we are participants in the creation of passion. We may, as experiencers, be even more able to be emotionally moved than the artist who creates, who is busy making choices, working and reworking the paint or words or musical notes. We, as experiencers, are able to appreciate the work in its finished form, as the one who created the work intended.

What is Passion?

What is this passion, the quality that I, and all these other people share?

I would define passion as, "devotion to activities, people and objects, interests and experiences that hold enduring excitement and purpose." Passion is both a feeling and an activity. It is the fuel that motivates you and gets you moving. When you have passion for something, you have the best chance of accomplishing it. You're motivated and willing to work hard to overcome obstacles. Sacrifice is not a big deal when you have passion. The Latin root of the the word "passion" is *pati*, to suffer. A passionate person is willing to suffer for that which they are passionate about. Even if you encounter hardship and defeat, you will experience joy when you pursue your passion.

Suffering has not been my experience. If I'm passionately involved, it's not suffering, it's joyful. I'm obsessed. I can't wait to get back to what I'm passionate about. Alice is a good example of sacrifice for passion. Alice has always loved to dance. For years, three nights a week, after a full day of work, she would brave horrendous Los Angeles after-work traffic for a two hour round trip to go to DanceHome, a dance studio where she would ecstatically twirl for a couple of hours before returning home. So, rather than passion being associated with suffering, I would say that more accurately, passion is associated with play.

Without passion, you'll probably tend to procrastinate, rationalize, have to force yourself into action. You'll need to be prompted by external motivation, such as monetary payment or fear of negative consequences or seeking for other people's approval. There is little joy when externally motivated. The pleasure you receive comes from obtaining the money, positive results or approval, not from the joy from engaging in the activity itself.

One can say that passion is the underlying motive force for both love and sexuality. A person can be passionately in love. And they can engage in passionate lovemaking. When you are passionate with your love and lovemaking, you show up with your whole self. You are present for your experience. Presence is a hallmark of passion.

A person who is passionate embodies aliveness. Aliveness cannot be hidden. It oozes from every pore. You feel it in yourself, and you sense it in the presence of a vital, alive person. You see it in their eyes, hear it in their voice. Aliveness has nothing to do with how old or young you are. It can be experienced at any age. A passionate older person is ageless. A young person who lacks passion is old before their time.

One thing that often kills off passion is fear, fear of the new, the challenging, the uncertain. Each time we give in to the fear, we start to wither and slowly die inside.

A Poem About Killing Passion

Here is a poem about passion. It is a catalogue of the many ways we kill passion, and in the process, kill our aliveness. And slowly die. It urges us to retain our aliveness by avoiding things which numb us, and to take on the new, the challenging, the uncertain.

The poem has been attributed to the Chilean poet, Pablo Neruda, but was actually written by Brazilian writer, Martha Medeiros. Translated from Portuguese.

You start dying slowly
If you do not travel,
If you do not read,
If you do not listen to the sound of life,
If you do not appreciate yourself.
You start dying slowly
When you kill your self-esteem,

When you do not let others help you.
You start dying slowly
If you become a slave to your habits,
Walking everyday on the same paths…
If you do not change your routines,
If you do not wear different colors,
Or you do not speak to those you do not know.
You start dying slowly
If you avoid to feel passion
And their turbulent emotions
Those that make your eyes glisten
And your heart beat fast
You start dying slowly
If you do not change your life when you are not satisfied with your job,
  or with your love, or with your surroundings
If you do not risk what is safe for the uncertain,
If you do not go after a dream,
If you do not allow yourself
At least once in your lifetime,
To run away from sensible advice.

My Experience Of Passion v/s No Passion

Living periods of passion in my life, versus times when I lack passion is a markedly different experience. During periods I lack passion, I am "at loose ends." I looked up in the dictionary the meaning of *loose ends.* "*You are at loose ends when you are bored because you do not have anything to do and cannot think of anything you want to do.*" That's kind of what it feels like to me when my ends are loose. I just sort of live from day-to-day, meal-to-meal. During these times, I'm generally feeling somewhat emotionally flat, few highs, few lows. Just living. At times enjoying, at times bored, but no real "juice" in my life. Seeking to be entertained. Watching the hands of the clock revolve, the pages of the calendar turn. Marking time.

It's a whole other ballgame when I have a project I am working on or am engaged in something I am passionate about. If I am creating art or writing, that experience infiltrates my life. I'll wake bolt upright in the middle of the night, put on my glasses and write (as I glance up at the digital clock now, it's 3:36 AM.) Or I'll stop in the middle of what I'm doing to go into the studio to make an adjustment to a clay piece I am working on. It can't wait till later. Inspiration takes precedence, and inspiration can attack at any time. This is what makes it exciting…it's unpredictable. I feel more alive, more engaged.

That's why, after I complete this book or finish the sculpture I am presently working on, I'll need to ask myself the question, "What's next?" Actually, I know what's next. Another book. But I have to put my notes for that book away in a drawer because the book I wrote before *Love And Time* is about to be released next month. And two video documentaries. And, and…

Passion And Purpose

At age 58, Alice was afraid. She looked in the mirror and saw the indications of age fast approaching. She watched with alarm as she viewed changes in her face and body, and ached with grief as friends and family fell ill or died. And she was concerned for her own health and life. The midlife questions kept recurring for her: Is this all there is? Who am I? What is the purpose of my life? In need of perspective, she searched for answers in the lives of elders who she admired, women who were living their lives with verve and meaning. She sought out these women, age 70 to 105, questioned them to find out what they believed made their life worthwhile. And she painted their portraits. What she discovered was that every one of these women had pursued some passion that played a central role in their lives. A part of that purpose for most of them was to be of service to others. The way they served was lofty or humble—one was a United Nations Ambassador, another was a pioneer of the Women's Liberation movement, another was a prominent psychotherapist, and another was a clown. But they were all of service, even if only by their inspiring presence.

The women were diverse. There was the celebrated ceramicist Beatrice Wood, 105 years old at the time Alice painted her, who, as a centenarian, was still in her studio producing art.

There was Happy Lucky Faun, 81, who, when in her seventies, changed her name to reflect her new mental state. Late in life, overweight and depressed, she took a yoga class. She became a contortionist and took clown classes so she could entertain at schools and nursing homes.

There was Dominga Reyes, 83, Buddhist nun, co-founder and President of World University, an accredited college whose curriculum specializes in promoting inner serenity and world peace.

There was Liz Bevington, 75, alias Skateboard Mamma, who every day after work, rain or shine, jumped on her skateboard and breezed up and down the Venice, California boardwalk. She was still at it well into her nineties.

There was Sosei Matsumoto, 83, who daily taught the ancient art of Japanese Tea Ceremony at the school she founded in Los Angeles. Hundreds of her students went on to become teachers. She continued teaching until shortly before her death at 103.

There was "Mamma Pat," Pat Patterson, 73, gospel choir founder and conductor, who's choir made goodwill guest appearances at services for African American churches throughout California. The gospel choir was composed entirely of Caucasian men and women.

There was Auntie Margaret, (Kakehuamaakaneoluluuonapali Ahuala Keilii) Machado 81, Kapuna, (honored elder), master teacher of Lomilomi, the ancient Hawaiian healing massage at her international school on the beach at Kealakekua Bay.

There was Betty Friedan, 75, activist, author, and pioneer of the Women's Liberation movement. Alice's portrait of her is on permanent exhibit in Washington, DC, at the National Portrait Gallery of the Smithsonian Institution.

There was Pablita Velarde, 79, born Tse Tsan, well-known Pueblo artist and author. She became famous for her depictions of Native American life. She broke tribal tradition to become a painter rather than a potter or basket weaver, traditional occupations of Pueblo women.

There was peace activist Sally Lillienthal, 77, founder and president of Plowshares Fund, a grantmaking foundation for the elimination of nuclear proliferation, with current assets of $35 million.

There was dancer Anna Halprin, 75, who founded the Tamalpa Institute for dance, and who was still giving dance performances in her 90s. Herself a cancer survivor, she worked with patients suffering from AIDS and cancer, using dance and movement as a form of healing.

There was lawyer/political activist Margaret Cruz, 81, who received her law degree at 62, and after her cancer diagnosis, founded the Margaret Cruz Latina Breast Cancer Foundation for underserved Latina women. She worked as an activist under every president from Truman to Clinton.

And there were many more. As of this writing, all the women Alice painted and was inspired by are dead. The last one died this year. And Alice is older now than all but five of the twenty one women were at the time she painted them. The paintings are gone, burned in a devastating fire. But the women live on in the pages of our book, THE ART OF AGING: *Celebrating The Authentic Aging Self*.

In the process of painting and writing, Alice discovered her passion and purpose. This project, WOMEN OF AGE, and her other art projects related to aging, have inspired her and have had a powerful impact on the path of her life. Now, at 83, like the women she painted, she herself is a woman of purpose and passion. She herself is an inspiration to younger generations.

Passion Reborn

Alice has always loved people. She loved to paint portraits and in time she became well known as a portraitist. Two of her paintings reside in the National Portrait Gallery of the Smithsonian Institution, and one was in the White House during the Clinton Administration. Alice and her portrait series was featured on Oprah, and a film about her work was screened at the United Nations during the Year For Older Persons. But she almost lost her passion for painting.

During the time of Covid, and after most of her paintings, over thirty years of her work, burned in the fire, Alice rarely went back into the studio. Her tubes and bottles of paint were gathering dust and spider webs. It seemed the flame of her passion for creating art was dampened, if not extinguished. In the almost three years since the fire, she had only painted two portraits, and one of me, which she had been working on and off for over a year, still not yet finished.

ALICE IN THE STUDIO
Alice surrounded by her PAINTING IN TONGUES abstract paintings

191

Then, one day about nine months ago at this writing, while sweeping the kitchen floor, an inner voice urged her to go to the studio. She obeyed, not knowing why she was there. She absentmindedly opened a drawer, and there was her colorful set of pastel chalks, art material that she hadn't touched in maybe seven or eight years. She found a black piece of drawing paper and started scribbling random designs. Then, without thinking or judging, she elaborated on those designs, and elaborated on the elaborations.

After I had not seen her around for several hours, I wandered into the studio, surprised to see her feverishly working on her second drawing. Alice was on fire, working in a medium she rarely used and experimenting with abstract art, which she had never done. Over the next few months, Alice produced dozens of drawings and paintings, each one alive and dancing with color and vibrant forms.

It was nearly impossible to get her out of the studio. I would sometimes have to prepare meals and bring them to her to get her to eat. Now she's painting on large canvases. They cover every wall of the studio. The latest is 4ft. by 6ft. She calls them "Painting In Tongues," because they come through her, without thought, from someplace beyond her mind.

Now, Alice is again filled with passion for her art. As she has said, "The well of creativity never runs dry." For her, at 83 years of age, the well is now overflowing.

Passion Is Ageless

Alice and I interviewed and videoed our neighbor, famed ceramicist Beatrice Wood in her studio when she was 100 years old. Every day she would go to the studio and throw pot after pot. Her hands would get tired so she would have her assistant prepare and soften the clay, but she herself would form the pots and apply the lusterware glazes that she was famous for. We visited her again in her studio when she was 103. By that time she had stopped working with clay because it was too difficult for her hands, but she was still creating. She spent hours writing and producing numerous drawings and prints. Beatrice told us at that time, "I'm happier now than at any other time of my life." She meant it.

Passion Is Infectious

In college, I took a course whose subject was the opposite of passion—logic. Not that I was interested in logic, nor, I suppose, were a good portion of the other students. The class filled a requirement and an available time slot. The instructor, Mr. Wertham, a sixtyish gentleman with grey hair, glasses and a bow tie, LOVED logic. He loved inductive logic, deductive logic, formal logic, informal logic. He loved disjoint sets and venn diagrams. And he loved sharing his love of logic with his students. Mr. Wertham's passion

When I get old, they're never gonna say, "What a sweet old lady!" They're gonna say, "What's she up to now?"

Wild Woman Sisterhood

infected the whole class. Pacing in front of the blackboard, wildly gesturing, scribbling proofs, telling stories, Mr. Wertham's passion held us captive. I unexpectedly found myself eagerly looking forward to the class.

There's not a lot of details I remember about logic. But I'll never forget Mr. Wertham's passion.

Passionate Presence In The Aged

Earlier, I described some of the functions and benefits of a passionate way of life. Passion as motivator, as fuel, as joyful, as being ageless. The tacit assumption is passion is associated with action, with accomplishing, with doing, creating. The above examples given were of artist, writer, dancer, musicians, activists, teachers, and myself, all actively creating. But what if one is very old? What if their *doing* days are over and they don't have a care about what can be obtained, created or accomplished? What if they are in the realm of *being*? The being state is receptive rather than action oriented. In being state, a person is aware, conscious, open to the moment. They are present. In presence is passion.

If you are a shut-in or have limited mobility, the power of attention plays an outsized role. At any age, places where you focus your attention and the strength of your focus determines the shape of your life. Though your environment is limited and you might be dealing with physical debilities, there are possibilities. If you are able, you could focus your attention on the life around you rather than only your own state. Looking outside yourself invites stimulation.

More than just being an observer, you could make that world, as limited as it is, a more inviting place. In her early nineties, our friend, retired chiropractor, Eve Venturi, (one of the women Alice painted), was having difficulty living alone in her home. Her partner placed her in a small facility, a home with six other elderly women. Until her death in her late nineties, she used her power of healing and love of touch to spread her care with the other residents and staff. According to the owner of the home, Eve's loving presence made a real difference among the caretakers and other residents. "I love to touch bodies," she would always say.

My dad's passion was walking. Into his ninth decade, every morning he would put the leash on Snoopy, the Chihuahua mix he loved, and set out at a brisk pace. He would do his rounds, check in with neighbors, wave to proprietors of businesses in the area and then head home. More than just the exercise, this involvement with the world kept him

JACK
My dad, in his mid 80's, striding

194

vigorous and connected to his world. I wanted to sculpt him and the pose I chose was, in his mid-eighties, my father striding along with energy and purpose, doing what he loved.

Aunt Sylvia, my father's sister, in her nineties decided to leave her comfortable home for an assisted-living facility. She decided to move, not because she needed assistance, but because she wanted the stimulation of being with other people. Sylvia was active and participated in all the activities of the facility; exercise, discussions, music, trips. She valued her independence and wouldn't let others help her unless she really needed it. If we extended a helping hand which she felt was not needed, she would sternly rebuke us with, "I'll let you know when I can use your help."

My Aunt Kitty was in her mid-nineties when she was in an assisted-living facility. Even there, she experienced her life in passionate ways. She was bedridden the last years of her life. When we visited her, she was always fully present with us, closely listening, participating and following conversations. All her life, Kitty was a passionate opera fan. We would bring her opera tapes with all the famous singers and all her favorite arias whenever we visited the facility. We knew not to play them while we were visiting because she would be so blissfully transported by the music that she would ignore us. We gave her the tapes only as we were about to leave. The minute we finished our visit and began walking down the hall, the sound of opera would blast from Aunt Kitty's room.

Aunt Kitty, Dad, Sylvia and Eve, in late old age, were fortunate to be able to be present the way they were. They participated in their lives, and, as their capability allowed, they followed their passions to the best of their abilities. The reality is, except for rare people, as one grows old, processes begin that can sap their passionate presence. Interest in things around them wanes. Often, they feel that they have done life. They deal with chronic pain. They get tired. Bored. Lethargic. Fall into the sleep of apathy. They are relieved when death takes them. But this does not have to be.

Passionate elders we have known have shown us that it is possible to resist and overcome this late-life lethargy. In spite of challenges, they can live and love as fully as they are capable, and they thrive even in limited environments in the late Winter of life.

A Moment Of Grandpa's Passion

I have a clear picture in my mind of my grandfather dancing. It was many years ago, at a family gathering, a wedding, I believe. My dad's father, an old man in his late 80s, was surrounded by a boisterous crowd, clapping in time with the music, shouting and egging on the usually quiet and reserved Grandpa Matzkin. There he was, in the center of the circle of friends and relatives, swaying and slowly revolving in response to the lively beat from the band, arms outstretched, face upturned, eyes closed, a beatific smile on his face. He was transported by the music. Though he couldn't move much, his old limbs plagued by arthritis, everyone could see and participate in the joy that radiated from him. I fantasied that in that moment, he imagined himself years ago in the Old Country, a young man in the Spring of life, twirling with abandon.

Staying Awake To Passion And Feeling

We seem to get more jaded as we've grown older. It's so easy, as we go about our daily life, to forget the mystery, forget the miracle, forget the privilege of being alive, and to numb ourselves and fall asleep.

"I thought (age) was a quiet time. My seventies were interesting, and fairly serene, but my eighties are passionate. I grow more intense as I age…"

Jungian analyst, Florida Scott-Maxwell. Written in her mid-eighties.

There is no blame. More so during old age, many of life's experiences are so painful, or so boring, so "done" or just so damn uncomfortable, that it is easy to fall into the habit of going unconscious.

I, too, am prone to numbing and mentally falling asleep in order to escape the sometimes harsh realities of being alive. This morning I read an email that our dear friends had lost their baby at birth just a few hours ago. I felt a wave of sadness, for them and for the unborn being, then I resumed what busywork I was doing. I waited until Alice had finished her yoga class before I told her the sad

196

news. She immediately burst into tears and wailed with sorrow from the depths of her soul. Alice had opened to the moment and let the sadness in, while I had walled off my heart to this tragedy by numbing my feelings and sidetracking my attention. Though I protected myself from feelings of sadness, this had left me unable to experience the depth of the pain our friends were going through. What Alice had experienced, by being open to allow the feelings to course through her, was aliveness, was passion. What I had missed, by shutting down my feelings, was aliveness and passion.

It's not like we should be all-feeling and walk around like an open wound. Nor should we be unfeeling, like a piece of wood. We should, however, try to keep our eyes and our ears, our mind and our heart and gut open and awake. The present moment, whether pleasant or uncomfortable, is where our passion lives. Devoting our time and attention to each moment as it arises, allowing the experience to enter us, is being awake to life. Being awake in this way is being youthful. Being asleep is being old.

Human life is made up of a collection of tiny moments, some moments of pleasure, and some of pain. Savoring the tastes of a delicious meal, feeling the ache in our shoulders from digging in the garden, enjoying the warmth of a lover's hand on ours, or feeling the depth of grief for our friend's heartrending loss of their newborn—these experiences are all part of life, all colors on the canvas that makes up the painting of our existence. We can selectively fall asleep, by numbing the present discomfort, or by blotting our awareness with our addictions, or by distracting ourselves by computer, phone or TV. Doing these things carves up our experience and takes us away from living, takes us away from connecting with others. And the painting on the canvas of our life, instead of being vivid technicolor, will be a drab black, white and gray. We will have slept through parts of our life. When our time is up, we will have realized, too late, what we had wasted by being asleep. This is good advice, from me, to me.

> *Better pass boldly into that other world, in full glory of some passion, than fade and whither dismally with age.*
>
> James Joyce

197

ELDERS LOVING WITH PASSION

Passionate love is fire. When out of control, it can be like a destructive forest fire that burns down everything in its path. When we think of passionate love, we think of youthful love, lustful love, with it's newness, it's excitement, it's uncertainty, it's ego, it's jealousy, it's clinging, it's consuming obsession. Passionate love by the young can transport them up to heaven, and in the next moment, crash them down to hell. I think many of us are familiar with that.

However, passionate love doesn't have to be like a conflagration. It can be a fire like a constant inner burning flame that elevates, inspires and fills a heart with love. This inner burning, loving passion is the kind many elder couples have. Theirs is a quiet love. They have been together for years. They thoroughly "see" each other and genuinely know each other, have been through tough trials, steadfastly supported one another, survived and made it through. This shared history strengthens the bond that these couples have, and fuels the inner burning flame so it will

OLD LOVERS HUGGING
An elderly couple in loving embrace

burn with more light, but less heat. So, though we don't usually associate passion with older couples, it's there, hiding beneath the surface in a more subtle form.

In What Ways Can Elder Love Be Passionate?

Love between elders who have been together for a long time, rather than boring, is often characterized by a special kind of passion. There are numerous reasons why that could be.

Passionate Elder Love Is Committed For The Long Term. One might think that if you know "you got your man" or "you got your woman," and you're sure that your partner will stick around no matter what, that confidence might lead to boredom and apathy and might dampen the passion you share, might even let you consider you don't have to be on your best behavior. Conversely, if you are uncertain of your partner's commitment, that insecurity might lead to a type of passion that is full of longing, jealousy, obsession and clinging. That may make for interesting material for romance novels and romantic movies, but it's not the kind of passion we're considering here.

The passion Alice and I have for each other is the slow burning, inner flame variety. It is stoked by the certainty of our commitment. I know it's not politically correct to feel you possess another person, but Alice and I know we "belong" to each other. She's mine and I'm hers. That belonging feels comfortable, feels strong, is forever. The strength of our enduring connection is passionate.

Passionate Elder Love And Passing Time. The most relevant factor determining value is scarcity. If there is lots of something, it cannot be valuable. That's why sand is not precious if you live along the coast. If you need some, you just go out to the beach with your shovel and bucket and dig some up. Not so if you live in Antarctica on an ice flow. That's also why diamonds are valuable, there's not a lot laying around you can pick up off the ground. When you are an elder, time is more valuable; you have less available. So time with your partner is more precious to you. You cherish them more and you cherish the time you have available to spend with them. Daily, Alice and I are cognizant of our ever shrinking time. We are often reminded of our last wedding vow at our renewal ceremony,

"May I always remember that this day may be the last we have together." There is no such thing as permanence, and we know that there will never be another day like this one. This recognition makes our days together more passionate.

Passionate Elder Love And Familiarity. Alice likes her back scratched. Yesterday, when I was scratching away, I realized that it was such a familiar thing to do that I felt as if I was scratching my own back. The "you" and "me" has grown into a "we." After all these years, we are witness to each other. We know each other. The old body, the sweet voice, the precious loving smile, all so familiar, so comfortable. Almost every time I look at Alice my heart melts. Some say that separation and distance creates passion. It may seem counter-intuitive , but for us, there is passion in familiarity.

Passionate Elder Love Has Been Tested Over Time. It's inevitable that if a couple has been together for long enough, they have faced some challenges, maybe in the area of health, finances, conflict, family, whatever. They've stayed together, supported each other, confronted their challenges and persevered. This has been written into their history. Their history of goodwill and mutual support has created an unbreakable bond. That powerful bond is held together with passion. The three months we spent, every day, all day at our son Jason's bedside at the hospital waiting for his heart transplant was a test we passed with flying colors; for Jason, for each other, for our relationship. After that, there will never be a question of our loyalty and dedication.

Passionate Elder Love Serves Each Partner's Well-being . I feel it every time we make the bed together, every time we do our separate tasks that pulls a meal together, every time we compromise divergent desires in order to make each other happy or support our relationship. It is a confirmation: we are a long-standing team. We are tasked to work together to serve each other, to serve the relationship and to serve our families and all we care about. Alice has shown, in many ways and at many times, she has my back. She knows I have hers. What a relief to know that, without a moment's hesitation, if we need a helping hand, a sympathetic ear, we have a steadfast partner who can happily fill that need.

Passionate Elder Love And Companionship. Being with Alice, just living our lives together, is a joy. I could go alone to an appointment at the dentist's office without Alice, no problem. Waiting in line at the post office, buying groceries, the Motor Vehicle Department waiting room, no problem. But to have a companion to keep us company on boring outings or just hanging out together, that's special. Nothing important to be said, small talk, gossip, comments about the news, observations about the lady with the funny hairdo in the seat nearby. But the sweetness of spending time with the old buddy of mine, that is incomparable.

The passion in elder love is not earthshaking rapture. It's found in the small things, the little everyday moments that, when added up, make for a joyful and meaningful life together.

Elder Love When Not In An Intimate Relationship

Much of this book is about aging couples in intimate relationships. The reality, however, is that many older individuals are living alone, either by choice, or they are alone because they have lost their intimate partner through divorce or death. If a person is without a partner, are they fated to a life without passionate love? In what ways can mature love be expressed in these individuals who do not have intimate partners? Can love between friends be passionate?

First, by way of overview, two stories. Otto and Vivaka Heino were nationally known potters and local Ojai celebrities. Vivaka was an extrovert, talkative and outgoing, always with a ready smile and friendly word. Otto was the opposite, quiet, somewhat dour, possibly reflecting his Scandinavian roots. After Vivaka died, Otto went through a transformation. It was as if her death released a part of him that had never been expressed. He became social and opened up to other people. He bought himself a silver Bentley, attended social events, and sometimes would monopolize conversations so much it was hard to get a word in.

Beulah, Alice's mother, had a close, loving marriage with Sumner, the love of her life. We had a good relationship with both of them, but their lives were entwined and naturally, their love for each other was their primary relationship. Beulah was a loving mother to Alice, but there had always been a distance between them. After Sumner's death, it was like Beulah allowed herself to be absorbed into the orbit of our love, and we into hers. Our relationship opened to a whole new level of love, spurred on by Sumner's absence.

In both of these stories, the loving energy that had been encapsulated in their intimate relationship was released at the death of their partner and flowed out into the world. They were able to share love in community rather than with just one other. The result was that both Otto and Beulah's life and love was actually expanded by the loss of their intimate partner. This is an important observation.

Now, about the question of the the possibility of passionate love without a partner. I think that a deep friendship can fulfill many of the same needs (but not all), that an intimate relationship does.

I believe the basis of a great love and a great relationship is not romance...it is friendship. Romance is the icing on the cake, the cake is friendship. In most relationships, the romance aspect is unsustainable and cools over time. Without that frantic emotional rush, friendship is stable and endures. Friendship, like love, is based on similar interests, ideals and values. Friends like each other. Liking is the basis for relationship. This is certainly true of Alice and me. Alice is my best buddy.

If you go back to the definition of love, you'll see that love and friendship have the same roots. *Love is my desire for the well-being of the object of my love and my willingness to commit my time, energy and resources to their safety and happiness.* You could substitute the word "friendship" for the word "love" in that definition and end up with a definition of friendship. You want the best for your friends and you are willing to do what it takes for their well-being.

This definition is about intention for action. It says nothing about who or what the target of that action will be. This is the behavioral aspect. There is also the feeling aspect, *cherishing*. When you cherish, *you hold the beloved in your heart as precious*. Similar to intimate relationships, you cherish your friends, enjoy them and want to be in their presence. That's what makes friends friends.

Love resides in the person who is loving. Love isn't about the object of love. The object is where love is focused. The most salient factor is the person who is loving. They are the source of love. It is the person's ability to love that determines the depth of the relationship, whether friend or intimate lover. If you deeply care about your friends, that is the expression of the openness of your heart.

Whether friends or intimate lovers, the three basic requirements of love still apply. A friend needs to be *safe,* they won't purposely cause you harm. They must have *appreciation* for you, value you for who you are. And they must be a mutual *connection,* a feeling of union and responsiveness.

So, taken together, it appears that many of the same mechanisms exist for love between intimate partners and love between intimate friends. Obviously, there are major differences.

The most obvious difference between friends and intimate lovers is that intimate partners share romantic and sexual connection while friends don't. Another obvious difference is place of domicile and amount of time spent together. Intimate partners usually live together and spend much more time together than friends. Another difference is interconnection. Intimate partners are often bound together by ties that friends are not. Financial, legal and familial ties are some of the connections that intimate relationships have, that even the closest friendships do not. Ties like these have strong emotional consequences on the relationship. These are all substantial differences between the love among close friends and the love of intimate partners. These differences have tremendous impact on the costs and rewards of relationships.

Can friend love be expanded to become fulfilling in some of the ways intimate love is? I believe so.

There is no doubt, the love between long-term, intimate partners is a special, incomparable bond. The intimacy and close ties are life enhancing. The differences between close friend love and intimate partner love are substantial. But I think it is possible for friend love to expand. I think it takes a conscious decision to cultivate deeper friend love.

Deepening friend love and deepening intimate relationship love both require the same thing—working on becoming the best, most loving, most mature person you can possibly be. As we will see in the coming chapters, having fulfilling relationships, and having a fulfilling life require one and the same thing—aspiring to be an admirable person and partner. If you cultivate noble qualities such as integrity, patience, generosity, authenticity, self-awareness and dependability, friends and lovers alike will be attracted to you and offer their love. These are qualities of a good friend, a good lover, and an admirable, mature person.

Intergenerational Loving Friendships

We've known Fallon for years. Every month or two, she'll make the hour drive over to our house and spend the whole day, morning to night, talking, painting, gossiping and eating lunch and dinner with us. We're always texting and emailing. She is 22 years old. The sixty-year disparity in our ages doesn't seem to make the slightest bit of difference. We love and admire her, and the feeling is mutual.

Many elderly people like to congregate together, like "birds of a feather." They're comfortable among those similar to themselves—old, sedate, satisfied with the status quo. They refuse to venture far from their "over 55 communities," members of whom hold common interests, gather at the usual haunts, and travel well-worn paths. To these seniors, the younger generations seem populated by alien creatures, their odd hair, clothing, music and their ways of thinking and behaving are easy targets of negative judgement and ridicule.

It can work both ways. Many young people are reluctant to hang out with "old fogies," who have widely dissimilar interests from their own. They're bored because they consider old people boring. Old people talk about their aches and pains, operations, their grandchildren and health insurance policies. Elders in young people's lives are most likely parental figures and teachers, persons in positions of authority, not the kind of people a young person can identify with. This disparity in generations is unfortunate. There can be fascinating cross-pollination of ideas, ideals and experiences between young and old. But this could happen only if each would take the chance and come together with an open mind and heart.

By hanging out together, Fallon and Alice and I learn from each other. The learning is not just one way, from elder to youngster. Fallon exposes Alice and I to new ideas and unfamiliar ways of seeing the world. After spending a day with each other, the three of us feel energized and loved.

Old People And Pets And Love

My elder brother, Steve, lost his wife to cancer six years ago. He eventually got a dog, Barley, a big, clunky, chestnut-colored mutt. Steve and Barley are best buds. Barley is always at Steve's side. Steve always takes Barley whenever he needs to go somewhere, unless dogs are not allowed. Of course, no animal can replace a lost human, but Barley fills up some of the empty space in Steve's heart. Steve and Barley share a beautiful love.

Until one has loved an animal, part of their soul has been unawakened.

Anatole France

Many old people have dogs and cats and birds, and these animals play an important part in their lives. This is especially true of elders who live alone. It's more than just having company or taking care of another living being—it's love.

This special love, that animals give, and people receive, and hopefully return, is passionate love. I believe this love is genuine, and is an essential part of many elder's "love lives." It also plays a central role in their physical and mental health. Many consider their pet a guardian angel. Interspecies love should be valued and honored as the important relationship that it is.

Love Lost

I'm sad to report that we've lost our beloved cat. It's been about five days since Roameo has been gone. Every morning, without fail, he would show up at the bedroom window, expecting breakfast. He had never been out of sight more than a few hours. We've inquired of neighbors, made signs with photos, called local animal shelters. We're facing the realization that he's not coming back. Chances are he might have been taken by a coyote. Roameo was part of our life. I'm afraid we will never see his beautiful furry face again.

Walking around this morning, remembering how he would follow me, join me when I sat, I realized, when I saw him, or when he would climb up on the bed for a snooze or a belly rub, I would feel love. Every time. It was an uncomplicated love we shared, simple, direct, pure. He loved my presence, felt happy to see me, knew he was completely safe with me, knew I would feed and take care of him. And I felt that simple, heartfelt love for him. He was a part of our family and part of our land for four years. We shared a good life together. We miss him. Now I'm contemplating the sad duty of removing his food and water bowls and getting rid of the cat box. We're preparing for a period of sadness as we grieve for our sweet companion.

Love Heals

I'm looking at some pictures of my daughter Angela, taken in her twenties and late thirties. She did not look happy then. There was tension in her face, around her eyes, in the way she held her body. A job that had ceased being rewarding, a few relationships, some good, some bad, some ok. She wasn't getting what she wanted, and not giving either. Then, in her mid-forties, she seemed to turn a corner. Her face brightened. Her eyes sparkled. What changed? She fell in love.

Bella was a white poodle mix, about two years old when Angela got her from the animal shelter. She was as cute as can be, with an adorable personality, engaging habits and a heart full of love. And so Angela and Bella fell in love. Angela became a helicopter mom, making sure Bella was safe and comfortable, with the softest, cushiest doggie bed, the best food, human food cooked to perfection, long walks, with plenty of time to sniff, extended petting sessions and scores of dog toys that filled every room of the house. The three most frequent topics of Angela's conversation was, and is, Bella, Bella, and Bella…what Bella did, what she ate, how she pooped.

Bella has brought love into Angela's life, or rather, Angela felt love for this orphan dog, and brought her love, her most caring love, to Bella. In the process of giving love, Angela healed her heart. Through that healing, she was able to bring her love to share with a real, live human, named Fred.

ANGELA AND BELLA

Our daughter with her beloved dog

Alone And Free

Not everyone is cut out for being in relationship. The single life can provide a freedom that intimate relationship cannot provide. Beulah and Otto's stories are examples of that. Time, energy and interests are bound up within a committed couple relationship, and this can be limiting. In a very real way, a person who finds themselves alone is blessed with an opportunity—the chance to look outside themselves and discover a world that is not limited by the desires and needs of another person.

So, then the question arises, "What to do with mature, passionate love when it is not bound in intimate relationship?" Besides inner exploration, and besides pouring that love into close friends, the choices of where to devote love are endless. You could be the best supportive parent and grandparent. You could fully devote your passion to your hobby or to honing a skill or learning something new. You could take advantage of your freedom and explore new friendships. You could do whatever makes you happy. It's up to you.

There is the possibility of expanding your mature, passionate love out into a world that can surely use your help, moving the expression of that love, from the dyad of "Us," to the openness of "We." If you are inclined, volunteering your time to church or charity, mentoring youngsters, serving on boards or town councils are examples. With love in your heart and freedom to do as you wish, even if you might be hobbled somewhat by your age, opportunities abound and the sky is the limit to express your freedom and generosity through loving actions.

PART 3.
MATURE RELATIONSHIP

A Child asks, "How can I get loved?"
An Adult asks, "How can I maintain and deepen love?"
A wise Sage asks, "How can I be a messenger of love?"

THIS LATTER PORTION OF THE BOOK, Parts 3 and 4, will be moving in a different direction. Alice read it and had some sharp criticism. "This is a book for older people," she said. "They have lived their life and tend to be set in their ways. They aren't about to make major changes. And it's too heady, too much didactic stuff." I've made note of her opinions, agree with much of what she said, and made changes in the manuscript. But our discussion helped me clarify the purpose of the book in a different way. Much of the first part of the book is about "what is,"– the myriad experiences of growing older. What the book focuses on in the final portion is "what can be." It's about the future, about possibilities. It examines what it takes for you to be an admirable, mature elder, what it takes to make all your relationships the best they can be, and things you can do to make the last years of your life rich and fulfilling. Part of that is to make the effort to grow to be your best and highest self.

QUALITIES OF A MATURE PARTNER AND MATURE RELATIONSHIPS

WHAT IS MATURITY? I looked up definitions of "maturity." Here are some of the dictionary definitions I found.

Complete in natural growth or development.

Ripe, as fruit, or fully aged, as cheese or wine.

A person fully developed in body or mind.

Noting or pertaining to an adult who is middle-aged or older.

We'll be looking at how maturity affects your life, your relationships and your happiness.

Evolving From Child To Adult

The way we are capable of relating to others is dependent on the level to which our personality and character has developed. If we have not evolved beyond a predominantly childish way of perceiving and acting in the world, we would be able to interact with another person only as a child would. We would be stuck in Spring.

It's no fun to be in relationship with a childish partner or even a childish friend. (I know, I've been both). A childish relationship is characterized by mutual need. Both partners are trying to get from each other, and this is a recipe for frustration and conflict. A fulfilling adult relationship requires the participation of two mature adults, both of whom desire to contribute to each other and strengthen their relationship.

Contemporary society has the prescription for what it takes to be an adult. This is usually stated in terms of tasks to be accomplished. A person considered to be entering adulthood has finished their schooling, separated to a degree or become independent from family of origin, obtained employment and earned money to provide housing and sustenance, formed a stable relationship, possibly married and had children, etc. Someone who has accomplished these things would have fulfilled societal norms and be considered an adult. However, a person could accomplish all of these goals and still originate from a childish mindset.

Children grow to be adults, and adults, through maturation and life and relationship experience, can normally evolve toward an adult mentality. Potentially, an adult has the skills and emotional makeup to be an excellent companion. Adults have become socialized. They've learned practical ways to get their needs met in concert with other people. Through cooperation and compromise, (the "I'll scratch your back, you scratch mine") mentality, adults have the potential to provide loving, peaceful, satisfying, long-term relationships. Not so with children, or with adults with a childish mindset.

Children, and adults who have not matured beyond a childish way of being, "want what they want when they want it," and they usually want it NOW. They experience discomfort when frustrated. Children and childish adults are often impulsive and lack the patience to expend time and energy to work toward future goals. Whereas Child (I'll capitalize Child and Adult states from now on), experiences impatience and anxiety when faced with frustration, mature Adults are able to tolerate discomfort and are even challenged by it, especially if they see that working with their frustration might lead to the satisfaction of some distant goal. They've developed patience, persistence and self-discipline, essential ingredients in the ability to reach future goals and get their needs met.

Child tends to be preoccupied with getting, rather than giving. They see interactions with others predominantly in terms of getting their own needs met. Others are seen as objects, as sources of Child's safety, comfort and satisfaction, rather than as individuals who have their own needs. Self-seeking of Child leads to conflict and competition. Adult, while being careful to not give more than is comfortable, enjoys giving of themselves and enjoys seeing others benefit from their generosity. They are practical and realize that giving will inspire others to be more generous in giving back to them. Balanced generosity leads to cooperation.

Child tends to be ignorant of the inner workings of their own psyche. Their thoughts, motivations and feelings hold little interest for them. They operate from impulse, from the surface, and do not care to delve deeper into their own mind. Mature Adults however, are tuned in to themselves. For the most part, they are sensitive to their thoughts and emotions, and aware of their motivations. This is a key element for successful relationships, because self-knowledge is an essential precursor to knowing others.

Because they lack self-reliance, understanding of how the world works and are dependent on others, Child may reject self responsibility and rely heavily on manipulating others in order to get their own needs met. Conversely, by becoming competent in the world, Adult has gained some expertise at controlling environment, self and others. With control comes more confidence and the elimination of the need to manipulate others. They are self-reliant, and are willing and able, if need be, to take on responsibility for others.

Without a clear sense of who they are, Child and childish adults tend to look outside themselves, to parents, authority figures, peers and partners to satisfy their need to feel they are good, valuable and worthwhile. Adults have a realistic sense of their strengths and weaknesses. Appreciating their own value, Adults aren't driven to prove their worth to anyone, not even to themselves. They have a stable, positive, reality based self-image.

Mature Adults have knowledge and experience for successfully navigating the real world. With emotional and mental focus and cooperative orientation, Adult is ideally suited to our contemporary Western culture. Adults know how to deal with people and get things done. They can solve their relationship problems and conflicts through intelligence, effective communication and compromise.

They have the internal and external resources to meet their own physical and emotional needs. Relationships between two mature Adults can be mutually fulfilling.

A Mature Person, Partner And Mature Relationship

What is it that distinguishes a mature person from an immature one? What traits do they display? How will their maturity be reflected in their relationships?

As I have for all the years we've been together, at least once a day I tell Alice I love her. Sometimes she'll jokingly respond, "What's wrong with you? Are you crazy? Why do you love me?" I've taken her response seriously and thought about the answer to that question. It's not just that she's beautiful, (in my eyes she is). And it's not just that she's smart. And it's not just that she has a great sense of humor. And it's not just that she's generous, creative and full of life. The short answer is that the main reason I love Alice is because she is a good person. I recognized her goodness within a short time of meeting her. It was her goodness that drew me to her and made me fall in love with her, and it's her goodness that keeps me loving her.

Goodness is virtue. And I also equate maturity with virtue. To my mind, a mature person is a "good" person. He or she has strength of character. They exhibit the following virtuous characteristics; integrity, commitment, presence, generosity, equality, acceptance, authenticity, communication, dependability, accountability, forgiveness, independence, stimulation, joy and several other characteristics. Bringing these qualities to their relationships, mature persons create mature relationships. Therefore, these qualities that describe a mature person are the exact same qualities that describe a mature relationship. Couples in a mature relationship demonstrate honesty and integrity with each other, are committed for the long haul, show up with their heart and mind for each other, generously give without expecting reciprocity, etc.

When I look at my marriage with Alice, I recognize that these are the qualities we both aspire to, qualities of personality and character that define a mature person. For us, these are the basic requirements for our extraordinary partnership. Though not perfect, we have strived to incorporate these qualities, individually and as a couple, into our lives and relationship. As much as we have been able to do this, so has our relationship grown and prospered. I believe that a person who can incorporate these qualities of maturity into his or her life, has the best chance of being able to achieve a fulfilling partnership. Following are short descriptions of these qualities of a mature person.

Integrity

Integrity is honesty and having high moral principles. It is a basic requirement for a mature person and for mature relationships. Integrity is essential for the development of trust. Trust is the foundation of any relationship. How could you trust a person who would lie, cheat, steal and manipulate? Through acting with integrity, trust takes time to develop. But trust can be quickly broken with a single lapse of integrity.

Commitment

Steadfastly choosing to remain in relationship is the foundation of a mature, committed partnership. A person who can commit is one who can use their will to overcome the easy tendency to run away when the going gets tough. A committed person has, what my Aunt Kitty called, "sticktoitiveness." A partner who is committed to the health of the relationship will stay through difficult times. Commitment also generates trust.

Presence

Presence is the ability to "show up," to be with another person with your whole self. You show up by bringing your full attention to them. You bring your heart, your feelings, your caring to them. You attend to them with mind and senses, listening, watching, feeling. Being present is one of the greatest gifts you can give to another person. By being present with them, it makes it easier for them to come into presence with you, and also presence with themselves. The prerequisite for being present for another person is to be able to be present for yourself.

Generosity

Selfish impulse is a major cause of the failure of most relationships. It is actually THE major cause. Lack of generosity is also the major cause of unhappiness in life. A person who thinks mostly about what's in it for themself, sends a message—"It's every man for himself. Grab what you can." On the other hand, generosity elicits generosity in others. So, in an atmosphere of giving, everyone can get their needs met. Cooperation has its source in generosity. Competition has its source in greed.

Equality

The conviction that each person is of equal value is the cornerstone of all mature relationships. People are not equal in the sense that they have different strengths and weaknesses, skills and education. But they are all of equal value, equal as human beings. Not higher or lower, better or worse, not deserving of more or less. Equality involves seeing everyone as soul, honoring everyone as soul. One soul cannot be better than another. Understanding this is the foundation of peace on an interpersonal as well as an international level.

Acceptance/Patience

Patience and acceptance are closely related. Patience is the ability to wait, tolerate discomfort and delay if necessary, and not react. Acceptance is fully acknowledging the reality of a situation without demanding it change. Both are essential qualities of a mature person and mature relationships. And both lead to the ability to attain future goals.

Authenticity

To be authentic is to display your real self, to not hide your "bad" parts you are ashamed of, nor to parade your "good" parts you are proud of. To show your real self, warts and all, takes courage. But if a person hides who they really are, they will never be loved for who they are, only for a false image they have presented to the other and to the world. Every truth about yourself you withhold from the other, every lie you tell, every effort to hide, is a weakened link in the chain of your love.

Communication

Communication is connection. The quality of the connection is as important, maybe even more so, than the accuracy. Yoga tradition has what is called, "The Four Gates Of Speech." They are posed as questions.
Is it true? If not, don't say it. *Is it necessary? Is it beneficial?* If not, don't say it. *Is it timely? Can the receiver take it in?* If not, don't say it. *Is it kind?* If it's harmful, don't say it. If people followed these Four Gates, there would probably not be much communication going on, but their connection would have the strength of clarity, integrity and caring. We tend to place more importance on what is said when we communicate. However, the ability to listen is of far greater importance and is the key to loving communication.

Dependability

A dependable person is supportive and one who can be depended upon. Their word is their bond. They say what they will do, and will do what they say. A dependable person can be trusted to follow through. Others have confidence in them. They have confidence in themselves. They generate trust and appreciation.

Accountability

A person who is accountable will not blame others for their own shortcomings. If they goof up, they will claim their failure. Claiming your own shortcomings is the first step in correcting them. Without accountability, there can be no correction. A person who is not accountable is not trustworthy.

Forgiveness

To forgive is to relinquish demands on how the past should have been, and is letting go of insistence as to how a person should have felt, spoken or acted. Holding on to those demands is like holding on to a hot ember. It burns the one holding it. Forgiveness releases both the person blaming and the person blamed.

Independence

An independent person is strong and self-sufficient. They are not in a relationship because of their need. If they were needy, they would constantly try to get from their partner. Independent people are in relationship to experience joy and growth and aliveness and connection. They encompass those qualities in themselves and make them available to share with the other.

Stimulation

To be a mature person is to be alive to the world. They have curiosity. Such a person seeks to be stimulated by new learnings, new friends, new experiences. They bring their aliveness to their partner, and encourage their partner's aliveness, which keeps the relationship ever new, ever evolving. The alternative is "the same old thing," which results in boredom and stagnation.

Joy

An unhappy person spreads their unhappiness to all they come in contact with. A happy person spreads their happiness. People who incorporate the qualities of a mature person have every reason to be joyful. The qualities of laughter, lightness, playfulness and humor they possess are life enhancing and lead to personal and relational satisfaction.

Spirituality

A spiritual person is one who perceives that there exists in their life and in the world, a power greater than themselves. They honor that power in any way they deem appropriate. They honor spirit in themselves, and they honor spirit in others. One who sees themselves in relation to a greater power has the quality of humility. Humility is necessary for a great relationship.

Expanded Love

For love to be real, it must be shared with more than just one other person. Love is a quality of the person who is loving. A loving person will bring their love to everyone and everything in their field of view—their family, friends, strangers, the tree in their backyard, even the neighbor's yapping chihuahua. All are deserving of being loved. To limit love to only one other person is being a love miser. True love expands beyond love for self (I), beyond close family and friends (Us), to (We), everyone and everything. This is the power and beauty of love.

Empathy

Empathy is the ability to understand another person's experience by imagining to be in that person's place. A person who is not aware of the thoughts and feelings that pass through their own consciousness, cannot be aware of another's thoughts and feelings. The person who is blind to other's thoughts and feelings means they are alone, they are an island insulated from humanity. So turning your attention inside, and being aware of the thoughts in your mind and the feelings in your heart, is the initial step toward loving another.

I should make the distinction here between "goodness" and "niceness." There is a world of difference between them. A person who is motivated to be nice does so out of a desire to please. They are impelled to cooperate and prevent conflict and maintain a calm atmosphere because they want to be accepted and want to avoid rocking the boat. Their motivation is external. A person who chooses a life of goodness does so for internal reasons, because they recognize goodness as beneficial, to self, others and the world. They choose goodness because it feels right and is an expression of who they truly are.

Many of these qualities of a mature partner form the core of the Loving Promises. (See Appendix 1.) I appropriated some of them from my book, LOVING PROMISES: *The Master Class For Creating Magnificent Relationship.* There, you'll find them in the form of vows you make to yourself as to how you will behave with your partner.

When you were born, you cried and the world rejoiced.
Live your life in such a manner that when you die,
the world cries, and you rejoice.

Native American proverb

Go to the Appendix and take the time to look over the summary of the Loving Promises. Three things to note about them. 1. They are the behavioral aspects of deep abiding love—what you *do* that expresses love. 2. They are qualities that are essential for a relationship to be truly mature—the way couples treat each other in mature relationships. 3. They are qualities that define a truly mature person—qualities they incorporate in their personality and character.

No matter what your age, strive toward becoming a person of integrity, kindness, generosity and joy. As you do so, you will have the possibility of attaining the mature relationships you desire. And you will have become an admirable, noble, mature person.

How It Works

How will taking on these noble qualities enable you to have mature relationships? There is a simple truth about the effect of the way people act toward each other that is so universal that it could be considered a law of behavior. It is usually spoken of as the "Law of karma," commonly phrased in a negative context, "You get what you give" or "What goes around, comes around." These are warnings—If you do people wrong, you will "reap as you sow."

The law of karma here is used in a more positive context, the tendency of people's behavior in relationships to mimic their partner's positive behavior. This is a simple concept, but a powerful one. For example; you are open-handed in giving to a person, they will tend to become more generous with you. You listen patiently, you will tend to be patiently listened to. You speak kindly, your kind speech will tend to be mirrored back to you by the person you speak to. The mirroring may not happen immediately, and it may not appear exactly as you envision, but karma works.

You have no direct control over any other person. You do have control over your own behavior. Why not use that control in a way that will guide yourself to be the best person you can be, help others be their best, while creating a beautiful relationship for you both.

Resistance: Our Devil

The above qualities of a mature person and mature relationships are ideals to strive toward. They are models of ideal persons and relationships, and it is a noble calling to aspire to them. When we have viscerally experienced the painful effects of behavior we wish to change, and/or have come to a clear understanding of the beneficial effects of the behaviors we want to adopt, we become ripe for change. Once we are ripe, mentally and emotionally ready to adopt the mature qualities, we can do so without encountering a lot of difficulties. However, if we strive to develop those qualities and are not psychologically ready, it's likely that we will encounter internal resistance—the tendency to give up or to act counter to our stated intention. In this case, change may never happen, or occur after much arduous inner work.

We're all familiar with the iconic image of a little white angel sitting on one shoulder, whispering in our ear, prompting us to be good, and on the other shoulder, a little red devil urging us to not listen to the angel. The devil is our resistance. He wants you to follow the easy, comfortable, immediate alternative. It is a reality of human nature that when our angelic side appears, our devil is not far behind. And the devil's arguments are so much more compelling. "Don't follow your diet and gnaw on that raw carrot," says the devil, "Have a delicious chocolate doughnut instead."

The way of conceptualizing love and mature relationships presented here, as various behavioral changes that are to be practiced and incorporated as habit, is an open invitation to our devil to arrive. The devil arrives in the form of the part of our mind that resists our stated intention. The devil's resistance is mostly unconscious, and has a dark life of its own. A prime example in literature is Robert Louis Stephenson's, *Dr. Jekyll And Mr. Hyde,* where a good and evil side exists in the same person. All the good Dr. Jekyll's willpower could not control Mr. Hyde's evil. In the same way, much of resistance is beyond our conscious awareness and power of will. That can confound our intended efforts to improve ourselves.

For example, say we want to improve the quality of generosity in our relationships (fortify our angel). So we give, and give, and give to our freeloading brother-in-law who lies around on the couch in our living room all day doing nothing but watch TV and drink beer. However, inside we feel resentful, unacknowledged and taken advantage of. So we find reasons not to give. (our devil) The devil will look for any opportunity to resist the impulse of generosity. The more we attempt to be generous, the more resistance our devil puts up, till we get tired of fighting our own resistance, give up, and kick the lazy bum out of the house.

Working With Resistance

As long as our resistances are below our conscious awareness, we will be in the dark as to how to work through them. As psychologist Carl Jung has written, *"Until you make the unconscious conscious, it will direct your life and you will call it fate."* He also wrote, *"One does not become enlightened by imagining figures of light, but by making the darkness conscious."*

Here then can be an initial step for dealing with our resistance—making an effort to become aware of the times our resistance becomes active. Once we are mindful when the unconscious process of resistance is activated, we can pause, take a step back and exert our will to choose our course of action. Working to acquire the qualities of a mature person and partner provides ample opportunity for your devil to emerge, and therefore, ample opportunity to become familiar with and work with your resistance with greater awareness.

Working with unconscious processes is not an easy task because they are beyond our awareness. Often, when under influence of resistance, the help of an experienced therapist is useful to navigate the dark forest of our mind and help us "make the unconscious conscious."

The dark forests of our minds are filled with traps and deep pits that can ensnare us. These are often emotionally charged remnants of our experiences from our childhood that have profound effect on our present feelings and behavior. (Suppressed fears, suppressed suffering, suppressed traumatic memories). Because we have never really addressed these experiences consciously, ancient feelings can be triggered and leave us helpless. Often, our willful decisions are of little use when we encounter these powerful unconscious processes.

The dark forests that comprise the landscape of resistance are fearsome. That's why we have avoided them for so many years. It takes courage to enter them. Often, in confronting our resistance, we will enter "the dark night of our soul," a period where we exit the safety of the known, and enter a period of confusion and discomfort. Here is where we encounter our dragons, the fears, the traumas, the old pain, the sense of helplessness that has kept us imprisoned in the forest. Confronting the dragons and overcoming them is how we can exit the forest and re-enter our present world, renewed, strengthened, and deepened by our experience.

The ability to turn within and become aware of repressed memories, feelings, and the machinations of our mind is an essential skill when exploring our shadow states. Meditation can be a valuable tool. The practice of some forms of meditation can be a way of developing the "mind-muscle" that can help more clearly and non-judgmentally examine the contents of our mind and soul.

Another helpful way of working with resistance is to hasten slowly. We see parts of ourselves that cause us pain and we want to get rid of them immediately, so we might undertake a major overhaul of our life. We take on too much, too soon, and in doing so, are overwhelmed and insure our failure. Without clarity, we invite our devil. If we want to make changes in our behavior, it's best to move in slow, baby steps. Then we can observe and will have more control of the process.

Results from working with qualities that will make us a good person and mature partner is usually not instantaneous. The work is characterized by practice, over and over, choosing the actions we want to accentuate, and at the same time, choosing to refrain from those actions we want to eliminate. With practice, new behavior becomes habitual. It is important to take this into consideration, realize we are probably in for a protracted period of practice, and understand that becoming a good person is ongoing work of a lifetime.

Most likely, the thoughts and behaviors we want to eliminate in our life will not disappear. They are embedded in our mind. They are like old friends who come uninvited. They come, but then they go. Nor will the positive behaviors we want to adopt instantly appear. A positive outcome of working with our resistance would be to come into a changed relationship with our shadow parts. Instead of blindly obeying impulses from our devil, we might acquire boundaries that limit our devil's power over us. And we might be energized by attaining the positive qualities we are aiming for.

I have struggled, to one degree or another, with every one of the qualities of a mature person listed above and with every Loving Promise. One of my most difficult struggles has been with becoming more generous. I grew up in a family where my parents lived through the Great Depression. For many years, as children growing up, their household was in fear of not having enough to survive. This was not uncommon for the generation that experienced the Great Depression. Mom and Dad hoarded throughout their lives, even though they were financially comfortable. I adopted the same carefulness about money, watching every penny and making sure to save and not overspend. Whenever it's time to open my wallet, thoughts of, "Do we need this? Can we afford it? Is there a cheaper model?" are triggered.

Year end is a test and a practice for me. We want to make generous charitable contributions. Right before December 31st, I sit at the computer with a long list of charities. Each charity presents me with a decision point as I decide the amount of each contribution. How much will I give? I try to be open-handed, fighting against my inherited tendencies, my resistance. This is just one part of my "generosity practice." Opportunities for me to practice generosity are endless and constantly arise. Do I give money to the beggar with outstretched hand, and if so, how much. Or do I walk by, pretending not to see him? Do I look for the least expensive product rather than one with the highest quality? Am I a miser with my time when a friend needs help, or do I offer a half-true excuse as to why I am busy? Each of these situations are opportunities to practice open-handed giving. When they arise, I try to be aware of my resistance and make conscious decisions. Becoming a generous person has been one of my goals for much of my adult life. I know I will be working with it till my dying day. It is a worthy goal, and I have made significant progress, but there is more to go.

Most goals are rarely reached suddenly, without lots of preparation. Intended results are achieved by gradually working towards your goals. If your aim is to be able to lift a hundred pound barbell, you don't start out with a hundred pound barbell. You start out with 40 or 50 pounds, or whatever you can lift without overtaxing yourself. Then you work with that weight, over and over, until it becomes easier, then you move on to a greater weight. Eventually, you'll find that 60, 70, 90 pounds have become attainable, and it's just a short jump to your goal. It is like this with any goal, including learning to be a more kind and loving person.

If we were to see the truth of the power of kindness, and see that kindness is a much more loving way of being in the world, then, with that unshakable understanding, choosing to be kind would be much easier. If resistance comes up, resistance comes up. In the face of your resistance, you still choose to be kind because you know how necessary it is to be a loving presence. Each of the qualities of a mature person encompass kind action. Keep working with them by choosing kindness, again and again.

Transformation/Change

Most of us would welcome being transformed, to be made whole, to undergo a radical metamorphosis, eliminate our defects and become the person we've always wanted to be. I've heard that transformation like this sometimes happens, but it hasn't happened to anybody I know. And certainly not to me.

I've changed though. I'm very different from the person I was before I met Alice. Very different, but in so many ways, I still have the same tendencies I had back then, still a bit shy, still a bit lazy, still a bit miserly, still a bit needy, still a bit greedy. Some things about me won't ever be transformed. The habitual patterns I've had all my life are too deeply embedded in my psyche to disappear. They remain, albeit in far less virulent form. What's changed most is the way I behave. I won't cut the pie unevenly and take the larger slice for myself—I'll share equally with Alice. I won't vie for attention—I can be content staying anonymous in the background. I can overcome my lazy impulse—I'll work hard for what I want. But my initial impulses to laziness, neediness and greed are still there, still waiting in the wings. My actions have changed though. When actions change, this can often bring on changes in thoughts and feelings. I'm working at it. I'm certainly not perfect, but I'm working.

Also different now is that I don't judge myself so harshly for all these weaknesses and imperfections. When they show

People often ask me what is the most effective technique for transforming their life. It's a little embarrassing that, after years of research and experimentation, I have to say the best answer is—just be a little kinder.

Aldous Huxley

up, I at least allow them to be without berating myself. This may not be transformation, but it is change. I don't demand to be transformed. I'll gladly accept the changes in me. They sure have made my character stronger, my relationships more rewarding and my life more fulfilling.

Relationship Problems As A Source Of Learning

It's easy to view the problems that come up in all our relationships, the arguments, frustrating behaviors, conflicting desires, as challenges we need to overcome in order to create harmony. The challenges are seen as obstacles to harmony. When we encounter obstacles, we usually think they need to be worked with and eliminated. Instead, I suggest reframing and welcoming problems as opportunities. The problems we have with each other, especially those that keep recurring over and over, are flashing neon signs that show us the places where we are stuck and need to grow. Where are we being stubborn? Selfish? Manipulative? Blind? How do we cut off communication? In what ways do we sow anger? What behaviors do we use to create distance? By viewing the problems that come up in life as a gift of valuable information, the rocky parts of our relationships become our schoolroom for learning how to love.

> *You can't always get what you want.*
> *You can't always get what you want.*
> *But if you try sometimes, well, you just might find*
> *You get what you need.*

The Rolling Stones, Mick Jagger and Kieth Richards

Is It Worth It?

You are in your 70s, 80s, even 90s. Do you want to lay back and enjoy your "golden years?" Does it make sense to start commitment on a self-improvement project that may involve a personality and character overhaul, and may engage you till your dying day?

I'm reminded of a true story I read many years ago that stuck in my mind. It was about a Jewish woman who lived in Germany or Austria during World War Il. During that time, she underwent extensive psychoanalysis with a famous analyst. It was a grueling, expensive and time consuming undertaking, and took years of dredging up painful memories. Finally, she finished her analysis, and felt liberated and released from her wretched past. Several weeks later she was rounded up by the Nazis and sent to her death in the gas chambers.

Was it worth it? Would she have done it if she knew her fate? Would you? Is there a reason to expend the effort, overcome resistance and cultivate the qualities of goodness, knowing that you are old and don't have a lot of time left?

It *is* worth it. It's worth it because if you don't try to be the kindest, most loving person you can be, you will have regrets. Lovingkindness brings purity to your life and to the lives of those around you. If you act with kindness and love, regrets won't burden you. To come to the finale of your life weighted down with a burden of regrets is a sad way to end a life. If you don't at least try to be a noble person there will be much you will regret in your last moments. That alone is reason enough to try to be the best person you can be.

I would like to make clear that this way of approaching mature relationships and mature elderhood is not THE way. It does not fit for everyone. Everyone is different. For some people, working through idealized personality and character ideals may be contraindicated. I urge you to always seek ways of growth that resonate in your own unique mind, heart and soul.

The Garden Of Our Life

Our life is a garden. In the soil of the garden of our life there are many seeds. There are seeds of generosity, of anger, of kindness, of prejudice, of integrity, of greed, of love. Many of these seeds were planted when we were young, by our parents, our culture, and as we grew, our teachers, our friends, our lovers, and ultimately, ourselves. The seeds grow to be plants, the plants of our thoughts and actions. We can select which of those plants we want to flourish in our garden. By watering, fertilizing and caring for the seeds of those plants, we encourage them to sprout and grow vigorous and sturdy. We can also choose to eliminate the weeds and vines we don't want in our garden by withholding water and fertilizer, so they will not sprout, or will eventually shrivel and die from neglect. Or, once we see they have begun to take root and are growing and overtaking the other plants, we dig them up. In this way, we eliminate plants we don't want, and encourage those we do. Over time, we create the garden of our life. As we grow older and our garden matures, we are able to delight in what we have grown, the bountiful harvest of nutritious vegetables and beautiful flowers. If, however, we have not tended our garden with loving care, we gather a harvest of spikey weeds and bitter, withered vegetables.

We are the garden, and we are the gardener of our life.

Which experiences do you want to grow more in your life? Which experiences do you want to die off? Which of your behaviors would you want to fertilize in your life? Which behaviors would you want eliminated?

The Fruit From The Garden Of Our Life

In our garden, we dig up the ground to loosen the dirt, add rich ingredients to make the soil fertile, plant seeds, apply water. And we continuously cull weeds we don't want to grow. Why do we do all this work? To enjoy beautiful flowers and delicious fruit and vegetables. What is it that we, as mature adults, find so valuable that we are motivated to do the difficult and time consuming work of planting seeds of commitment, generosity, forgiveness, integrity and all the rest? What is the fruit of the garden of our life? The fruit is goodness, being a good person and having a wholesome, joyful life. The fruit of goodness is love, loving relationships, loving family, the beauty and joy of a love-filled life.

The goal in life, according to most people's opinion, is to live with ease and comfort, to be showered with praise and adulation, to be loved by everyone. Though this would be pleasant, in a way, it is a childish goal, and not realistic. Everyone must face painful challenges in their life. The point is not to avoid those challenges, but to encounter them, work through them, use them to become the best you can be. Your struggle with pain, failure and loss offers you the opportunity for a level of strength and depth you cannot obtain any other way. Encountering and working through hardship is how you become an expert gardener of life and the way you receive the bounty of your harvest.

OLD LOVERS STANDING IN SWEET EMBRACE
*An old couple with the man lovingly embracing
his beloved from behind*

SOME THOUGHTS ABOUT MATURE ADULT RELATIONSHIPS

Immature love says, "I love you because I need you."
Mature love says, "I need you because I love you."

Eric Fromm

AS WE GROW OLDER AND MATURE, so do our love and relationships mature. Our present ability in Winter to love and relate to other people is far different now than when we were in Spring and Summer. Aged love has the potential to grow wide and deep. The following are some random thoughts on maturity and mature relationships.

Two Halves Don't Make A Whole

Two halves don't make a whole. Two halves make two halves. An immature couple who are incomplete within themselves and attempt to complete themselves through their relationship, will end with an incomplete relationship.

Your relationship will be incomplete if you don't love yourself, and attempt to find self-love from being loved by another, if you tend toward melancholy and must rely on your partner to raise your spirits, if you lack self-control and need your partner to set boundaries for you, if you feel emotionally empty and want your partner to fill you up. You are seeking wholeness through another person.

Mature relationships consist of two people who are relatively whole within themselves who bring their wholeness into the relationship and soar together, not two individuals who bring their needs into the relationship in hopes that the other person will fulfill those needs.

Childish Beliefs

In the Bible, the Apostle Paul writes about growing up and putting away childish things. Children, as they are growing up and unable to take responsibility for themselves often assume that others will take responsibility for them. At a young age, this is appropriate because children are in need of the protection of an adult. However, as we grow to adulthood, we must take responsibility for our own life. If we don't, our passivity will get in the way of meeting our needs in life and relationships. The following are some assumptions and expectations concerning the power that you give to other people that keeps our relationships immature. By giving away your power to others, you dilute your own power and lose the ability to author your relationship.

You have the expectation that another person has the power to make you happy...	Other people cannot "make" you happy. Ultimately, you alone are responsible for your happiness or unhappiness, and you must work toward your happiness on your own.
You have the expectation that another person has the power to protect you from the pain of living...	Along with tears of joy, life inevitably dispenses tears of sadness. While other people can accompany you and support you in your time of need, your pain is yours alone to experience. The power to safeguard your being lies in your own hands.

You have the expectation that another person can provide you with a sense of your own self-worth…	While other people have their opinions about you, your self-esteem is something you develop on your own. You cultivate self-esteem by gaining knowledge and skills, accomplishing goals, appreciating your accomplishments, etc., also by understanding that, just being human, you are worthwhile beyond measure.
You have the expectation that you will be the center of another person's universe…	You are the center of your own world. Other people in your life are the center of their own world. If you want to be their center or if they expect you to be theirs, you're both in trouble. Though we may be surrounded by many people, ultimately, each of us is alone in our own universe.
You have the expectation that the state of your relationships, your partners and yourself will remain stable, even without your continuing positive behavior…	Change is the only thing that will never change. Even the best relationships are subject to change. It is the behavior of the partners that creates stability or flux. How you act with another person determines the state of your relationship with them.

A key sign of maturity is the willingness and ability to take responsibility for yourself in your life and your relationships. It will be very difficult to have a mature, fulfilling relationship with others if you hold these immature beliefs and continue to give away to them, the power you should assume for yourself.

Seeking Authorities

Another variety of immature belief is that there is some person of authority who possesses secret knowledge, a storehouse of wisdom, is the holder of the key to your happiness. You just have to find them, sit at their feet and follow what they say, and then… all will be revealed.

If you pay attention, each moment of your life is your teacher.

There is such a supreme authority in your life, but that teacher cannot be found outside yourself. That wise authority is you. The way you are taught is through life itself as it unfolds. The occurrences in your life provide all the learning materials you'll ever need. You merely have to pay attention, listen, feel. Your gut will tell you what is right or wrong, good or bad, destructive or beneficial. You don't even have to travel far. Your schoolroom is your relationships, your family, your workplace.

Earning Our Life And Our Relationships

An adult comes to understand, *there is no free lunch.* Happy or sad, fulfilled or unfulfilled, you've earned the life you have. You've earned it through the energy you bring, the time you spend, the resources you expend, the wisdom you glean. If you are a student, you study hard and earn a degree. As an employee, you work hard at your job and earn your salary. No study—no degree. No work—no salary. No free lunch.

This is especially true with adult relationships. People respond to the way they are treated. You earn your good relationships through treating those you care about with generosity, integrity and kindness. And your bad relationships you earn with greed, dishonesty and unkindness. Good relationships are joyful. But they cost you. Are you willing to pay the price?

Part of the price of maintaining a good relationship is that not only must you treat the other person in loving and caring ways, you must do so consistently. By that I mean you don't let up on your integrity, your presence, your commitment, etc.—ever. Letting up even one time, can cause irreparable damage to trust in the relationship. Lie once and you plant a seed of doubt in the other person's mind, "Are there other times they have lied to me?" Same with breaking your commitment to monogamy, to non-manipulation. to accountability. You can have 20 years of flawless commitment, and one breach can destroy all those years of accumulated trust.

Grownup Persons And Mature Relationships

Maturity doesn't just happen. It is a choice. When Alice and I were in Mexico, we purchased a little alter that held a tiny sculpture of an old skeleton walking with a cane. On it were written the words, *Envejecer es tu destino. Madurai es tu decision.* A friend fluent in Spanish translated. "Aging is your destiny. Maturing is your decision."

In the end, the destruction of love is not the work of a single cataclysmic event but the cumulative effect of countless small erosions.

George Blue Kelly

The truth is that everyone grows older. But not everyone grows up. Growing up is not simply adding up birthdays. To grow up is to grow deep. Look at a tree. As it gets taller, it's roots grow deeper. A magnificent tree needs a deep root system to nurture and support it. To deepen, to mature, takes work, takes attention, takes commitment.

For any relationship to be healthy and fulfilling, both people need to continually cultivate their maturity. A mature partner paired with an immature partner is unstable and invites conflict. Such a relationship is like a bird with one wing. However, when two mature partners find each other, they are able to soar.

Seeking Approval

Here I am, writing about mature relationships, and I note how some of my behavior around Alice is not mature at all. It's infantile. I notice that at times, I want her approval. I want her to see what a sterling, capable, heroic, strong, manly man I am, (even though I may not always believe it myself).

"Look Alice, I fixed the vacuum. Look Alice, I'm really serious about my exercise regimen. Look Alice, see what a good boy I am." It's not just with Alice. I notice my approval seeking behavior can come up anytime.

This feels like I'm a seven-year-old, back with trying to please my mommy and daddy. I don't like it. But I can't simply cut it off. This tendency toward approval seeking is such a deep part of me. Ancient history.

What to do? I realize I can't simply willpower this deeply ingrained mental habit away. So I try to simply be aware. I try to make note, without judgement, "There's my little boy again, trying for approval." I try to let him be as he is without judging myself too harshly if I can. I figure this hungry little boy is not going away anytime soon. He'll be around me in some form for the rest of my life. Might as well make friends with him. Hating him will only tighten his grip.

Stages Of Long Term Relationship—A Couple's Life Journey

It might be helpful here to look at what could be some typical stages that a couple in a long-term, committed relationship might go through over the span of their time together. (Inspired by Susan M. Campbell's book, *The Couple's Journey*).

Relationship is like a journey. In many ways this is a useful comparison. Being in loving connection is an adventure, an ongoing voyage of discovery. Over time, each partner learns about their mate, themselves and the process of living with and loving another person.

Typically, as couples grow together and become more comfortable and committed, their relationship will mature and they will progress through a series of stages. Each stage of a couple's journey represents new tasks to be accomplished, new challenges to be encountered, new learnings to be absorbed. Once the tasks of one stage are achieved, the opportunity to move onto the next stage comes into view. Successive stages firm up and deepen the couple's connection.

Honeymoon

New love is exciting, romantic. Holding hands, a first kiss, surprise gifts, confessing love. So many new things to learn as the stranger begins to become familiar. Both are on their best behavior. Neither person is aware of, or will tend to minimize the other's defects. Egos and bodies bask in the warmth of new love.

Disillusionment

Reality sets in as partners relax and allow more of their real, unvarnished selves to come out. He's a bit of a slob, she is sometimes lazy, he flies into rages when frustrated, she talks on the phone for hours with her girlfriends. The excitement has begun to wear off. Annoyance and resentment start to grow as partners become aware of each other's imperfections. Here is where work on the relationship begins.

Power Struggle

Partners express their dissatisfaction with each other's supposed defects and try to get the other person to change. They will try reasoning, arguing, criticizing, manipulating. Anything to get him to clean up after himself or get her off the phone. It's also about competition and establishing pecking order. Who will win, who will lose, who will be the one in control? If disillusionment and power struggle persist, it could lead to withdrawal or breakup of the relationship.

Truce

Power struggle is upsetting. It's unstable. After a while, if the relationship persists, couples settle control issues and negotiate a peace treaty, eventually becoming resigned to parts of their mate they don't fully accept, appreciative of the parts they do. Since many parts of the relationship are working well, they are willing to "live with" their mates supposed imperfections.

Acceptance

For the most part, the couple is happy enough with each other. They're getting their needs met, working together to create a happy, safe and secure nest. While things may not be perfect, they are certainly good enough. They've gotten real with each other, accepted and appreciated who they are, given up concentrated efforts to try to change the other. This stage could last for a long time or forever, and most couples remain content in this non demanding, comfortable and peaceable stage. This is what many people would call, a "good relationship," and in a sense it is good.

Conscious Commitment

The couple who have reached this stage is not content with a "good enough" relationship. They want their union to be great. They are willing to do what they can, as individuals and as a couple, to further their own and their partner's physical, intellectual, emotional, social and spiritual unfolding. They make mutual fulfillment the central goal in the relationship, and are willing to sacrifice some of their wants and needs in order to grow their partnership. It is here, in the Conscious Commitment stage, where individuals grow to maturity, and where their relationship can deepen into passionate, generous, conscious love.

Realize that this description of the stages of a relationship is just a simplistic sketch. Each stage contains so much more than what is abstracted here. For example, a couple in Power Struggle stage may be jockeying for position, yet at the same time, be deeply in love with each other.

Not all couples will go through these stages, and those who do, may not go through all of them, and not necessarily in this order. It's interesting to see this as an aerial view of long-term relationship.

An Alliance For Serving Others

There is another stage in long-term relationship. It is quite rare, but very powerful. It occurs when a couple has achieved a degree of Conscious Commitment and has the desire to bring out into the world the love and generosity they have found in their relationship. Martin Luther King Jr. and Coretta Scott King, Bill and Melinda Gates are examples of couples who have made meaningful contributions. But shared service doesn't have to be on an expanded stage. A couple can team up to serve their neighborhood, community or extended family. When a couple is in alliance with each other, they can work together to create a better world.

Goodwill And Conflict

Conflict is a fact of life. Even the most loving couples and stalwart friends who are together for many years can become embroiled in conflict. When two people get together, there will always be times when needs, beliefs and intentions do not match.

Often, people think that when they are having conflict there's something wrong with their relationship, that conflict is a bad thing and should be eliminated. The absence of conflict does not indicate that a relationship is healthy, nor does the presence of conflict indicate that a relationship is in trouble. Actually, the collision of desires and wills is an indication that the relationship is real and on track.

One thing I am certain of—when mature adults are in conflict, if one person wins—both will lose. The only winner of the conflict should be the relationship. The relationship wins when both persons have goodwill toward each other and goodwill is the foundation of the way they resolve their conflict.

When Alice and I have a disagreement, maintaining goodwill is uppermost in our minds. As unusual as it sounds, we want our conflict to be a positive experience. Alice genuinely wants me to be satisfied with the outcome and I want her to be satisfied too. We want the conclusion we arrive at to be balanced. We don't want each other to lose. We are unwilling to take advantage of each other in any way. We want the process of coming to resolution to be harmonious. Neither of us wants angry arguments, hurtful words, manipulation or power struggles. We want there to be no lingering ill will. We want, as much as possible, for there to be no under-addressed issues, no leftover resentments, no unexpressed bad feelings and no unspoken expectations about the future. Basically, we want our conflicts to be an expression of our goodwill and love for each other. When this happens, conflict draws us closer together rather than pulling us apart.

You Will Find What You Look For

There is a saying that is very true. *"When a pickpocket meets a wise man, all he sees are his pockets."*

What you look for is what you'll find. If you look for faults in others, you will find them. If you look for their fine qualities, you will find them.

Alice is not perfect. I'll spare you the list. (I'm sure Alice has a list of her own.) Fortunately, neither of our lists are very long. I turn a blind eye to those few imperfections I find in Alice. She is not my improvement project. I require enough of my own self-improvement to take a lifetime. So I do my best to accept her as-is. I ignore the things I think she needs to improve, unless it's harmful to her, to me or to the relationship.

I find that when I look for her fine qualities and praise her for them, those qualities seem to grow more prominent.

Anger Mixed With Love

Anger, conflict and arguments shouldn't close down your heart. I often tell the story of an argument that Alice and I had years ago. I don't remember the issue. We had been driving when our conversation became heated and I pulled the car off the road and parked. We were facing each other, nose to nose, screaming at the other at the top of our lungs. In the midst of our fury, we both looked down at the same moment. We were holding hands, maintaining our loving connection. The anger dissolved into laughter.

Loving concern endures. Like clouds floating in a clear blue sky, anger will dissipate and pass. The clear sky of love remains.

A Love Nest

A pair of sparrows have built a nest in the rafters over our front door. It's a sturdy nest. Sparrows mate for life, and this pair worked on the nest together. The bowl-shaped outer support is made of sticks and brambles, but the inside is soft and neatly lined with grass and feathers so it will be warm and cozy for the eggs and the baby birds.

We identify with these two tiny feathered friends. Alice and I, lovebirds that we are, have created our own nest. We've gone to great lengths to make our home a comfortable and inviting nesting place. Our home and the surrounding garden is an extension of ourselves and a reflection of our relationship. Every niche and cranny, inside and out, reflects our love for each other. All the pictures on the wall and every knickknack and piece of furniture holds a sweet memory. Our home is our love nest.

I believe that every person's living space reflects their mind space and heart space. I've been to a party at a multi-millionaire's palatial mansion, sumptuously decorated by professionals, no expense spared. Valuable antique furniture graced every room and priceless Old Master paintings hung on the walls. The property was surrounded by high fences, topped by razor wire. There was a guard at the tall steel entry gates, and armed guards roamed the property to protect life and objects within. That living space felt cold and totally devoid of soul. I've also been in poor people's simple living spaces that are overflowing with warmth and love.

Alice and I were in a taxi in a rural part of India when the driver told us that we were about to pass his house. He asked if we would like to stop in for tea. Of course we agreed. We pulled up to an adobe-covered, boxlike, tin-roofed structure, about the size of an average living room in America. Inside the house, the single room was divIded by blankets into kitchen, living, storage and sleeping areas. I didn't see a bathroom and assume it was a communal one outside, shared with neighboring houses. The driver borrowed chairs from a neighbor so that we would not have to sit on the dirt floor. His wife prepared the tea in the "kitchen," boiling water drawn from a community well simmered on a small gas burner that sat on the floor. Their baby gurgled contentedly in a woven basket suspended

241

from the rafters in the ceiling. The dried mud walls had colorful pictures of Hindu gods, Ganesh and Laxmi, and several family photos. There was one small window, and on that windowsill was a glass jar with a flower. The couple were bursting with pride about their humble home and were delighted to show it to us. Their simple room was suffused with love. This was their love nest.

Neatening The Nest

I was born during a time when there was a sharp demarcation between men's work and women's work. The "little lady's" domain was the house interior. She was the one who cleaned and washed, cooked and took care of the kids. The man went out into the world and worked to bring home the bacon, carried heavy objects and fixed what broke. Dad wouldn't think of picking up a broom, neither would mom consider mowing the lawn. This was the way it was with my mom and dad, and I thought this is the way it should be with me. I learned differently when I got married.

A couple's living space is a shared venue. It is also the crucible where love lives. Home is also each person's refuge, a place where they can close the door to the frantic outside world and rest and restore themselves. I believe it is an act of love for both partners to participate in keeping their home clean and neat, and to share other duties that maintains their life together. It doesn't have to be the exact equal amount of sharing, but taking care of house and hearth should be a shared enterprise. I write this in the early afternoon, after having just washed my hands from cutting up fresh fruit for fruit salad for lunch, cleaned the drainboard, scrubbed the pot I boiled eggs in and folded the laundry. It feels to me like I wasn't engaged in household drudgery. I was performing acts of love dedicated to Alice, to myself, to our life together, and to our sweet home.

"Soulmates"?

Is there such a thing as a soulmate? A one and only? A match made in heaven? Each of us could have probably had any number of partners that would fit hand in glove with us. It doesn't matter. In any mature relationship, always, always bring your best self to the relationship you're in. Sometimes, even after being in a long term relationship, we'll experience "buyers remorse." Especially after a conflict, we might feel that maybe we've made a mistake and there might be a genuine soulmate out there. That may or may not be true.

However, whether your relationship has lasted one day or a lifetime, you owe it to yourself to treat the person with whom you are in connection, with as much integrity, goodwill, kindness and care as you can. Don't withhold part of your lovingkindness and save it for some future time with an imagined soulmate. Don't compromise when it comes to your heart. If you show up with less of your loving self than you are capable of, you cheat yourself as well as the one you're with.

Appreciating Past "Imperfect" Relationships

I love Tiana, my second wife. Alice loves her too. She is like a sister to us. We have taken vacations together and she comes and stays with us several times a year. We are fortunate to have each other in our lives.

In the distant past, beside good times, there was much pain Tiana and I inflicted on one another. That's gone. There's only love now. We're both sorry we had to go through the pain, but we understand it was necessary and valuable for us to do that. We were immature and too blind to learn any other way than through suffering. Same with my third wife, Susan. She doesn't travel much, but I'm glad we keep in touch by phone. It's good that we share each other's life and love. I feel good having extended family with years of intimate history behind us, even though some of that history was imperfect.

Alice has had a few "imperfect" relationships of her own. One in particular she especially appreciates. They haven't spoken in decades, and never will again. Alice appreciates this man because he taught her so much. He taught her what she didn't want in a relationship. He taught her that she deserved to be respected and treated well in a relationship. What a wonderful gift he gave her when he left her for another woman.

Puppy Love For Old Dogs

When we envision mature relationships we probably envision an elder couple, grey hair, wrinkles, looking very adult and sedate. However, I believe mature relationships should be able to include childlike innocence and unbridled enthusiasm. True maturity must encompass the ability to be "as simple as a blade of grass," as well as being as solid as a rock.

In the early seventies I had the honor of playing drums backing up the legendary bluesman, John Lee Hooker for several concerts. John Lee had a song, a slow blues he would sing called, *I Want To Be Your Puppy, Baby.* Some of the lyrics go, "I want to be your little puppy dog. I want to wag my tail and come runnin' to you. Put a leash around my neck, baby and lead me anywhere you want to go. I lay down at your feet. You pop your fingers, I'll keep running to you. Baby, I just wanna be your puppy dog."

The image of innocent surrender. The picture comes to mind of coming home after a days work and being greeted as you open the door. Your young dog has awakened by the sound of the key in the latch and is excitedly racing around, tail wagging, jumping up and down, blissfully happy to see you back. That's the way we both feel when Alice and I have been separated for even a few hours and are reunited. It's puppy love, even though we're both old dogs.

Being an uninhibited young pup around the ones you love is not just for youth. It might even be a marker for mature love.

Suitcase Packed

Looking back at past relationships, I realize that with every one of them, I lacked the commitment to stay around if things got uncomfortable. I always gave myself an "out." Metaphorically, my bags were packed and sitting by the door, ready, just in case the relationship got too real.

This was not so with Alice and I. Without the slightest doubt, she and I were in it for the long haul, and this made all the difference.

Commitment is a jail. Committing to a person, a job, an ideal, is to foreclose an exit. It is willingly entering a cell, locking the door and throwing away the key. Why would a couple do that in a relationship? Making the commitment to stay and work through difficulties allows each partner to dig deep beneath the surface, past the old hurts and immature bs. Deep within is where they will find the buried treasures of compassion, unity and self-understanding. Deep within is where they will find true love.

A person can dig many shallow wells, but if the water lays far beneath the surface, it only takes drilling one deep well to find it. Commitment is that deep well.

How To Fall In Love With Everyone

Can romantic love be manufactured? In 2015, author Mandy Len Catron wrote an article titled, "How To Fall In Love With Anyone, Do This," which was published online in the "Modern Love" section of the New York Times. It became one of the most popular articles of the year, and within a month, garnered over 8 million views. The article was based on a series of 36 questions developed by psychologist, Dr Arthur Aaron and his team, designed to allow pairs of strangers, who took turns answering the questions to each other, through self-disclosure, to foster closer interpersonal relationships between strangers within a short time.

The questions started out innocently enough, and then became increasingly personal, so that by the time the final questions were answered, the pairs knew very intimate information about each other. The experiment ended with the pairs staring into each other's eyes for several minutes. What generated interest was that some of the couples actually fell in love. And a few even got married. Mandy and her partner, who barely knew each other at the time, were one of those couples who fell in love and are happily married.

My takeaway—when you and another person open yourselves and honestly reveal genuinely intimate things about yourselves, you both become more lovable. It may not be true with everyone, for example, if the person were an axe murderer. And it may end in intimate friendship rather than intimate love. But I think that in general, if a person opens themselves to you, you will tend to feel more close to them, and more inclined to open yourself to them. To know someone is a precursor to caring for them. And in order to love someone, you must know them. This applies to old and new relationships, intimate partners or friends.

Intimacy, as the old statement says, is In-To-Me-See.

Communication

Clear communication is considered very important for good relationships. Often, many hours of couples therapy is devoted to helping couples better communicate with each other.

I wrote a book for men about love and relationships, titled BECOMING LOVE-ABLE. There is a whole chapter about communication. It consists of only one short paragraph, which I reproduce a portion below.

"Not that being able to communicate your thoughts and feelings openly, clearly and succinctly isn't important. It is. But what's more important is the impulse behind the communication. If you don't have love in your heart or if you aim to lie and manipulate, your communication will serve to facilitate those ends. Even if your communication is sloppy, if you are coming from love and kindness, somehow those feelings will be received. What I am saying is, become more love-able. If you do, communication will take care of itself."

Defensiveness

When we act defensively, what are we defending? We are protecting an image of ourselves that we believe is true, or, more often, protecting against an image we believe is false (but have a sneaking suspicion is actually true). That suspicion? We are wrong, bad, less than, screwed up or in some way, a flawed human. Bottom line: we feel we are not lovable. We don't want others to know, and we want to avoid rejection and deflect criticism and not feel shame or hurt, so we become defensive.

Defensiveness works because it creates a side skirmish that takes the spotlight off of true feelings.

A feedback loop ensues whereby the other person, feeling blamed, becomes defensive in turn. Mutual defensive feelings and responses cycle back and forth, often increasing in intensity. True feelings are lost. Neither person feels heard. Problems are not resolved and conflict escalates further.

The antidote—making the choice to act like a mature adult. When feeling defensiveness beginning to arise during conflict—listening to the other, expressing genuine feelings and accepting responsibility. This allows the balm of truth and caring to enter the interaction, and ends the need to defend.

Farts

It was shortly after we met and fell in love. We were peacefully lying in bed, when suddenly, Alice let out a big fart. She looked at me sheepishly. I let out a fart of my own. Stench. We smiled. No suppressing. We are starting off our relationship being real with each other.

Polishing Rocks, Polishing People

People's relationships can be compared to a rock tumbler, a device consisting of an electric motor connected by gears or a belt to a tubular metal cylinder that slowly revolves, sometimes continuously for days. You put ordinary looking rocks in the cylinder, and the rocks will constantly rub against each other, smoothing out all the jagged, uneven edges. When the tumbler stops, what were once ordinary stones, have been polished into beautiful, shiny, jewel-like gems.

This same kind of thing happens in a committed, long-term relationship. Through their years of loving and arguing, resistance, honesty and compromise, a couple who have chosen to remain together will have their hard edges polished smooth. The friction will have done its job. Then they, and their relationship, become beautiful.

Sympathetic Joy

Shared pain is half the pain. Shared joy is twice the joy.

German proverb

Sympathetic joy is rejoicing from another person's good fortune. It is experiencing happiness for another person's well-being, unadulterated by self-interest. Your friend wins the lottery, you're genuinely happy for them. Another example, a mother's pride and happiness seeing her child progress in school. The opposite of sympathetic joy is jealousy and envy. Jealousy and envy is fueled by greed. A coworker gets a promotion and we put on a false smile and congratulate them, but inside we feel, "Why couldn't it have been me?"

Sympathetic joy is an essential aspect of mature relationships. It's natural to feel happiness when your partner or friend experiences good fortune. You are tied to them by your caring: their blessing is your blessing. However, some couples or friends feel competitive with one another. If one person wins, they feel they have lost, as if there is a limited amount of good fortune to go around. The greed and envy they feel is the opposite of sympathetic joy. Sympathetic joy is the antidote to greed and envy.

Buddhists place great value on sympathetic joy. Their name for it is *mudita*. They have many practices and meditations that are aimed at increasing *mudita*.

The Dalai Lama has said, "If I am only happy for myself, many fewer chances for happiness. If I am happy when good things happen to other people, billions more chances to be happy!"

Love And Acceptance

Our beloved asks us, "Love me as I am, accept me for who I am." This acceptance is an aspect of unconditional love. Unconditional love is held as an ideal, as the best kind of love. But does this love without conditions always serve our partner? Might we fully accept our partner, yet still hold out for them to be a better version of themselves?

For example, let's say that I've had a strong work ethic and valued getting things accomplished, but suppose lately, I've gotten fat and lazy. My "to do" list has grown to unmanageable proportions, leaving important tasks undone while I lay around on the couch, eating bon-bons, drinking beer and playing video games. If this were the case, how could Alice hold me in "unconditional positive regard," while still kicking my ass to get me to take care of necessary business?

There lies the conundrum. We can love and accept our partner for who they are, yet also see the potential for them to follow through with their positive intentions and be their best and highest self. To hold that vision for them, and apply pressure to motivate them, is a beautiful way to serve them. If we can do this without blaming or putting them down, what a way to inspire them, what an invitation for them to grow.

It's a real slippery slope. As soon as we insist that our partner change, that sets up a resistance. The stronger our insistence, the greater the resistance. Alice has things (not many, she says), that she would like to change about me, and sometimes she is quite vocal about it. But I know that Alice deeply loves and accepts me, and if I didn't change a bit, she wouldn't love me any less. I'm the same way about Alice. I think that's as close to unconditional love and acceptance that people can get.

Compassion

As we look upon our world and our life from the perspective of the many years we have lived, we may be fortunate to have acquired a quality that has the ability to enlighten the darkest of our judgements—compassion. Compassion, similar to empathy, is our ability to feel for another's pain, and to have some understanding of the sources of that pain. In addition, compassion includes an action component—a willingness to be of service to help alleviate that pain.

The sources of pain in people's lives varies with each individual, but at bottom, the source is the same—injury. People are hurt, by insult, by poverty, by betrayal, by the judgements and unkind acts of others. They retreat their innocent, vulnerable heart to a place where they feel protected. They turn away and wall off their feelings. But sometimes the injury is so severe and the pain so intense, that they strike out with vengeance and force others to endure the same injuries that they have endured. They cause others harm.

The Dalai Lama was speaking to a Tibetan monk who had been recently released from a Chinese jail, where, for 18 years, he had been isolated, and often beaten and starved. The monk said that he had repeatedly experienced danger. "What danger?" the Dalai Lama asked. The monk replied. "The danger of losing my compassion."

How, as mature, caring adults, shall we look upon such injured people? One way is, *with the compassion of a loving mother toward her errant child.* A loving mother sees her child's ignorance, pain and immaturity. Her compassion prevents her from judging too harshly, or meting out punishment that will create harm rather than benefit.

Though we might have that depth of compassion for people who harm others, we should remember, evil exists and is dangerous. We shouldn't minimize the danger and destruction such people present to self and society, and we should take measures that will protect ourselves from them. But if we could see all people with an eye of compassion, even those who purposely hurt others, our heart will not be so burdened by the weight of blame and desire for retaliation and revenge. This will release us, and allow our kindness to continue to flow, and maybe to even be of service to an injured soul. Isn't this what we want?

The Spiritual Aspect Of Relationship—Self to Self

I had written before that I considered relationship to be in the spiritual dimension as well as the mundane. As we develop more as spiritual beings, all our life and all our relationships take on a holy aspect. That means that everyday problems that arise in relationships and life are also spiritual

We are not human beings having a spiritual experience. We are spiritual beings having a human experience.

Pierre Teilhard de Chardin

250

problems, to be approached with spiritual solution. Working to transmute our ordinary ego self, (with its obsession about "I, me and mine,") into an expanded Self that taps into the mystery and majesty of the universe, is a primary goal of the spiritual quest. This quest will have a powerful effect on all our relationships. It will be most noticeable with our intimate relationship. We will tend to view our partner as more than just their physical body and collection of mental and emotional complexes. We might even come to see them as an emanation of divine energy, as a god or goddess in human form. (Or, as Mother Teresa would say, "Christ in one of his many disguises.") Seeing this aspect of our beloved as a spiritual being, we will treat them with utmost honor and respect. As we are able to see the divine in our beloved, so we are capable of seeing the divine in ourselves. When we see the divine in our self and our beloved, could it be that difficult to see the divinity of all others?

To welcome people, to love people, is the greatest worship of God.

Swami Muktananda

As our expanded Self evolves, we become more able to access our spirit nature. All the relationships we develop begin to evolve from the ego realm of *self-to-self*, to the spiritual realm of *Self-to-Self*. This sharing of spirit is the flowering of the highest and deepest level of relationship, the deepest level of love. This is the apex of mature love.

The Little Things

Last night Alice was cold. I got up out of bed, put socks on her feet and brought a blanket and tucked her in. This afternoon, Alice noticed the sun was in my eyes. She walked to the car and brought my hat.

It's not the words or thoughts or the grand gestures. It's the small things done with great love that express love the best.

Not all of us can do great things. But we can do small things with great love.

Mother Teresa

> *Every gesture is a seed, and the seed determines the harvest.*
>
> Wayne Muller

This Shared Journey Of Our Aging

Alice and I look at each other, watching with wistfulness and curiosity as our faces and bodies age day by day, month by month. Smiling, we call each other "old man" and "old woman." Often, we accompany each other for grocery shopping, or on visits to doctor's offices, making sure we go out to lunch before or after so that the chore becomes a shared excursion. At night, we lay in bed, together, but alone, reading our respective books or looking at our laptop. Or we'll gossip late into the night… holding hands. Then we'll cuddle into each other's warm bodies like the little mammals we are. This shared journey of aging is so poignant, so sweet.

What a privilege to share my life, my home, my bed, my heart with Alice, a privilege made sweeter with the knowledge that our time together is growing short. We think of our friends, so many of whom have lost their beloved partners, or have divorced, or have never had a long-term relationship, and we value, even more, our precious time.

Having this person in my life, knowing her as I know myself, being known by her, caring for her as I care for myself, being cared for by her, is to come to the realization that we are not alone in the universe. In this life, in this time, as each of us passes through the "vale of tears," we have a fellow traveler to keep us company. This makes all the difference.

OLD FACE

PART 4.
PREPARATION FOR WINTER

Life really does begin at forty. Up until then you are just doing research.

Carl Jung

BEFORE GOING INTO BATTLE, a good general spends much time and effort in preparation. He works out his battle plan. He consults with his officers and other experts. He considers what moves the opposing forces might make, and what he can do to counter those moves. He makes sure of his artillery and supplies, his transport of men and material, his air support, etc.

In a sense, preparing for old age is like preparing for war, a war with time. We enter the war knowing we might win a few battles, but ultimately, will lose the war. Knowing that, if we do not stand up and fight "the good fight," we will have lost before we have begun. To fight the good fight well, we must prepare well.

Broken Air Conditioner Unit

The summers are hot where we live here in Ojai. The days of 100-plus-degree Fahrenheit weather would leave our house sweltering without air conditioning. So when our fairly new whole-house AC unit was not working as it should, I called the company that installed it less than a year ago. The technician came out, put on a gauge to test the pressure, and just stood around while the pressure in the compressor kept climbing far higher than it should. There was a loud bang, as a part exploded. Not only that, the high pressure might have damaged other parts of the unit. The company wouldn't take responsibility, and wanted over a thousand dollars just to replace the part their worker ruined. Even then, once that part was replaced, was the whole unit defective because of the extreme pressure?

I was incensed. I spent hours researching on the internet. I got estimates, spoke to other technicians, and there was consensus—the company screwed up and should take responsibility. (Be patient, there's a point to the story.)

For almost a month, I wrote well-crafted letters to the company, made phone calls to the manufacturer, consulted with experts, did online research into the complex intricacies of AC technology. More letters, more phone calls. Still, the company kept lying and would not take responsibility. I explored legal remedies, Small Claims Court, the Contractors Licensing Board.

The frustration was taking over my mind. Righteous anger would burst into my meditations, and they became meditations on air conditioning. I found it hard to fall asleep at night without obsessively thinking about it. And when I did sleep, my anger would play out in my dreams.

I consulted a lawyer friend who had worked on multi-million dollar contracts with the federal government. He read the fine printing of the contract. Even though the problem was caused by their employee, there was nothing I could do. They won.

Why am I writing about this? And why, in this section about preparing for old age?

This incident led to an important realization for me. My mind was out of control, racing around like a wild monkey. With so little control over my mind, provoked by a relatively minor incident like this, how much more mental suffering might result if I was confronted with a serious one.

What if Alice got sick, or died, or I contracted a serious, debilitating illness? How mentally prepared was I for these eventualities? Apparently, not very. There's a litany of all the ills common in old age: arthritis, dementia, chronic pain, stroke, blindness, cancer, heart attack, and on and on. What's the chance that we'll both escape all of these and live out the Winter of our lives to a hearty old age, pain free and illness free? Not impossible, but not likely. When these events would happen to Alice or me or family and loved ones, what will be my response? Will I have a monkey mind to contend with? Judging by my reaction to a broken air conditioner, probably. This incident showed me that I needed to work with my mind, so that I will be prepared in advance for difficult circumstances when they occur.

Preparation is essential. When Winter is about to come to our mini-farm, we prepare our home. We make sure the roof is secure, stow wood for the fireplace, protect plants that are not cold hardy, try out the generator and check the gas cans, etc. We should do the same preparation with our life as we enter old age.

The things that will happen with our physical body are determined by our genes, our circumstances and our luck. We do have some control. It's obvious that we should take care of our bodies, with healthy food and proper exercise, using care as we walk and drive, securing our finances, nurturing our relationships. But it is mostly our mind that will determine how much we suffer. It's not the events in our life that will cause us the most suffering, but our attitude toward those events. So it is of prime importance that we work with our mind so that, when we encounter the cold winds of Winter, we will be protected from its most painful blasts. These and related topics will be the subjects of this, the final section of the book.

First we'll look at some of the things we usually consider negative aspects of aging that actually have positive properties. Then we'll explore things we can do that can help lessen the impact of the infirmities of old age and make this last stage of life more fulfilling.

A CHALLENGE AND A BLESSING: UNEXPECTED GIFTS OF AGING

When we courageously confront the past, we discover how much we have gained from apparent losses. Once we get beyond our anxiety, we glory in the hidden benefits that accrue from what we took to be painful failures.

Rabbi Zalman Schachter-Shalomi

WE GET OLD. WE LOSE PASSION. We get feeble and sick. We hurt. We die. It's a bad plan. Is this our inevitable fate as we age? Is weakness, slowness, illness and dependency inherently always negative? Is there any upside to this cruel plan? I hope so. I'm old, and it's inevitable that I will be growing older day by day. In spite of the considerable challenges from growing old, I believe the passing years hold the ability to reward us with life-enhancing gifts, even in old age. We can begin to receive them by opening our mind and letting go of preconceived negative judgments we hold about aging. *Aging gracefully is finding grace in our aging.* There is grace in growing old. It's not obvious. It is sometimes hidden. I believe it is important to search for the gifts of age.

Many of the gifts I recount here, at first view, seem more like burdens that aging forces us to endure. It's a paradox—that which causes us great discomfort can also have aspects that are a blessing.

Who in their right mind would want the gift of suffering, or losing your youthful appearance, or the gift of bad memory? These losses hurt, and the pain should not be minimized. There is no possible way a devastating loss, like a debilitating illness or death of a partner can be compensated for. But there are rewards. However, if you focus solely on the negativity of aging, you'll make yourself miserable and you'll miss the gifts. As you explore them more deeply, you can see how rich and potentially rewarding these unexpected gifts of aging can be.

The Gift Of Perspective

There's a hike we like to take that is not too far from our home. We drive our car up a winding country road that climbs for about 15 minutes, till we reach the end at the summit. We park, pass through a gate, and begin our walk. Shortly, after rounding the first curve, we are treated to a spectacular vista. Range after range lay beneath us, all the way to the ocean, and stretching beyond, a series of islands, the Channel Islands, are visible. Until we got to the vista point, all we saw was trees and road.

When we first moved here, we had just a vague idea where our house was situated, where the town lay, where the neighboring city was located. Our knowledge was gained from maps, but that gave us a superficial understanding of the terrain. Standing on the peak of Sulphur Mountain, with its panoramic views, provided us the actual experience of where we were. Looking back, we could also see parts of the road and the trail from where we came. Looking ahead we could see where the trail led. This is the advantage of perspective. Perspective allows you to scope out the territory, where you are, where you came from, where you are going. Perspective from the experience of living helps you scope out your life.

Aside from the obvious advantage of still being alive, a real benefit in having attained old age is the gift of accumulating perspective. Growing older gives you the possibility of a panoramic view of your life, a panoramic view of your generation, a panoramic view of what it is to be human. From the vantage point of age, we are able to observe origins and development, follow trends over long periods, see potential dead ends or opportunities before they occur. This is knowledge younger persons are not privy to.

As an elder, you have weathered storms. You have a storehouse of experiences and feelings. With years under your belt, and with mistakes made, problems solved, pain endured, joy celebrated, people loved, you have a greater understanding of the meaning and purpose of your life. You see the events that have happened as figures in the tapestry of your life. Your life-long experience has given you an appreciation of the complexity of human life and human beings, a tolerance of frustration, and a sense of lightness born of detachment.

With a lifetime of experiences, there are things an older person knows that a younger person has yet had time to learn, things that can only be understood by having lived years of a life. Yet, let's be clear, perspective is not the same as wisdom. It is an aspect of wisdom, but wisdom takes more than seeing with wider perspective. Perspective is the raw material. Wisdom is integration of that material into your heart, gut and mind. Wisdom uses perspective to gain understanding. With understanding, we choose to act in ways that foster highest good for self and others. Without perspective though, there is a deficit of understanding, and therefore, a deficit of wisdom.

The Gift Of The Passing Away Of Youthful Physical Beauty

You might have noticed, age changes your physical appearance. Day by day, more wrinkles, more bulges, more grey hair. There are ways to delay the ravages of age, such as surgery, hair dyes, Botox injections, tummy tucks, slimming salons, vitamin supplements and makeup and various creams and lotions. These may work for awhile to keep the old appearance at bay, and for many women, this is a choice they are happy with. (And for men too. There are cosmetics for men, steroids to build muscle and surgical procedures to enhance men's appearance, and these are being used with greater frequency.)

I hold no opinion, one way or another, of people doing all they want in order to be able to look younger. Actually, it's great to look youthful. But I've noticed that when people are attached to looking young, and in fear of looking old, the stronger the attachment to their youthful appearance, the greater the chance they will suffer as they age. There's no escaping time. As they grow older and the years take their toll on their youthful appearance, people who place primary importance on looking young have the opportunity for continuous self-torture. Each wrinkle, each blemish, each new gray hair, will be a cause for suffering.

We earn our face and body. Our life experiences, our personality and character are impressed into our flesh. This is our real beauty, not society's jaded view, with its emphasis on youth. (Probably the average age of Vogue models is late adolescent or early twenties.) When I look at these young women, I see surface perfection, but I don't see soul. It takes time to develop inner beauty. Time and heart.

I remember when I was in my early twenties, I saw a photograph of the famous artist, Georgia O'Keefe. That photo left a lasting impression on me. She must have been around eighty years old at the time the photo was taken. Her face was a mass of wrinkles, probably from years living in the Southwest sun. What blew me away at the time was that I saw the incredible beauty in her face, her inner beauty. I was attracted to her, and that surprised me, given that, up until that time I had only been attracted to youthful beauty.

The choice, as I see it: take good care of your appearance, but don't make it your reason for living. Surface beauty comes and goes, inner beauty remains. Surrender to the forces of age on face and body and relax and appreciate the beauty of the moment. Every season has its beauty. Is Summer more beautiful than Spring? Is Autumn more beautiful than Winter? Enjoy your appearance in whatever age you're at. Look upon the changes wrought by aging with curiosity and appreciation. The alternative is to wage continuous battle against the inevitable losing war with time. You'll temporarily win a few battles, but you'll lose the war. Fight the war as you will, and lose with grace. Meanwhile, enjoy the physical appearance you've earned. Your inner beauty impressed on your face and body is a gift that time has given you.

Go right now and look at your face in the mirror. Really look, but try to do it without looking for the imperfections, the wrinkles and sags. Look beyond those and see the brightness that shines through your eyes, the patina of wisdom that age has given your face. You'll smile at your image.

The Gift To Life Of The Recognition Of The Nearness Of Death

Death draws nearer as you age. Each day you live is one day less you have to live. We fail to understand that when the Grim Reaper knocks on our door, he is also bearing a great gift. The realization of your mortality that he brings is the greatest motivation for you to wake up…or go to sleep. For many people though, the sleep of ignoring the closeness of death is a choice they make. The thought of the annihilation of their personhood is too much to contemplate. So they keep thoughts of death at arms length, and never receive the gift.

As you grow older, more and more, death has a way of injecting itself into your consciousness. Family and friends die and you attend services, maybe even in the first row. You hear of the death of icons like movie stars and political figures, and feel a part of your history has been erased. You get ill or receive a grave diagnosis and the thought of your demise becomes much more real. You rearrange your priorities. The realization that you do not have limitless time is a wake-up call that pushes you to live more in the immediate moment. You can focus more on enjoying the little things—an intimate conversation with a friend, the taste of your morning coffee, a slow walk in the park.

With the reality of your death staring you in the face, you may be motivated to prioritize what is important to you. You may search for more meaningful answers to the question your recognition of impermanence brings up, "What should I do with my remaining time?" This is a good question, an essential question. It's one that should be asked at any time of life, but it is especially relevant in the later years.

Time feels more precious as it keeps running out. We're more careful now to not waste it on things we have no real interest in, people who bore us, and places we don't want to be. We have no time for bullshit. We want our life to be real, to be meaningful. We want to pursue things that we had put off, things that give us joy. That is the gift the nearness of death has for us.

Our friend Bill woke up in the hospital after having a life-threatening heart attack. The first thing he did was summon his wife to his bedside and tell her he wanted a divorce. No more time for bullshit. He wanted his life to be real, and knew that if he would remain in his OK, but lifeless marriage, he would continue to slowly die inside. And so would his wife. So he chose life. His experience of being close to death is what cemented that choice.

The Gift To Relationship Of Recognition Of Nearness Of Death

As Alice and I have grown older, and as our time is getting shorter, awareness of our deaths has been a great gift to our relationship. It has made our life together more precious and our love more deep. There is a realization we have of the reality of "the last." Our planned vacation up to Northern California in coming months might be our last. Our making love last night might have been our last. The dinner we are preparing for tonight might be the last one we have together. Knowing about "the last" has made the moments of our life more precious. More than any other time in our lives, we savor our time together.

Say you have a large jar full of jellybeans, and you are a jellybean connoisseur. At first, with that full jar, you think nothing about reaching in and grabbing a handful of beans and popping them into your mouth. After awhile, the jar is half empty and you start thinking about conserving. When you are down to the last few beans, you take one at the time, maybe save for a special occasion. And that last bean…you hold it in your mouth till it melts and you savor the last of the slowly vanishing flavor. Those beans are Alice and my diminishing years, and there's getting to be fewer in the bottom of the jar.

When we first got together, we enjoyed our life. We gave no thought to the future and believed we would live forever. But not now. The nearness of death is often on our minds. Yes, there is sadness, profound sadness, but in the sadness is gratefulness, and poignancy, and the delicious savoring the moment of our experience together. We love each other more now than we ever thought possible. Thanks to the gift of our recognition of the nearness of our death.

The Gift That Can Come In The Time Before Dying

In the weeks before he died, Riley sat in his chair or lay in his bed while visitors filed in and out of his room to hang out or say goodbye. Family, psychotherapy clients, old friends and neighbors would drop by to say goodbye in any way that felt right for them. Some would play cards with him or watch TV. Some would reminisce. Some would cry. But we all felt the preciousness of these moments, the last we would see of this incredible man.

These were times which stood out in our minds and hearts because they were so real. Death is real, it wakes us up. No time for bullshit.

Riley's wife, Rhoda, gave and received bounteous gifts during the time of his dying. Rhoda stepped up. She and Riley were both strong personalities, unafraid to assert their opinions and individual desires. But with Riley ill, Rhoda's needs became secondary. Her only mission became to serve him and make him comfortable. I had never seen her so dedicated and so surrendered, and so loving.

I had known Riley for almost 38 years. The hours I spent with him before his death were the most intimate moments in all that time. Riley and I spoke candidly of our love and appreciation for each other. It was a beautiful way to reach completion and say goodbye. These last weeks were a gift to both of us.

At the end of his life, Riley, was able to harvest the love he had planted throughout his lifetime. A gift to him and to us.

The Gift Of Not Having A Role

I have retired. I am no longer seeing clients or leading groups. I am not *"A Psychotherapist."* My ears are damaged. I no longer play drums in a band. I am not *"A Drummer."* I rarely sculpt anymore. I am not *"A Sculptor."* If I am not these roles anymore, who am I?

When we retire from our work, our career, our function, what is our role? Maybe we play a bit of golf, grandparent our children's kids, go on a cruise. Who are we? We go to a cocktail party, engage in conversation with an affable stranger, the inevitable question comes up, "And what do you do?" How do we answer that question when we've lost our role?

But our role consists of what we've done. It's of the past, ancient history. Who we are without a role, is *who we genuinely are.* If we are brave enough to let go of our role, we stand up in front of the world as we are in this moment, unclothed in degrees and titles, without the veneer of our "specialness." What we present to the world and what the world sees of us is what they get. And we can simply relax and be who we are.

The Gift Of Bad Memory

I look back fondly at the time, so many years ago, when I traveled alone in Europe and North Africa. How exciting, being a young man, just out of school, on an adventure of a lifetime, seeing places I had read about, meeting fellow travelers, feeling the exuberance of youth. The photos I took confirm what a great trip that was.

Yet, if I dig deeper into my memory banks, I am able to dredge up a more complete picture of that trip, a forgotten picture that includes scenes of sitting lonely and depressed in my room in France, being afraid at night in the streets of Tangiers, Morocco, getting lost in a small town in Germany

A clear conscience is usually a sign of a bad memory.

Steven Wright

264

and being accosted by intoxicated strangers, sitting in the hospital emergency room in Ostia, outside of Rome. These unhappy experiences don't easily come to mind.

There is one gift in having a bad memory, probably the only gift. I notice, and friends corroborate this in their own experience, that I have an excellent memory for the pleasant things, the joyful times, the life-affirming events. It's much harder to recall the uncomfortable, painful, forgettable times. It's not pleasant to remember misery, so, reflexively, those memories are dimmed. With unhappy experiences dimmed in memory, looking back, I seem to have lived a stellar life.

If only my actual past was really as sweet as the way I remember it now. Forgetting the unpleasant is the gift of my bad memory.

The Gift Of The Decrease Of Sex Hormones

Our bodies are perfectly timed. When we enter childbearing age, our sex hormones are at full bore. We have the desire to procreate and our organs are primed. Coupling and mating are of primary interest. When we meet another person, our hormones prompt us to categorize them in one of two ways—"Would I want to get them into bed—or not."

As we get older, past childbearing age, other interests, other needs take precedence, at least with most of us. Our desire for sexual expression is driven more by a desire for close emotional connection and sharing physical pleasure, rather than by hormones. By middle age and later, sex increasingly takes a back seat, either from loss of interest or by physical debility. Also, we are emotionally settled and less driven by ego needs – to have to be loved and admired, to be seen as a "stud" or a "femme fatale," to have a "trophy" partner, to have to "perform." What a relief! We're no longer in the mating game, a game based on seduction and attraction.

I'll tell you. The amount of free time I have because I am no longer obsessed with sexuality is...well I can't even tell you.

Ram Dass

265

There is a kind of peace in this. With rutting season over, we are free to enjoy the opposite sex, (or the same sex, if you prefer), as people, as personalities, as souls, and not primarily as bodies and as objects of desire. The connections you form, without the hope or expectation of a sexual encounter, can be far deeper than two bodies rubbing together.

There can be another benefit from the gift of the calming of sexual desire. As the spiritual teacher, Osho, has said, "The declining energy of sexuality can become rising energies of spirituality." Obsessing about sex keeps our energies tied to our body, not our heart and soul. This is the reason many spiritual paths recommend celibacy for monastics. Celibacy, or sexual restraint, especially if chosen later in life, can be a heart opening discipline that can lead to a deeper, wider, more spiritual love.

The Gift Of Being Dismissed As Old

A dotty old lady, feeble-minded, quirky, an old codger, an eccentric old fool, in second childhood, these are dismissive terms sometimes used to describe old people. Young folks might not expect so much from grandma and grandpa cause, you know…they're old. Old people are thought to lack useful, productive functions in society, so the world passes them by and they are left out of the mainstream. They live in the past. They are deemed irrelevant. Odd. Passé. This can be beneficial, as long as the elder doesn't take other's opinions personally. The truth is, who really wants to always be a serious adult all the time and be confined by adult convention. It's good to be able to unleash our quirky, childish, goofy self.

Since the time we've entered adulthood, most of us have had to act like a grownup. We've had a job, had to present a sober image, wear a suit and tie or uncomfortable heels, please the boss, preserve decorum. Now, because we are out of the spotlight and don't have to fit in, elders like us can be free to be more of who we really are. We can be eccentric. We're under the radar. At this stage of our lives we don't have to be tactful and we don't have to be so concerned about what others think. They don't notice us anyway.

Now, there is nothing left to prove. The compulsion to compare ourself to others dwindles. The need to compete with others evaporates. The desire to win approval, to fit in, to not be seen as different, all these become less important. Thus, we don't have to hide behind a mask of propriety. We are freer to say what we think, act how we feel, and not conceal from the world the unique individual we really are.

We can be like Beatrice Wood, who was decked out in bright-colored saris and silver bangles till the day she died at 105. Or Skateboard Mamma, who, into her nineties, had fun zipping up and down the Venice, California boardwalk on her skateboard, dodging pedestrians. How undignified. Or ceramicist Otto Heino, our Ojai neighbor, who hit it rich from a certain ceramic glaze he invented, bought himself a new silver Bentley and, in his late eighties, delighted in driving up and down Main Street on Saturday night, with the other teenagers. These elders didn't take themselves seriously, nor did others. They enjoyed their eccentricity, and they enjoyed the freedom that eccentricity afforded. It allowed them to be their authentic, old selves.

The Gift Of Boredom

The world that shaped us has receded into the past. A new world has taken its place. It's so easy to remain a relic of the past, easy to be comfortable to travel the same familiar roads, follow the same old routines, meet with the same friends, eat the same foods, enjoy same entertainments. While there is value in maintaining connection with the familiar past, there is also a cost. Too much of the same and we become fossils. We avoid challenges, are unwilling to try anything new, and we force ourselves to stay within the safe confines of our comfort zones. We sleepwalk through life. We fail to grow. We become bored with our life and with ourselves. And we become boring.

There is a potential gift in our boredom. For most of us, boredom contains an element that can be uncomfortable. That uncomfortableness can motivate us. It can push us to put in an effort to try new ways, bring in new friends, sample new experiences. Boredom can be a motivation that wakes us up from our lethargy. Boredom can be the precursor to creativity. But it can only do this if there exists somewhere within us, the remnant of a flame of adventure. Without that flame, there is no gift from boredom.

Life isn't always exciting. It has its hills and valleys. One thing about boredom is true—if you're bored, you are facing a void. You have spare time and space to fill what is empty. So to receive the gift of boredom, fill the void with new and interesting experiences.

The Gift Of Bodily Suffering And Limitation

I've lived a charmed life and not suffered a lot. As of now, I'm relatively healthy, not in need of a great deal of money, living in a great house, with a great woman, in the richest country in the world. Maybe in a few years, maybe less, if I'm alive and possibly have suffered some serious pain and losses, this would be a different book. I can only write from my perspective as of now. My perspective now, with the relatively little experience of suffering I've encountered, tells me that there are gifts that can be derived from suffering and loss of function.

The most obvious gift is that suffering and loss can lead to positive change. There is nothing more motivating for you to want to change than for you to be in pain. My son, Jason loves certain foods that are not good for him. We tried over and over to convince him to alter his eating habits and eat healthier, to no avail. But then he ended up with an ambulance trip to the hospital emergency room with an excruciating pain in his gut that was directly attributed to consuming the forbidden foods. Bottom line, Jason got the message and forevermore, avoided the offending food. And never again was he to experience that pain. He was motivated to change his eating habits. Pain has a way of doing this.

What if there is no choice you can make that will alter the amount of pain and limitation you are experiencing? Alice and I had a conversation with the spiritual teacher, Ram Dass. This was not too long after he had a massive cerebral stroke that left him partially paralyzed, aphasic and in constant pain. Speaking haltingly, Ram Dass referred to his stroke as "Fierce Grace." He felt it was a gift of grace because the stroke opened up his world, deepened him and gave him valuable teachings he could not have obtained any other way.

Ram Dass, formerly Richard Alpert, lived a charmed life. Born into a wealthy family and educated at Stanford, he went on to become one of the youngest tenured professors of psychology at Harvard. His life turned around when he traveled to India and met an Indian guru. Eventually he became a celebrated teacher in his own right, gave popular workshops and wrote many influential spiritual books. Life was going well for him. He was a spiritual celebrity. And then, the stroke.

Ram Dass had written a book titled, *How Can I Help*. He told us that after the stroke, he would now be able to write the book, *How Can I Be Helped*. As a cripple in a wheelchair, with little he was able to do on his own, he learned by experience how to be helpless. It also taught him how to be old. It was an experience of humility, especially useful for a man who had been filled with pride and ego. And it propelled him to another level of spiritual growth. That, he told us, was a priceless gift for him.

There are many ways a person can approach bodily suffering and loss of function. One can, as all of us do, seek medical solutions. This is well and good, and an important part of becoming whole again. But only part. There is another dimension, which Ram Dass championed, that would have us turn inside and learn from the suffering. In that case, the suffering and limitations of age can be a great teacher. It can teach us humility. Forced by painful circumstances to accept our limitations, we must give up false pride, become more humble, more understanding of the limitations of others. Suffering can break us down, but it can also break us open. By being broken and brought low, for the first time, we are able to truly feel the suffering of others. We are able to recognize the suffering of others because we feel it in ourselves. This makes us more human.

Being broken-down, broken-open, and surviving, we learn how strong we are. Without the challenge of suffering and limitation in our life, we cannot really know our strength. It is unfortunate that we must learn through pain, but pain is a powerful teacher.

When the body breaks down, refuses our commands, causes us pain and limits our abilities, we see clearly that this "flesh puppet" we occupy is an unreliable vehicle. If we turn our awareness inside, to our heart, our mind and spirit, we can learn that there are much more reliable foundations. External suffering, as difficult as it is, pushes us to turn within, to a realm that is beyond this physical body and beyond our worldly concerns. This is the only place where we can find lasting peace and inner strength. Though it be "fierce grace," suffering can be a path that will help to lead us to our spirit.

Although suffering can be a gift that can lead us to more expanded awareness, many people refuse to accept that gift. Those people become bitter in the face of suffering, and do whatever they can to avoid feeling. Very different from a tradition that was held in the Buddhist monasteries in Tibet. There, the monks daily recited a prayer asking for more suffering. From suffering, they believe, comes the gift of compassion and wisdom.

The Gift Of Surrender To The Effects Of Aging

Aging is an exercise of being out of control. Though we humans try, we are never really "in control." As time progresses, losses accelerate. Most people lose some of their physical abilities, and lose some of their mental abilities as they age. There's not a lot you can do to stem those losses. Loss comes with the territory of being an aging human. There are things you can do to delay your disintegration for a little while, but only a little while. You are not in control.

I put my time in at the gym, yet I find it more difficult to lift the 50-pound bag of chicken feed like I used to a year ago. Even though I moderate my food intake, my belly keeps expanding. I take my brain supplements daily, yet I keep losing my keys and forget names of people I've known for years. I am not in control of my aging.

After you've done and are doing all you can, there is no other option, other than fighting a hopeless battle, than to surrender to the reality of your aging. Surrender is a word that holds a negative charge. An army surrenders when they are losing, a wrestler surrenders when he is helpless in an armlock, a fugitive surrenders to the police. Surrender, in this sense, is giving up because you're weak or outclassed by an opponent who is stronger or smarter.

However, there is a positive meaning of surrender, and that is what I am referring to here. Surrender is a clear-eyed recognition and acceptance of *what is*, recognition of the reality of your situation. When you recognize the truth of your aging, and have explored all options, done what you can, then allowed yourself to surrender, a peace will overcome you. *Peace follows surrender*. No more fighting. Peace follows the recognition that you have done, and are doing the actions that are appropriate for your situation. Peace follows your acceptance of your aging, and the realization that you have minimal control. You do what you can to maintain health and vitality, but you are at peace with your age. A peaceful, undisturbed mind is the gift of surrender.

The Gift Of Needing Less

The early part of your adult life you tend to acquire things, the latter part you tend to get rid of things. As you grow older, you learn the true meaning of the word, "Enough." Actually, you experience the true meaning of the words, "too much."

Think of it. How much "stuff" do you really need? Probably not much. Especially when you're old. Before I met Alice, I lived for awhile in a friend's pool house, the place where they showered and changed clothes. The room was so small I could almost touch the walls when I spread my arms. I stayed there with all my worldly possessions—a few changes of clothes, some plates, glasses and cooking utensils, a box of books, important papers, a few more things, and that was all. I was content. Now, if Alice and I needed to move all our "stuff" it would probably take three large moving vans.

We've made a commitment to not acquire anything unless we really need it. When Alice buys an article of clothing, she's made an agreement with herself to remove a similar article from her closet. There are things I think I might need that I've packed away in the barn. But I've got boxes there unopened since we moved here thirty years ago. We've gotten along without them for thirty years, I suppose there's no critical need for them now. One of these days we'll rent a dumpster and clear out all the excess stuff. Our kids will be grateful.

We evacuated our mini-farm when the fire threatened several years ago. My brother called later that day to tell us that he had heard on the radio that our street was on fire and we had probably lost our home. My first reaction surprised me. "OK, new life. We could get a small apartment in town. We'll be fine." And we would be. We didn't really need all that stuff.

The Gift Of Slowing Down And Waning Energy

As you get older, you "run out of juice" sooner. You just can't run and do all the things you used to do. Your "get up and go has got up and gone. "Where's the gift in that? If you are sedentary to begin with, there's no gift in having less energy. However, if you had been running around in circles all your life, doing, doing, doing, the aging body forcing you to slow down has the potential to be a real benefit.

My mom always had been active. She was a traditional busy housewife, cooking, cleaning, shopping, taking care of my dad and us kids. As she got older, she slowed way down. We got her help so there was a lot less for her to do. At times, when we visited, I would notice her sitting in her easy chair, doing nothing but staring into space, a faint smile on her face. I feared she might be getting dementia. When I sat down next to her and asked what was her experience, she paused and said, "A thought comes and goes. I watch it. Then another thought comes." Mom was engaged in wakeful meditation. Without intending, she was practicing mindfulness. Slowing down, she had become a more peaceful person.

In the Summer of life we measured our value by how much we produced, how much we accomplished, how much we acquired. Now that the Winter season is here, there is a time for rest. The body slows. The mind slows. Energy ebbs. There is no need to rush, no tight schedule to follow, no deadline to meet. Because there is a lack of constant external demands and a damping down of frenetic energy, an elder is more able to slow down, and smell the roses, absorb the smile of a child, slowly savor the hot cup of coffee on a cold Winters day. They are able spend more of their time just *being*, rather than *doing*.

By *being*, an elder is present, not in the past, not in the future. Washing the dishes after dinner, they simply wash, scrubbing caked food off the pots, feeling the warm, soapy water on their hands, drying, stacking. Not wanting to, or having to rush through to some more pleasant task or an important appointment. Aliveness is in the present moment, this very moment, nowhere else. If the moment is washing dishes, that's where aliveness dwells.

The unrushed elder has a mind that is not so filled with minutiae, not so swept away by the ramblings of an unhinged brain. He or she walks slowly, and at that leisurely pace is able to see beauty that would be missed by a person who is rushing off to some important task. A bird on the wing, a fragrant flower, the smile on a child's face…seen, taken in and appreciated.

An unrushed elder is able listen to and hear the quiet inner voice that speaks with truth and simplicity. That inner voice speaks for the soul, not for the mind. An elder who is able to slow down and listen to their inner voice and enjoy the beauty of a leisurely walk has received the gift from their quiet life and waning energy.

The Gift Of Being Humbled

When I first arrived at the ashram in India, I was full of pride and ego. I was an important person, the Manager of the Los Angeles Ashram. I expected to be treated royally. Instead, I was given a simple cot in a dormitory with fifty other ashramites. Everyone is given a job to do. I expected I would perform some administrative work, instead, the job I was given was cleaning toilets. Eventually, I graduated to the job of washing dirty rags. I was incensed, but soon recognized how perfectly appropriate it was that I had been treated this way. My ego was so inflated, I needed to be humbled. That was a gift.

Aging is a humbling experience. It is humbling to have your youthful beauty taken away, your health, your energy, your career, your memory, your sexual vigor, and all the other things that the mounting years can steal from you. Gone. Your ego takes a hit. You once were a strapping, vigorous youth. You were a force. A beauty. Proud, important. People would look to you and admire you. Ask your advice. Now you're old and wrinkled. Instead of being a somebody, you've become a nobody.

But humility is a strength. Now, as a nobody, you don't have to look to others in order for you to be appreciated. You don't have to create an image to impress people, hide your defects, put yourself forward and seek others approval. With an ego that was like a balloon, punctured by the sharp pin of age, you don't have to be anything or anyone, but to be the person who you truly are.

When your aging has enabled you to become free to be your simple, essential self, you are free.

The Gift Of The Helplessness Of Grief

In the modern world we believe there is a solution for everything. A pill, an operation, a product. But if there is a loss for which there is no solution, we are at wit's end, we are helpless.

Roameo the cat is gone. It's been weeks now since we last saw him. We've done the right things, talked to neighbors, scouted the property, posted signs. Nothing. He was only a cat, but we shared the special kind of love that can happen between species. We miss him and still moments we imagine he will come greet us when we come home. His sudden absence has given us a deepened understanding of life. This is grief training for losses later on.

How lucky I am to have something that makes saying goodby so hard.

Winnie The Pooh

We are in grief. The one characteristic of grief that stands out clearly is helplessness. Whatever loss is the cause of grief, there is no way to bring things back to the way they were. And so there is a profound sense of helplessness. In that helplessness, for me, is a coming to visceral understanding of the nature of the world and of human life…*we are not in control.* A death, an illness, a calamity can happen, and we are at the mercy of fate, or karma, or the Big Guy upstairs. We don't get a vote. Understanding we are not in control is a gift, it is an initiation into reality. We can deal as best we can, but we are forced to face the reality of the helplessness of our human condition. This is real, this is life, and the only thing we can do is grieve.

The Gift Of The Loss Of A Loved One

My friend Carol asked, "Is there any way to lessen the pain when a partner dies?" My response, "Yes there is. Have a terrible relationship."

When we love, we become vulnerable. We are vulnerable to the death of the one we love. This is the great disadvantage of loving—the painful heartbreak of loss. Shakespeare's "Parting is such sweet sorrow." Except it isn't sweet.

'Tis better to have loved and lost, than never have loved at all.

Alfred Lord Tennyson

It takes great courage to open ourselves to the possibility that we might lose the person we love most. That possibility is always there. If we try to protect ourselves by closing our heart, avoid feeling love or prevent ourselves from opening to another, it will work, we can become invulnerable. But our invulnerability comes at a cost. It leaves us cold, loveless, lifeless, encased in a protective shell.

When one who we love dies, a part of us dies. But in the sadness and the grief, we are able to taste the depth of our love. It is as if the truth of our love is brought to its apex by our loss. Through the death of a beloved do we know how much we love them. Through their death we feel how grateful we are for them to have been in our life. Through their death do we learn how much we have lost. And through their passing, we are able to see how capable we are of love. This cannot begin to make up for the emptiness.

It is true that old age is a time of loss. With each loss we examined, we found a corresponding gift concealed within. These were genuine gifts. From loss of outer beauty, we found the potential to appreciate inner beauty. From the withdrawal of external interests, we found the energy to expand inwardly. From the recognition of the nearness of death, we found the zest to savor life in the present.

A challenge and a blessing, that's what getting old is. Being able to see some aspects of the losses from aging as a gift is mind-bending. It allows you to see with a more accepting perspective. It can help you alter the way you perceive your growing old.

LEFT

An elderly woman in bed grieving her recently departed beloved. The sheets and pillow indicated where his presence remains

INNER TASKS FOR
THE LAST STAGE OF LIFE

PREVIOUSLY, I WROTE ABOUT GROWING OLD as opposed to growing up. Growing old is easy, you just celebrate your birthdays, one after another. However, it takes work to grow up, to live fully, grow wise and love deeply. As I see it, in order to grow to be a conscious elder, one must, even in the Winter season of life, do the mental, emotional and spiritual work that can lead to a more uplifting, creative and fulfilling old age.

This same inner work can be seen as essential preparation for dealing with the pain and sorrows of old age. Nobody knows what the Winter of their life will bring. More than likely there will be surprises and most will be challenging to mind, body and spirit. The following "tasks" can be seen as ways that will help an older person to navigate some of those difficult challenges and protect themselves from some cold blasts of this, the last season of their life.

Below, I have outlined over thirty-five of these inner tasks that I felt were the most important.

I have not gone into much detail in describing these tasks. Whole books could be written on each one, and if you look, you'll find them. My purpose here is to bring these essential tasks to your awareness, not to describe in detail how to accomplish them. There are extensive resources available for that. I won't be suggesting resources on the various topics here. I'll leave that up to you to check out. I hope you'll see the value and investigate on your own.

There is no life period which is preferable for these tasks to be undertaken. Some people might begin in middle age, some in youth, some in old age. The sooner, the better. You don't want to wait till your house is on fire before you start digging your well. As you grow older, you become clearer and more motivated because you have lived some and life has provided greater clarity about your needs, and there is usually more of a sense of urgency…you recognize time is growing short.

There is no level of importance or order that these tasks should be tackled, or even a requirement that all or most must be worked with. Also, it's not like you complete a task, then you're through with it. The work is ongoing. It's a process. Often you'll work with a task, circle back around after ensuing months or years and revisit the same task, but with a deeper understanding because you've lived and experienced more.

It's all personal, all unique to you. Some tasks will be so meaningful to you that they'll shake and wake you, some you will connect with superficially, some you'll have no interest in at all, and some you've already accomplished long ago. What comes up and moves you is there for a reason. We'll start with an essential task—gratitude.

Appreciating And Celebrating Blessings

About a year ago, I walked out the back door of our bedroom, smack into a large rattlesnake coiled and ready to strike from three feet away. I rushed back into the house, grabbed my pistol and shot it. In my panic, I neglected to use ear protection, which resulted in major loss of hearing in both ears. At first, I was sad and bemoaned the fact of the loss and the necessity of wearing hearing aids. I still occasionally grieve the loss. But now, every time I put my blessed hearing aids in my ears, I feel grateful. I am reminded, I can hear! What a blessing.

As I've grown older, my eyes have gotten dim and more blurry. All I have to do is slip on my blessed glasses and I can see clearly. I can read, see sunsets, see the wrinkles on my wife's beautiful face. What a blessing.

"You don't miss your water till your well runs dry." And when you finally get a cup of water, you really, really appreciate it. Age can dry out your well. So when you realize the dwindling years you have left and add up a list of limitations and losses, hopefully, you'll focus on what you still have. There's still plenty left to savor—a taste, a smell, a beautiful sunset, a sweet interaction with a loved one. These become more enjoyable when you take the time to appreciate and be grateful.

You have much to be grateful for. You've been born a human being, and not a flea or a goat. Be grateful. You're probably an older adult and you're alive. Many people in the world don't make it out of their teens. Be grateful. You're educated, or else you would not be able to be reading these words. Many people in the world are illiterate. Be grateful. You probably have retained your senses, though they may be less acute as you've aged. Many people in the world are blind or deaf. You go to bed with your belly full. Many go to bed hungry. Some don't have a bed. You want to take a hot shower, you turn a handle. Some must walk miles and carry their water. Miles to carry wood to heat the water. Be grateful for these things you have.

You have a body. How blessed you are that you can still move and love and feel pain. Thank your legs for moving you around, though maybe not as fast as before, thank your eyes for seeing, maybe not as clearly, thank your ears for hearing, maybe not as loud. Thank your tongue for tasting, your skin for feeling. And if there are one or two or three things you cannot do or feel, don't concentrate on those. Pay attention to all the things you can do and feel.

Gratefulness is a protective shield. By being grateful, concentrating on what you have, your heart is full, and negativity has difficulty trying to find a way to enter. By contrast, ungratefulness, concentrating on what you don't have, opens the door to negativity, and negativity closes the door to receiving.

I recount the things in life I am grateful for as part of my meditation practice. But gratefulness won't just happen by counting blessings. That's just words. Gratefulness, in order to have real impact, often needs the contrast of struggle and sorrow. I will never really know how fortunate I am to be healthy until I contract a chronic, debilitating illness. I will never really know how fortunate I am to be living in America until I have spent extended time in a country that is experiencing famine or a brutal dictatorship or in a war zone. If I had experienced these things, every day I would fall to my knees in gratitude for the sweet life I am living now.

More than just feeling grateful for the blessings in your life, celebrate them, enjoy them, savor them. Like everything in life, they won't last.

I am looking now at the half drunk bottle of wine that sits on the dining room table. The dark red color, the aroma, the rich taste of the Cabernet Sauvignon is superb. But I savor every glass even more so because of the month I spent in Winter, 1975, working in the vineyards of the Napa Valley of Northern California. The backbreaking work pruning grape vines so many years ago reminds me of the calluses on my hands. It gives me a sense of appreciation, as I drive past fields of workers, for those men and women who labor so hard to put food on our table. And it makes each glass of the wine taste more delicious to me.

Reviewing And Accepting The Past

Who we are today is a product of our past. Everything that happened to us, every thought, every feeling, every experience contributed to make us the person we are now. To be able to look back at our life, accepting the lows, appreciating the highs, allows us to savor the life we lived. And it allows us to more easily move on unencumbered into our future.

For many people, looking back at one's life is considered nostalgia, something old folks do. It's true that some old people live in the past, live in their memories. They repeatedly celebrate old loves, high school sports victories, past accomplishments. These folks are steeped in nostalgia, living in a time gone by. For them, memories of the past can be a trap, not a gift.

Looking back and reviewing your life isn't always nostalgia. It can be an important part of growth in old age. It is a summing up, a tying up loose ends, a finishing touch which can be like the period at the end of a sentence. It is a coming to truth of who you had been and who you have become, the good, the bad, the ugly, the beautiful. Life review can be a part of creating a sense of fulfillment of a life. It can heal. It can lead to insight.

One can review their life informally, just spending time looking back at their history, but it is more fruitful to approach life review in a more formal manner. There are books and workshops that provide a useful framework for delving into the past. These use guided visualizations, paper and pencil exercises and any number of techniques to help you bring up key events in your life and examine forces that changed you.

The value from remembrance of your past has a lot to do with how you do it. If you look into your history, searching only for where you went wrong, the mistakes you made, people you hurt or hurt you, things you wanted to do but didn't, you'll be inviting remorse and depression. Conversely, if you close your eyes to negativity and search only for the happy memories, you'll be dining on confections and leaving out reality, the meat and potatoes of your life.

Your tendency might be, like mine, to go for the confections. So much more pleasant to recall the good times, the triumphs, success, adventure, travel, young love, the times we showed courage, the times we were at our best. In order to be an exercise in healing though, life review needs to include darkness as well as light. The losses, the wrong turns, painful experiences, maybe even more than the joyful times, may have left a more enduring mark on our life. Recalling these painful memories may be more difficult, but a more fruitful part of life review. This is especially true if we understand that each failure is a steppingstone to wisdom.

The painful memories might consist of our own failings, in which case we need to forgive ourselves in order to heal. But they may also include our failings toward others, where we may need to seek forgiveness from them, maybe even offer to make amends, if appropriate. Our memories might include other's failings toward us, their hurtful words and damaging actions that caused us pain, in which case we might seek to release the offender, and ourselves through forgiveness.

Ultimately, it is compassion, acceptance and forgiveness toward self, and compassion, acceptance and forgiveness toward others that allows us to move forward in our life, unfettered by ghosts of the past.

The purpose of life review is not to simply rip the scabs off old wounds. The purpose is to understand, integrate and accept undigested experiences from the past. It is an attempt to find answers to the important question, "What was this all about?" Your answers might lead you to see patterns that were invisible before. You might discover that some negative events that happened, some of the experiences with people you considered traumatic, actually were the cause of opening you in new and positive directions.

So, paradoxically, by consciously looking backward, into our history, we are also looking forward, into our future. Life review can be preparation for a good life. And it can also be preparation for a good death.

Claiming Old Age

Only recently have I started to describe myself as "old." Before, I was reluctant to claim myself as an old person. Now at 80, I am genuinely an old man, an octo-gen-arian, and now I am not at all reluctant to define myself as such.

Because "old" has so many negative connotations, it's easy to see why people are reluctant to claim to be old, even when they obviously are. The reluctance is widespread. You can find many books on aging, but when you start reading, you discover that they are actually about *anti*-aging.

A popular concept of aging in these books is to extend middle age values into old age. Be physically active, with lots of exercise and sports. Be busy, with lots of events and activities. Be youthful, with lots of supplements, serums and plastic surgery. This approach doesn't value elderhood. In fact, it disparages it. It attempts to deny getting old. And it shames those who don't buy into this idea of a "youthful" old age.

When you're old, you're old. To try to deny or hide it is denying reality. To try to return to an era that is past, is to be out of sync with where you are now. The worst part is that by denying your "oldness" you miss out on the riches that old age can provide. There is much to explore, much to learn, much to be gained by embracing your age. Instead of valuing "youthfulness" as a goal as you age, why not value "freshness." Freshness implies curiosity, a sense of adventure and openness to experience. Freshness is the essence of youth. And it is ageless.

Many cultures have ceremonies and rituals that mark the entry into old age. These celebrations are rites of passage that honor a person as an elder, and officially designate his or her passing from one stage to another. The ritual confers on the elder, separate, elevated status, with new duties and responsibilities. And through the ceremony, the community has the opportunity to officially recognize the elder's new position.

A friend who has been leading safaris in Africa for many years, gifted me with a *rungu*, which was given him by a tribal elder. A *rungu* is a short, carved wooden staff that could be used either as a weapon or as a symbol of authority. He told me that once an elder male of the Samburu tribe has reached a certain age, he trades his weapons in for a *rungu*, and takes on the function of judge and honored holder of tribal traditions.

The closest we have in our culture to such an aging rite of passage is the retirement ritual, where the retiree is given a luncheon, a plaque, a watch and a hearty farewell…and then…nothing.

Without "sugar coating" the challenges aging presents us, claiming your age is an initial step in changing your perception from the idea of getting old as a tragedy, to seeing it as an opportunity. The opportunity lies in understanding your challenges as a way to discover your best and highest self. Then you see your waning energy, your decrease of sexual drive, your declining youthful physical beauty, as the potential gifts they can be. You can use these challenges that aging presents you in order to wake up and turn within to discover the riches that lay inside. This can be the impetus to practice these tasks of aging and to do the inner work to discover your radiant spiritual being.

What claiming your age entails is to embrace the reality that you are old, to celebrate that fact, and as an elder, to live your last years with as much depth and heart and soul and wisdom as you can muster. By claiming your age, you proclaim to the world that you honor your years and are blessed to have lived so long and so well, and intend to continue to do so till you run out the clock. By claiming your age you claim the bounty of depth of experience that can only be obtained through years of living.

Completing Unfinished Business

Alice and I went through a process of completing unfinished business many years ago. We were about to embark on a year-long journey around the world, one that would take us to many unfamiliar lands. There was a sense of uncertainty for our future. Would we return? So we decided to complete, as much as we could, that which was left undone and unsaid in our lives. We paid all the outstanding bills we could, tried to make amends, when possible, to those we might have harmed; forgave, either in person or mentally, those who hurt us, and we told those we loved that we loved them. This allowed us to enter the coming year with a clean slate and a lightened burden from the past.

The young have a bright future to live. The elderly do not have that luxury. Their future is abbreviated. That means that at some point they will have to let go of dreams, let go of uncompleted projects, let go of unhealed wounds. Some things will have to remain unfixed. Words spoken long ago in the heat of anger cannot be taken back. Past friendships neglected will probably remain neglected. Debts unpaid to friends long gone remain unpaid. We will take some of these things to the grave with us.

Because we don't have the luxury of an unlimited future, we elders have an urgency to take care of business now. Decide what you can let go of. Decide what is important to complete. Let go of what cannot be changed. Do what is necessary to finish what is unfinished and needs finishing.

By taking care of business now, there will be less unfinished business that you will carry into your old age. By not taking care of unfinished business, you will be incapable of freely embracing the possibilities of the present moment. Your energy will be sapped by old wounds, angers, grudges, self-judgments. Part of you will be mired in the mud of the past.

Of special importance is tying up loose ends so that your family won't have to do so after your death. Alice and I have made arrangements for things like removal of our bodies after death and for our cremation. We have put our financial records in order. We have made out our wills. We are in process of going through our "stuff," so our kids won't have to. We want to make the trying time after our deaths to be as easy as possible for our family. And for the one of us who survives.

They found our neighbor and friend, Roy Patton's body propped up in bed, by his living room window. He was ninety years old. Apparently, he had died of natural causes sometime the day before. He had pulled his bed to the picture window where he could overlook his beloved rural property. For a long time he had known he was dying and had spent the preceding weeks cleaning up the land, pruning bushes, making sure the watering systems were working, etc. All bills were paid, all things borrowed returned, preparations made, all papers were in order.

They said, when they found him, he had a serene smile on his face. Life complete. No unfinished business.

Generating Continuing Growth And Aliveness

When Alice and I took our trip around the world, we set out with a spirit of adventure. We didn't plan in advance. We made up our itinerary day-by-day. We were explorers. Each day we set out in the morning with the intention to get lost and see what the day will bring. Each day was an adventure into the unknown. To live life as explorers invites growth and aliveness.

A pioneer of conscious aging, Rabbi Zalman Schachter-Shalomi often used the verb "eldering" rather than the noun "elder," or "senior," because the noun denotes something static, an unchanging state, while the verb "refers to a state of growth and evolution, a process with endless possibilities." As we are "eldering," we are generating adventure and continuous growth.

Alice's mother was special, an "elder." Up until the last

Explorer and writer Alexandra David-Neel was born in 1868. She died in 1969 at 101, a few months after renewing her passport.

few weeks of her life, until her death at a few days shy of 88 years, Beulah was ageless. Late in life, with her flaming, dyed red hair, high heel boots and leopard patterned tights, and her "try anything" attitude, Beulah attracted devoted friends and admirers of all ages. When Alice gave Beulah her old oil paint set, Beulah, at age eighty, with no art training, started painting the first of hundreds of beautiful florals. She was an avid reader. She would attend Elderhostel classes on history and art all over America and Europe, even into her eighties.

Unfortunately, Beulah is not the norm. A word that can be used to describe too many old people's approach to life is, "stagnation." Stagnation describes a body of water like a pond that is static: there is no inflow or outflow of fresh water. After awhile, the water in the pond becomes brackish, lifeless. It starts to stink.

As we grow older, the increasing pressure of entropy can come into play in our lives. We can lose interest, try to conserve our energy, avoid new and different experiences, stay within safe, comfortable boundaries. We resist change and have no interest in novelty and adventure. By staying only within the boundaries of the safe and known, we avoid growing, and by avoiding growing, we can stagnate. That which is stagnant lacks aliveness. We become bored and we become boring. We die before we are dead.

Be assured, the reason you are feeling bored and are boring is that this is a choice you have made. When you choose to be safe and comfortable, you choose to be on autopilot. If you want to live a life of continuing growth and aliveness, you have to grab your hammer and build the life you want. Does your "old story" bore you? Build a "new story." Have you run out of things on your "bucket list?" Start adding to the list.

One key to generating aliveness is maintaining curiosity—curiosity and willingness to put out the energy to expand. The dictionary defines curiosity as *the desire to know*. With curiosity and energy, you'll take classes and workshops, meet new people, try things you've never done before. In the words of Loving Promise #28, *"I will instigate and participate in uplifting activities, learnings and adventures which inspire (me) to evolve physically, intellectually, emotionally and spiritually."*

When you follow this Promise, you are *investing* yourself. The word "invest" is meaningful. When you invest, you give something valuable in order to receive value back. Invest your time, interest and passion in order to grow and uplift yourself. The return you will get from your investment is aliveness.

Letting Go Of The Need To Be "Somebody"

If you're not somebody in this contemporary world, you're nobody. And often, when you're old, you're nobody.

When most people get old, they become less central to their world and "the" world. When they reach 65 or so, they retire, (or are retired) from their work, thus losing their role and title. Children grow up and move out of the home, and mothers are no longer actively "moms," and dads no longer actively "dads." In general, as elders have less power and position, wield less influence and thus are less depended upon, they lose prestige. They no longer have a role. They become less "somebody" and more "nobody." They can see this as a curse or as a blessing.

Society, especially in Western culture, tends to cast older people aside, put them out to pasture to make room for the up and coming generations. Old people, having grown up and educated in a different era, supposedly hold outmoded ideas and are not up to date with the technologies and culture of the contemporary times. They seem like another species to the nascent generations, relics that are a bit out of place and a bit uncomfortable to be around…too much like parents. They stand on the sidelines as the world is passing them by. They are obsolete. They retire. People spend two thirds of their life working hard for the privilege of spending the last third doing nothing.

Here's some dictionary words related to retirement—withdraw, remove, depart. Not very impressive, especially

If you're still becoming somebody, it's too early to start the process of becoming nobody. You really have to solidify your somebodyness. Then, when you're established in somebodyness, then explore your nobodyness.

Baba Ram Dass

if people see retirement as "retirement from life." We've all heard stories of people retiring from their jobs, then ending up watching a lot of TV, drifting around for awhile, and then dying. Their life was their work, and when they lost their work, they lost their reason for living and they lost their identity. And when they lost their reason for living and their identity, they were nobody. There was no sense in continuing to live, so they lost their life. I personally have known several people who died within a few months or a year of retirement. Theirs was death by boredom, death by not being "somebody."

Actually, retirement is a fabulous opportunity. You're free. You're not saddled with 9am to 5pm of busyness, 8 hours of your life in salaried servitude. No need to work, produce, get ahead. No need to spend hours to commute. Your job now is not to please your boss or the owner of the company. Your job now is to please yourself and those you love. Your time is freed up to do what you want, go where you want, be who you want. You are free to spend all day feeding the ducks at the lake, read books at the library, volunteer at the homeless shelter. If you have the energy and are healthy, the skies the limit. By having the freedom to be a nobody, you become somebody.

It's true. It's so much easier being a "nobody." Even the "Somebodys" of the world are actually really nobodys like us, many of them trying to act like somebody. Truth is, in this world, somebodys are nobodys. Even the greatest somebodys among us are actually smaller than a tiny grain of dust. If these important somebodys were to suddenly disappear, the world will go on without them. A handful of people might mourn for a short time, but soon enough, they will forget.

When you don't have the need to try to be "somebody," you'll find it so much easier to just to be yourself—the *you* that you really are.

Getting Rid Of What Is Not Needed

When we packed for our trip around the world that was to last more than a year, Alice wanted to make sure that we would have everything we needed. We had bought two large backpacks with numerous pockets. Alice filled all the crannies and all the pockets with clothes and shoes and camping supplies and dry goods and utensils and first aid and beauty supplies and pharmaceuticals and stuff we might need for any eventuality. However, we could barely lift them, and when we put the packs on, the weight made it easy for us to tip over backwards. If we needed something near the bottom, we would have to undo half the pack, then it would take a long time to put everything back together. After our first few days in mainland China, we shipped literally half the stuff back. There is no reason to bear the weight of carrying around with you what you don't really need.

Two opposing processes are at play in our lives, *attachment*—holding on, and *surrender*—letting go. Attachment is more prominent at the beginning of our life. We acquire physical strength, knowledge, objects, friendships, family, honors and position. We accumulate material goods and struggle to hold on to and increase what we have acquired. Surrender is prominent in the latter part of our life, when, one by one, we must let go of all that we are attached to. It's not just that we *must* let go of these things. As we get older, we *want* to let go. By living our years, we have gained perspective and a greater understanding of what is important and what is not. We are more able to make the discrimination between what we need and what we don't. That understanding makes it easier for us to part with what previously, we thought we couldn't live without. Our burden becomes lighter.

Taking Responsibility For Preservation Of Health

If you're not healthy, your universe is not healthy. Your illness can be the point around which your life is organized. Illness is no fun. That's why every blessing that people confer on each other always includes a wish for good health.

Physical health is not a given. What we do in our life has a tremendous effect on our body. The body is a machine, and like any machine, the parts will wear out over time. We can extend the useful life of a machine by regular maintenance—keeping it cleaned and oiled, using high quality fuel, and by correct usage—using it in the way it is intended, like not overworking or allowing it to overheat. In the same way, if we take care of how we feed and care for our precious body, we have the best chance of living a long, vital and healthy life.

Long, vital and healthy. The trajectory for the life of many elders is, as they age, increasing illness and disability over an extended time, until death overtakes them. A lot of years of suffering. The ideal trajectory is to live long and healthy, then after a short period of illness, a quick death. I think for this to happen, people need to invest in their health.

On Tuesdays and Thursdays, Alice attends an hour and a half yoga class, either online or in person. She has been doing yoga since before I met her. On Wednesdays and Saturdays, she attends an hour stretch class. Alice has been investing her time and energy. The payoff for her investment has been a healthy, strong and vital 83-year-old body. A good investment.

The thing is, if we don't invest, we enter a downward spiral of physical health. Entropy takes over. For example, if we neglect to keep up an exercise routine, we become less strong. Because we are less strong, exercise becomes more difficult. And because it is more difficult, we cut down and find excuses to neglect it even more. You can see how it's easy to spiral downward and end up spending our evenings on the couch in front of the TV. And our days in the doctor's office.

We invest in our health for our own benefit, but we are not the only beneficiaries of a long and healthy life. Our beloved is also concerned. I think of Alice having to deal with my potential extended illness and death, and the pain that would cause her. So I get my butt to the gym, join the stretch classes, eat the right foods, take my vitamins. I do this not just for love of my own life, but also for my love of Alice.

"Finishing" Important Relationships

I'm using the term "finishing" here not in the sense of ending, but in the sense of completion. When you have constructed a wooden table, the last thing you do is apply a finish coat. Then the table does not require any more work. With the application of the final finish, it's finished.

The important relationships in your life—life partner, parents, children, close friends, most likely contain places from the past that are "unfinished." Hurt feelings that were never talked about, lies that were swept under the rug, love and appreciation never expressed are examples. The relationship may never feel complete without saying that which was left unsaid, doing that which was left undone.

It's not like everything unfinished must be worked through. Sometimes it's better to not reopen old wounds. Sometimes the person has left or died. No matter. The finishing is about you, not them. And often the finishing can be done by you alone, in your own heart and mind.

There were things in my history with my father that I felt unfinished with. I thought about these things and decided I would not confront my father. The incidents were old, he was old, he would not understand. It would be unkind to confront him. I chose to work through on my own, and to let go. As I did this, it created room in my heart. I felt compassion for Dad instead of blame. I felt love for him. With these feelings, the raw parts of my relationship with him were finished, and we would move on in a fresh and loving way.

That's the thing about important relationships that are finished. There is no more work to do. All that's left to do is to enjoy giving and receiving love.

My dad and his brother had an unfinished relationship. He and Uncle Al had an argument and, even though they lived a couple of miles apart, they didn't see or speak a word to each other for over ten years. When Uncle Al became ill and needed to undergo a serious operation, he finally called my father because he feared he might not survive the surgery and wanted to mend their relationship. This call revived a loving, brotherly relationship that lasted until my uncles death seven years later.

Addressing Regrets For Mistakes And For Life Unlived

"I could have…I should have…I would have…I shouldn't have."

It can be difficult when you've grown old and you look back at your life and see things you wanted to do but never did, mistaken choices you made that caused you and others pain, an opportunity passed up, a life unlived. You were afraid so you compromised and played it safe. You were busy and never made time for what you really wanted. You followed the wrong advice and chose a path that turned out to be unfulfilling. And now you're old and your feelings of regret keep recurring.

It seems to me that the best preparation for death is a life fully lived.

Frank Ostaseski

Is it too late? That's a question you need to ask yourself. Maybe it is too late, maybe it's time to accept your unlived life, make peace with your past and move on. Or maybe it's not too late. Maybe there's still time and inclination to correct past mistakes, take the path not taken. Either way, by addressing regret, you move to come to resolution of a place within you that was stuck.

There's nothing sadder than to arrive at the end of your life with the helpless feeling…I could have…I should have…I would have…I shouldn't have.

Embracing Aloneness

We are born alone, and we die alone. This is true no matter how many friends we have, no matter how close and loving our relationships are. At our birth we are completely alone, and at our death we are completely alone. We do it by ourselves. The very old know this. Many of their friends have died or moved away. Perhaps their intimate partner has died. They are left to deal with being alone. Many become lonely. This is a source of great sorrow for many old people.

Being alone can result in loneliness. People who suffer from deep-seated loneliness constantly need the company of others. If they are by themselves they'll feel agitated, unhappy, incomplete. Often, they will seek a diversion—call someone up on the phone, go to the refrigerator for a

"Paradoxically, the ability to be alone is the condition for the ability to love."

Erich Fromm

292

snack, view porn, turn on the tube, have a drink or smoke a joint, anything to distract them and fill up the void of emptiness they feel. Actually, it may be that the response people have to their lonely feelings may be more distressing than the feelings themselves. Perhaps most detrimental of all is the lonely person who is driven to become embroiled in a relationship, even a destructive one, in order to escape from their lonely feelings. In truth, there is no way another person can fill up the deep-seated emptiness a lonely person feels. That feeling of emptiness is a bottomless pit. As the philosopher John Paul Sartre has said, "If you are lonely when you are alone, you're in bad company."

Loneliness is endemic in our society. The percentage of people who describe themselves as lonely in the U.S. has doubled in the last twenty years. Loneliness is a source of stress. It is a major factor in the development of a variety of physical illnesses. Research shows that lonely people tend to get sick at younger ages and die sooner of their illness. And the elderly are subject to loneliness at much higher rates than younger persons.

The healthy quality of *aloneness* should not be confused with loneliness. Aloneness is very different. A person who doesn't have a driving need to be around others, who is comfortable in their own skin, who enjoys their own company, engenders the quality of aloneness. They feel complete within themselves and don't have the constant need to have other people around to fill up their time.

Aloneness is a solid foundation that cannot be destroyed. A person who is comfortable with being alone and who can just sit and be present within themselves will have the ability to withstand emotional pressure. Pressure from late-life losses are common sources of stress, and those elders who have the inner resource of aloneness to deal with stress will be able to use their own self as a sanctuary in order to navigate their world with greater ease.

Periods of alone time have been used for millennia by people as a way to deepen and discover themselves. The Buddha, Jesus, Moses and the founders of most religions, went on prolonged solitary retreats, and returned with insights that formed the foundation of their respective religions. Many indigenous groups include a solitary "vision quest" in their rites of passage. Rabbi Zalman Schachter-

Shalomi, pioneer of the conscious aging movement, received many of his insights about aging during a forty-day retreat he experienced in late middle age.

We all benefit from periods of solitude. Being alone can be healing. In the crucible of silence, our true thoughts and feelings are free to arise, unimpeded by the noisy pull of the conflicting needs of the outside world. That silence and aloneness, be it in meditation, or contemplation, or in just a solitary amble down a country road, allows us to hear the quiet voice within, the most subtle urgings of our heart.

All of us have a quiet inner core. Our busy activities, our manic mind and the cacophony of sights, sounds, touch and tastes we experience in the world can draw us away from that center. A healthy balance between that inner world and the outer world is essential, as is the ability to easily float between the two worlds when the need arises. The balance is dynamic. A period of solitude can be balanced by a period of external activity, and vice versa.

If a person finds themselves overly embroiled in the outer world, in mental chatter and compulsive busyness, they don't have to sequester themselves in prolonged retreat. Sometimes all that is required in order to bring back balance is a few moments of solitude, like a walk alone in the park, listening to relaxing music, reading a book, or a short meditation. Those moments of solitude can be healing.

Being alone in nature is especially healing. Years ago, I was going through a period of sadness and distress. I needed the balm of aloneness in a natural setting. So I took myself to the country, to an oak forest adjacent to a friend's property. In the early afternoon, I found a small glen and sat down to meditate in the dappled sunlight. Within that timeless hour, the agitation drained from my body and mind. Refreshed, I was about to get up to leave. I heard footsteps in the dry leaves behind me. A fawn had entered the clearing, not noticing me sitting there. I could have reached out and touched her, she was that close. For a few magical moments, I held my breath and didn't move a muscle. After munching on some grass, suddenly, she caught my scent, and in a fraction of a second, bounded away into the forest. I sat for minutes in awed silence and felt renewed by the precious moment I had just witnessed.

Maintaining Relationships

Taking comfort in being alone is a healthy thing. However, some old people, as time goes on, take being alone to an extreme. They isolate themselves and become hermits. Their living space becomes their fortress, and they maintain contact with none but one or two others, or they avoid contact with everyone except those who provide basic services. Social withdrawal and isolation is the opposite of loneliness, but is based on the same mechanism, *fear*. Fear-based isolation like this is not healthy. Mental health requires maintaining relationships.

Maintaining *real relationships*, not just maintaining connections. On social media, people maintain hundreds, maybe thousands of connections. They call them "friends." Most are superficial, if even that. These are not relationships. Relationships require direct social interactions, face-to-face interactions, where people communicate what's real for them.

Direct social interactions with people you like and who like you provide multiple benefits. Direct interactions with friends bring joy, aliveness and variety to your life. Friends offer help when you need it, and emotional support and comfort when you're down. Having friends improves your sense of self-worth and overall confidence. Friendships create community and provide you a feeling of belonging.

The power of the influence of community cannot be underestimated. Community is the atmosphere in which you are immersed. If that atmosphere is enlivening, you are uplifted. If it is deadening, you are poisoned. Positive community can be found everywhere, in religious groups, sports activities, social clubs, civic groups, volunteer organizations. In the real sense of the word, relationships and community are *nourishing*, to the heart, the soul, the mind, and to the health of the body.

All my life I have had the tendency to be a recluse. It's always been my natural tendency. Thankfully, Alice is the opposite and thrives on social intercourse. Due to her urging, we have an active social life, engage in daily interactions with many friends and maintain friendships with a multitude of people of all ages and interests. My social life would probably be threadbare without Alice's influence.

Our friendships have enriched me. Connections with those in my life who I love has helped me be a member of the human family and feel the humanity in myself.

This evening, on the spur of the moment, we cooked dinner and had friends over; Bob, a neighbor and his grown daughter, Alyssa, and Liz, visiting from Northern California. When we served our food and sat down to eat by the flickering candlelight in the darkened room, we held hands in silent blessing, as Alice and I have done at every meal since we met. In that minute of wordless communion, there was a tangible bond that affirmed our loving connection. Everyone felt it, and the peaceful connection endured throughout the evening.

It's been said that the problems of the world come down to one thing—feelings of separation people have toward each other. In that moment of communion around the table, there was no separation—only love.

Not Abandoning Your Body Awareness

I hurt more now than when I was younger, lots more. I am not alone in this. As we grow older, it's highly probable that we will be experiencing more bodily pain. Aching joints, sore muscles, nerve pain, digestive issues and more may plague us. Because we hurt, we might tend to shut down awareness of our body, or at least some parts that are causing us discomfort. We ignore, divert or anesthetize consciousness of our precious body. But by shutting down our bodily awareness, we also shut down our aliveness, presence and vitality. There's danger we'll take up residence in our head, not our body. We can become dis-embodied.

Two times a week, Alice and I attend a stretch class, called Somatic Stretch®, developed and taught by our friend, Meredith. It's an hour of turning awareness within, through gentle stretching. The effort is to get to know our body, from the inside. The movements are slow and gentle. We don't compete with ourself, trying for some external goal, like seeing how far we can twist or how deeply we can bend. With each stretch, we come up to the edge of our pain boundary, but don't exceed it. Pain comes from the body trying to protect itself from overstretching. Before we exceed our stretch limit, the bodily sensations are actually pleasurable. The point is to become familiar with our body, to make friends with the sensations that arise, rather than push through them or try to avoid them. With gentle awareness comes presence. With presence, our bodies come alive.

I think it's important for elders to take time to focus bodily awareness within. There are many ways to do this, such as the slow, conscious movements of yoga and stretch, and Oriental practices like *tai chi* or *qi gong*. The more aware we are of this physical being we occupy, the more embodied we become.

Awakening To The Reality Of Your Death

We were all together in the doctors office when we heard the words from the doctor about Sumner's diagnosis. Sumner, my father-in-law, age 71, was in good health. A burly, ex-navy man, he was not the kind of guy to get sick. Some tiredness, some minor pain, some bleeding. We thought it might be something easily fixed and Sumner would be

THE STRUGGLE
An old man, terrified as he is being chased
and captured by DEATH

297

back to his old self. But no… late stage liver cancer, inoperable, little chance of survival, a few months at most.

Until this time, for the last two years since we met, Alice and I had been living a dream. We were in love. Everything was rainbows and butterflies. We were in a protective bubble, where nothing bad could touch us. Madly in love, abundance of creativity, work humming along, our families happy and well. A death, especially Sumner, who was not the dying kind, shocked us to our core. It was an alarm bell that woke us to the reality of the fragility of life. Life would never be the same for us.

It's not just a death that can remind us of the temporary nature of our human life. Sickness, onset of physical debilities, advancing birthdays, New Years, our kids and their kids growing up, parents getting old, a glance of our aging face in a mirror, these are all reminders that we will not be here forever.

My parents lived into their nineties. I live a much more healthy lifestyle than they did. I eat well, exercise, take vitamin supplements, live in a healthy environment, have no serious health issues and I am emotionally sound. Actuarial tables give me about nine more years, but since I am in excellent health, I assume that I will outlive the age of my parents. WRONG!

Though it may be comforting, I think it's a mistake to assume you will live a long life. It's more prudent, on some level, to believe that it's entirely possible that you'll die tomorrow. Or today. With your imminent death in mind, you will covet and won't squander the time you have left. You'll squeeze the flavor from every minute, and consciously strive to live your best life. As the saying goes, "Live your life as if each day will be your last. One day it will be."

I just this moment had a wake-up call that makes this task of awakening to my demise a lot more relevant. Alice and I recently took a cardiac scan that tests for arterial plaque. We just got the results a half hour ago. The results were definitive. My diagnosis: "Severe plaque burden, left

There are tiny vessels found in Roman and late Greek tombs called lacrymatory jars. These were thought to be for saving tears of sadness. Why save tears? Because tears are precious. When your heart breaks and you weep from sadness, you care, you love. The tears of grief is simply love that has no place to go.

anterior descending artery. Clinical Interpretation: High likelihood of cardiovascular disease. Precursor to the "Widowmaker" heart attack. Maybe I won't live longer than my parents as I had assumed. Interesting to see how I digest this information.

Update. I just took a cardiac stress test. Artery allowing blood to flow to the heart. Relief. But, calcium plaque doesn't go away. I am subject to heart attack and stroke. Hmmm.

Mining Grief

Every life has a storehouse of sorrows—betrayals, hopes upended by fate, love broken or unrequited, damage caused through carelessness by self or others. A major cause of sorrow is loss.

Old age, more than any other period of life, is a time of loss. Loss of friends and loved ones, loss of physical and mental abilities, loss of positions of authority, etc. Normally, loss is accompanied by sadness, and sadness by grief.

After a loss, we, especially men, are encouraged to "Keep a stiff upper lip." "Suck it up." "Grin and bear it." We are allowed a short time to quietly mourn our loss, and then are encouraged to put it behind us and get back to normal life. We're told by people who are uncomfortable with our grieving and want to help us stop, "Everything happens for a reason." "It's God's Will." "Time will heal." "Keep busy." "Get a dog." But these words are not helpful. They draw us into our mind, take us away from our soul

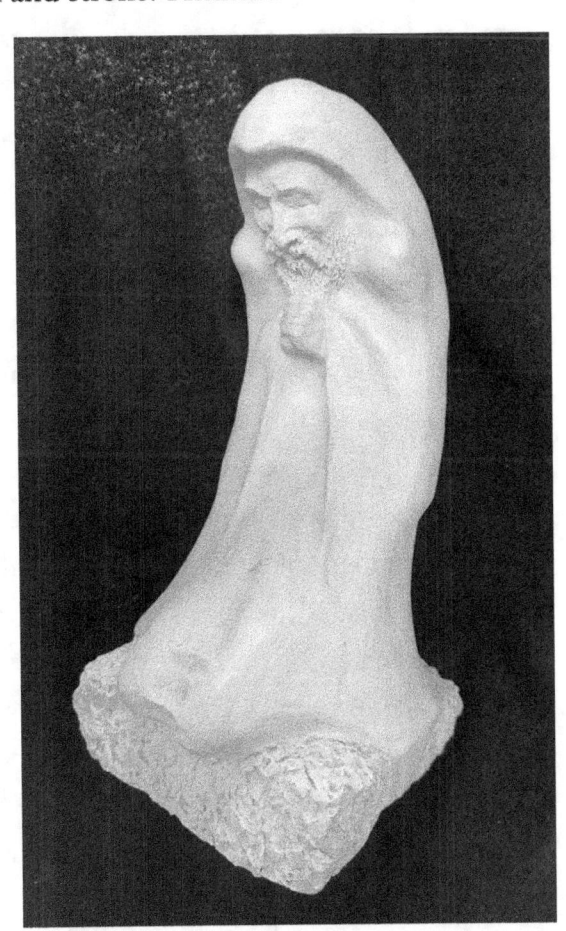

BENT FIGURE
Man withdrawn in grief and prayer

and our gut. That's where our grief resides. We can push grief out of our awareness, by ignoring, by medicating, by explaining it away. But if we do that, thus short-circuiting the grief, it remains a white hot ember in our soul and eats away in our belly.

Actually, grief is not something to be overcome. It is to be integrated into your life. Mourning ends, but grief remains. You don't "move on" after someone you love dies, you move forward "with" them inside of you. Grief is to be integrated into the fabric of your life. If allowed to stay, just stay, without being pushed away, it will bring you deeper, make you more human.

Some things can't be fixed, some wounds are not meant to heal. The wound becomes a precious part of you. Such is grief, even grief that is "worked with" and expressed. The sorrow is there, will always be there. In a sense, embracing grief is an affirmation of life.

Grief is painful. It doesn't just evaporate. You cannot control it. You cannot will it away. All your tears may temporarily release some of the pain, but can never wash it away. Grief will have its way with you. The helpless pain of grief can soften and open you. Or it can be so emotionally overwhelming that you shut down, harden your heart and go unconscious. That is how I had dealt with grief most of my life. I was no expert on doing grief, but I was expert at holding grief back. Anesthesia. Don't feel. There have been times that I have even boasted about being able to dismiss my grief, as if that was manly, a mark of strength. Actually, allowing yourself to feel the grief, allowing it to wash through you, allowing grief to express itself as it will, that is real strength.

I attended a large meeting where my guru was holding a celebration of the birthday of his guru, who had died several decades earlier. Speaking about his guru's attributes, Muktananda suddenly choked up. This man, who had undergone years of rigorous spiritual practices, and was considered by many to be an enlightened master, started bawling like a baby. Between sobs, tears running down his cheeks, he spoke of his grief. "I feel him with me every day," he said, "but I miss his body."

It's been months since Roameo the cat disappeared. Time has softened the sharp pain of grief, but we miss his presence. Every once in awhile, I'll see a movement out of the corner of my eye or imagine that I see him at the window as he appeared for breakfast every morning, and think, "It's Roameo!"

only to be disappointed. As a memorial, I've painted a reclining concrete cat with Roameo's coloring and placed it by the birdbath where he used to hunt birds for hours, usually unsuccessfully. Warm thoughts of him whenever I fill water in the birdbath.

Engaging Suffering

> *The art of happiness is also the art of suffering well.*
>
> Thich Nhat Hanh,
> Buddhist monk

Suffering is a fact of life. Of all stages of our lives, the last stage is likely to include the most suffering. The possibility of chronic pain and physical disability, memory issues, feeling useless, loneliness and depression from loss of loved ones, these and more add to the burden of suffering in old age.

These issues are real, and they get our attention. When they occur, our first thought is, "This hurts. How can I get it to stop?" We look for some secret, some magic solution that will change our situation or heal our body and make the pain go away. Oftentimes there is no magic solution and we are stuck with our pain.

We could become victims. Our physical and emotional pain could grow in importance. Our life could become about our pain: will it stop, what can I do, how is it impacting my life? Poor me, poor me. We suffer and allow our suffering to define us.

There is a difference between pain and suffering. Pain is inevitable, suffering is optional. Pain is what happens to us. Suffering is what we do with our pain. Therefore, *there can be pain without suffering.* Buddhists call suffering, "The Second Arrow." We're shot with the first arrow—that's the pain. The second arrow is the suffering brought on by the emotional

> *The foundation of all mental illness is the unwillingness to experience legitimate suffering.*
>
> Carl Jung

reaction we have in response to the pain. It's the stories we tell ourselves about the pain—"It's horrible, it'll never stop, I'm miserable."

Pain is a signal. There's physical pain, mental and emotional pain, and spiritual pain. These are signals that things are not right. Pain has causes, and the physical causes can be worked with or addressed by a physician, the emotional causes by a therapist, the spiritual causes by clergy or a spiritual teacher. In most cases, the pain itself can be worked with. Medical science has developed effective medications for numbing or eliminating pain.

If, instead of directly addressing the sources of our pain, we bemoan the fact that we have it, let anger overtake us, get caught up in negativity, lamenting, hating, jealousy, complaining…we suffer. (The Second Arrow) Or we'll try to numb it with drugs, food, work or sex. (Ineffective ways of dulling pain) These themselves become addictions and only serve to create more pain and suffering.

One thing is certain: pain is real. Hoping it will disappear or trying to numb it away is not a realistic solution. Pain and loss must be engaged. In addition to tackling the causes, the engagement with pain can take the form of being present for the pain, maintaining our awareness on it rather than running away. This may seem counterintuitive, but by turning toward the pain rather than away, focusing bare attention on what hurts, we move to eliminate the sources of suffering. *The first step in healing is feeling.*

No one says it's easy to put our attention on our painful feelings and sensations, but that is a time-tested approach to work with suffering. It's not just that we put our attention on what pain we feel; the quality of our attention makes all the difference. If our attention is fraught with panic, hopelessness and catastrophic expectations, these become the subject of our attention, and that kind of attention can amplify these qualities. Ideally, when we attend to painful experiences, if we can instead look with a calm mind, a sense of curiosity, and an openness to any outcome, this can allow us to approach our pain with breathing space. Approaching this way opens the possibility for healing to take place.

We had a conversation with Ram Dass over five years after he had his debilitating stroke and was enduring consistent pain. He said that even in spite of the pain, he felt serene. I asked him, "How is that possible?" He replied, "When the pain becomes severe, I meditate, and I use the pain as my object of meditation. Then I don't as much experience pain, but I am a separate witness to it." That degree of separation helped him to disidentify from his pain. It becomes more "the" pain, less "my" pain.

There are times when nothing will help, and focus on the pain becomes impossible. At those times, distraction is an alternative. Placing attention on something other than pain, something pleasant or engaging, might give temporary relief. If nothing works, you'll just have to suffer through and feel terrible. One consolation is, if you are lying at the bottom of the well, you can't go any farther down.

There is an approach to our pain that can help us get through it and grow. Joseph Campbell says it far better than I can. "Whatever your fate is, whatever the hell happens, you say, 'this is what I need.' It may look like a wreck, but go at it as though it were an opportunity, a challenge. If you bring love to that moment – not discouragement – you will find the strength is there. Any disaster you can survive is an improvement in your character, your stature, and your life."

The ability to feel the depth of your suffering can enable you to feel the height of your joy.

Cultivating Courage

Aging is not easy. It has been said, "Growing old is not for sissies." Awakening to the reality of your death, mining grief, engaging suffering and other tasks that we encounter in the Winter of our life requires courage. Facing aging, loss, illness and the end of our life, we enter unknown territory. It's all new for us, there are no familiar markers, little we can control. We see the end in sight, and the end ain't pretty. There is much to be afraid of as we grow old, and even the most courageous among us are fearful. Running away and hiding our head in the sand like the proverbial ostrich is not an option. Aging and death will eventually catch up with us. We need to turn and face our fears. Facing our fears is what defines courage. As John Wayne said, "Courage is being scared to death, but saddling up anyway."

It takes courage to keep awareness of our death in our consciousness, courage to look back at our life and admit where we've fallen short, courage to show up with our best and highest self, when lying and avoiding responsibility is so much easier, courage to fully open our heart to the unbearable pain of the loss of a loved one, the loss of our health and vitality, the loss of all we hold precious.

How do we cultivate courage and face our helplessness, fear and sadness? We just do. Knowing that confronting our demons is the only avenue that will bring us the possibility of a peaceful old age, we stand straight, gird our loins and confront them. We "saddle up" with the knowledge that in order to live our remaining time as an admirable elder, and in order to have a chance at a good death, we welcome our challenges with a resolute heart and mind.

Releasing and Being Released Through Forgiveness

There is an amazing book, *The Sunflower,* written by Nazi concentration camp survivor, Simon Wiesenthal. Wiesenthal was summoned from his camp work detail to be at the bedside of a dying SS officer who was haunted by guilt. The officer wanted absolution from a Jew, any Jew, for the murders and torture of innocent people he had taken part in. In one incident, he participated in rounding up a group of Jews, men, women and children, into a large building, setting fire to the structure, and shooting them as they ran out the door, trying to escape the flames. As he confessed, it was obvious that this man was genuinely suffering from remorse. Should Wiesenthal, out of compassion for another human being's suffering in their dying hours, offer forgiveness? Or should he speak from truth and justice and add to the officer's pain? Or should he remain silent?

In the final section of the book, many prominent political leaders, writers, psychologists, theologians, jurists, human rights activists and survivors of genocide give answers as to what they would do if faced with this situation. What would you do?

Forgiveness is relinquishing demands for how the past should have been. It is letting go of insistence about the way another person should have felt, spoken, or behaved. It is releasing your anger, resentment and righteousness and relinquishing the desire to punish or gain compensation for your pain. Should you carry feelings of anger and blame to your grave, or should you do what you can to release it and move into the future with a lighter heart and mind? Blame is of the past. Forgiveness looks to the future.

Forgiveness is a healing balm that heals both the one being forgiven, as well as the one who forgives. Forgiving another person who has hurt you is an act of kindness toward them. It helps release them from guilt over their misdeeds and unbinds them from obligation. It restores balance and equanimity. It helps them be around you without shame. Forgiveness is also an act of kindness toward yourself. It releases you, because holding on to festering anger and resentment is a painful, self-imposed prison. The unforgiving heart shuts down and the hurt and anger are walled up inside where they fester because they cannot be freed.

Letting go of blame when you've been hurt is not instantaneous. Forgiving is a process that sometimes takes a long time. If you've been hurt, especially by someone who had been close to you, the caution and distrust can remain for years. If you're older, you don't have years. That's why it's important to examine situations in the past that are deserving of your forgiveness and make a judgement as to your readiness to forgive. Are you able to be the first to make the move of extending your hand? Ready to give up seeking retaliation? To give up your righteousness? If you are ready, it may be time to forgive.

Forgiveness must be done wisely though. As psychologist Thomas Szasz has written, "The stupid neither forgive or forget; the naive forgive and forget; the wise forgive but do not forget." If you are in the company of hurtful people, it makes sense to remember who they are.

Are there actions so hurtful, so heinous that the perpetrators are not deserving of forgiveness? Look at Wiesenthal and the Nazi officer. What if someone has done something unforgivable directly to you? Should you demand revenge? Demand restitution? Demand apology? Demand remorse? Turn the other cheek? Or simply forgive?

Our friend, psychic Gary Spivey, chose forgiveness. He was tortured by a father who hated him, forced him to work menial labor even as a very young child, and who beat him bloody with thorn bushes and shot his beloved dog in front of him as punishment for a minor offense. He was an evil man and inflicted his evil on his defenseless child. Yet, in his last years, Gary bought his father a home, paid all his medical bills, got him a caretaker and made sure he was safe and well taken care of. He never even received a "thank you," from his father. Why would he do this for a man who treated him so badly and didn't have an ounce of appreciation? Gary realized that the one who receives the most benefit from the act of forgiveness is the one who forgives. By letting go of the hate and blame he held toward his father, Gary was released from the painful emotions he held in his heart.

Forgiving Yourself

Forgiveness is not just for others. Sometimes it is we who judge ourselves the harshest. So we, too, need the soothing balm of forgiveness. We, too, are in need of being forgiven…by ourself.

There are times in my life when I've done things so stupid, so hurtful, so embarrassing, that I wish I could erase the images completely from my memory banks. But I can't. When these memories come up, as they occasionally do, vividly and in living color, I shrink in shame. It's like I've been kicked in the gut. But I'm the one who's doing the kicking. I've not forgiven myself.

Recently I've come to an understanding that has helped to dull some of the sting of self-blame and thus made it easier for me to be more self-forgiving. I understand now that, for many of the mistakes I've made, *it's not exclusively my fault.* So many times when I caused hurt to myself and others, I just didn't know. I just didn't understand. Looking at my history, I realize I was subconsciously influenced by my parent's ignorance, my society's ignorance, my own confusion. Knowing this, I'm not placing blame on my parents or on society. They too are ignorant. And knowing that I was influenced by others doesn't make me free of blame. I still caused pain. But seeing my ignorance does allow me to blame myself less and forgive myself more. And now my looking back and seeing my past harmful actions as ignorance is an indication that I have evolved to a wiser level of understanding.

We have all failed, hurt others and ourselves, said and done things we're ashamed of, things we wish we could take back. No one of us is perfect or anywhere near. This recognition of the universality of human frailty, and by deduction, our own frailty, can be the beginning of self-forgiveness. It takes humility to face our weakness, hurtfulness, immaturity and greed. Recognizing we're not so special is a good beginning. That's where the work is, accepting ourselves as flawed creatures and equal members of the human race. Once we've done that, we can move on to forgive ourselves.

The willingness to forgive ourselves for our failings and the openness to be forgiven, makes the task of forgiving others easier. Forgiving others starts with turning our compassion inward and forgiving ourselves.

Asking For Forgiveness, Making Amends

We can forgive others who have hurt us. We can forgive ourselves if we have caused hurt. What can we do and say to others if our hurtful actions have caused them pain? If we have wronged someone, discord, hard feelings, and incompleteness will remain until we make the effort to make things right.

Before we got together, Alice went through a period when she had very little money. A man she owed money to for yard service would come to her house for payment, and she would hide and not answer the door. He finally gave up and stopped coming around. Over a year passed. Alice and I went into a local drug store and there was the man, helping customers behind the counter. Alice immediately went up to him, apologized, opened her wallet and paid him what she owed. He had hardly remembered the incident, but for Alice, it was an important unaddressed feeling of guilt that had weighed on her all that time. As soon as we left the store, Alice broke down in tears of relief. She had no idea of how heavy was the weight of her guilt, and how relieving the lifting of that weight would be for her.

There are hurtful things that I have done to others that are sticking in my gut and the discomfort won't go away by itself. I have sought out those I hurt in order to take responsibility for my actions, apologize and make amends when possible. I felt a rush of relief with those who I found and with whom I was able to ask for forgiveness, and forgiveness was granted. They did too. With one person in particular, my reappearance would cause more hurt, so I made no effort to contact them. For those I have been unable to reconnect with, the discomfort remains, and probably will for the rest of my life, in somewhat diminished form. Diminished, because my intention to ask for forgiveness itself is healing.

Accepting Help When Helpless

Of all the losses of old age, the need for being helped by others, perhaps especially for men, is one of the most demeaning. Our body may have become frail and weak. We may need another person to help us with the simple tasks of getting dressed, eating, wiping our butt. This happens. Losing independence and becoming a burden to others is especially challenging when we highly value self-reliance and control. To require help with simple physical needs is humiliating and reflects on our self-worth.

Years ago I used to have extremely painful and debilitating back spasms. One of these episodes came on when I was attending an important business meeting. By the end of the meeting, I was in extreme pain and could not even bend down to tie my shoes. Reluctantly, I asked for help. Two women each got on their knees, tied my shoelaces, helped me to stand, and supporting me on each side, helped me walk out of the building. All my fears and judgements of helplessness and dependence were triggered. Though I felt a measure of appreciation for the women's help, the embarrassment and humiliation for needing that help was overwhelming for me.

A much different, more skillful example of accepting and working with helplessness came from an acquaintance when we were living in an ashram. His spiritual name was Mahadev and he was a victim, from childhood, of muscular dystrophy, which left him wheelchair bound, with useless legs and limited use of his arms. "Victim" is not an accurate term for him. He was not a victim of anything. He radiated warmth and lightness. Mahadev had a way of, not really demanding, but expecting that you would be happy to help him when he requested it. No embarrassment, no shame, no extended thank-you in appreciation for your help. If he needed assistance, he would simply ask for it. If you could help, great, if you couldn't, no big deal, he would just go on to ask someone else. He didn't let his being unable to have full control of his body define who he was.

Mahadev was able to receive with grace. I think part of what made him so light about being helped by people was that he saw that those who helped were receiving benefit from helping him. He, in his helplessness, provided those who assisted him the opportunity to be of service, and they benefited by serving. Their heart opened a little by being of assistance to this man who was obviously in need. Mahadev made it easier by being unattached to whether it was you who helped him or not.

I hope that, if and when I am in need of assistance when I grow older, that I can have Mahadev's lightness about helplessness, and not let false pride prevent me from reaching out when I am in need. I hope I could accept that help with grace and appreciation.

Facing The Reality Of The Need To Relinquish Control And Independence

My dad was a stubborn guy. This could be good or bad, depending on the circumstances. Often, though, his stubbornness was problematic when he got older. His hearing was declining, so we got him a high-end set of hearing aids. He didn't wear them, insisting instead we yell in his ear when we wanted to communicate with him. He had always been on top of his financial dealings, but when he began dropping the ball, he wouldn't allow anyone to help him, even though his negligence was costing him money. His driving was abominable. He was a danger to himself and others on the road, yet he rebuffed all efforts to take his car away...until he had a fender bender and finally allowed us to sell his car.

I don't want to be like him. I want to face facts. If I am falling, forgetting things, losing my way, in need of help, I don't want to let my desire to be in control and my pride dictate my decisions. Aging is relentless and can force you

It is often a long hard slog to achieve independence, but equally hard, at an appropriate age, to surrender it.

Ann Orbach, psychoanalyst

to make uncomfortable choices. Facing the truth is viewing your situation without prejudice, weighing alternatives, and choosing appropriate actions. Easier said than done, especially if you cling to being in control. Letting go of control is a difficult decision to make. And, especially for many men, among their greatest fears is to be helpless and having to be taken care of.

When I am a danger to myself and others and it is appropriate I give up the freedom my automobile provides me, I will surrender my driver's license and get rid of my car. I affirm that I will do it. If I am feeling sick and in pain, I will not automatically assume I will get better, as I had in the past, but if it is appropriate that I explore the health issue with a medical expert, I will do it. If and when I become confused and cannot handle my financial affairs, and it becomes appropriate that I relinquish that responsibility to others who are knowledgeable, I will do it. If it is appropriate that I must leave my beautiful home and move to a facility where I will be protected and cared for, I affirm, I will do it.

It is difficult to know when it is the right time to give up independence, let go of control, or relinquish activities that are no longer in accordance with reality. It's even more difficult to actually do it. The trick is in having the wisdom to recognize what is "appropriate." To follow through and "do it" takes courage.

Learning To Become A Caregiver

Friend and associate, psychotherapist Jed Diamond, found his world suddenly changed when Carlin, his wife of thirty-three years, slipped and broke her hip. She needed a partial hip replacement and was incapacitated for quite awhile. Formerly busily focused out in the world, Jed took on the unfamiliar role of becoming her primary caregiver. He learned a lot and wrote glowingly about the joys he experienced by taking on caregiving duties with Carlin. "In this time of caregiving for Carlin, I am once again experiencing the beauty, joy and unspeakable love that passes between us and connects us both to the mystery we call God."

By having lived long, there's a good possibility that at some point in your life you will have an opportunity to become a caregiver. As you grow older, intimate partners, family and friends will age along with you and might be in need of help. The task may fall to you.

You could be a caregiver at a distance, and hire someone with knowledge and experience to provide care for the loved one in need. That may be fine if you can afford it, because not all folks have the disposition to be a caregiver. And some circumstances require a professional. Also, some people who need care might prefer hired help rather than inconveniencing a loved one.

Being a caregiver is a serious undertaking and requires more than simply providing efficient service to one in need. In addition to serving, caregivers provide a listening ear, a reassuring shoulder, informed advice, encouragement and an open heart. That kind of care requires sensitivity, generosity and patience. Also, compassion for another's suffering. Without bringing your generous heart, loving touch and patient disposition to the work of caregiving, you might be radiating an attitude of impatience, disgust, boredom, resentment and martyrdom. These are not the best conditions for healing to take place, neither for the person being cared for, nor for the caregiver.

Being responsible for the health and well-being of a loved one can be very stressful. There might be lots of tasks to juggle, from helping with the mechanics of daily living, like cleaning, dressing and feeding, to organizing medications and arranging transportation. Also, being with another person and bearing witness through their adversity and suffering is not easy. It is difficult for us to remain present psychologically and emotionally. But our loving presence can be the most healing gift we can offer.

Caregiving can often be draining and outside your comfort zone, but it can also be very rewarding. You benefit personally and develop character by summoning your best humanity and performing generous, selfless acts. As with Jed Diamond, serving a loved one in need is a gift that can deepen the bond between you. Trust builds and walls come down. And both of you can feel grateful for the acts of serving and being served.

Done with the right attitude, caring for another can be a spiritual endeavor. A traditional path to enlightenment involves performing service with no demand for anything in return or expectation of congratulations. Serving with this attitude is generosity to the nth degree.

By caring for another person in their time of need, you are strengthened and deepened. And as a valuable bonus, you gain insight into what's important when there comes a time in your own life when you will need to be cared for by others.

Serving As A Guide

We don't usually look to the young when we want to know wisdom and character and justice and compassion. These are qualities valued by living years of life. Look to the young if you want to know achievement, acquiring, winning, looking good. These things are what many in the younger generation value and know lots about. Their interests lie in building and short term goals, while elders, with their greater perspective, might

I am not wise until someone asks me to be.

Rabbi Zalman Schachter-Shalomi

hold concerns that value sustaining well-being for society for the long-term. Their impulse might include a desire to deepen, preserve and inspire into the future.

As with each previous generation, the power brokers of younger generations hold political, social, technological and financial power now. They are often covetous of that power and often filled with arrogance and pride, not inclined to listen to "has beens" and "old fogies" (the elders of the older generations). They are busy in the world and have little patience for "Big Questions." However, wise elders, by having lived a life and gained perspective, can be mentors and give the up-and-coming generations what they need most, guidance gained through lived experience, lived truth. That guidance from elders, if accepted, can be a light on the path, and can help save succeeding generations from making the same errors they have made. In these

The Great Law of the Iroquois people is that any decision of importance should be made with consideration of it's effects seven generations into the future, so that decisions made now will also benefit descendants.

312

times where so much power remains in the hands of so few, and some of those few are "irresponsible boys in men's suits," errors can have consequences that can have widespread effect, possibly mean the destruction of civilization.

We elders know the world. We have lived through war and know the suffering that violence brings, and are clear that there are no winners. We elders have seen politician's greed for money and power and know full well where corruption and lack of integrity leads. We elders have observed the devastating effects of hate, prejudice and injustice. We elders have experienced one group's thirst for revenge over another, and know that an eye for an eye, tooth for a tooth leaves both sides blind and toothless. We elders know these things. In our lifetime we have experienced the folly of chasing after short term, profit-driven goals and, because of our extended, multi-generation perspective, see how our assault on the environment will wreak havoc for future generations.

We elders are the memory of our generation. Thus we can serve as prophets and truth tellers for those coming after us. That is a priceless role we can play. Our responsibility as elders, rather than fade away, is to assume the role of sage guide and model the best and highest qualities of human beings. In this sad world, with its greed, violence and lack of kindness, we have a choice as to how we will act. Will we withdraw in silence, or will we rise to the occasion and speak out from a place of caring. If we don't step up, from where will the guidance come? I urge you, don't fade away. Stay engaged. Be visible. Be vocal. The Earth needs you, people need you more than ever now.

Yes, the world needs elder wisdom, but don't expect the demand to come from the young. Ram Dass wrote, "We cannot expect the young to beat down our doors, begging for our wisdom, reminding us of our responsibility to society.

You think I am waiting to die...
But I am waiting to be found.
I am a treasure.
I am a map.
And these wrinkles are
Imprints of my journey.
Ask me anything.

Samantha Reynolds
Portion of the poem,
I Am Not Old

As older people, we will have to initiate the change by freeing ourselves of this culture's bias, and remember the unique things we bring to the table."

OK, so all this is well and good, but how many of us will serve as a guide on the world stage? Not many. It would be great if our wise counsel could move multitudes, but that's for the Mother Teresas and the Nelson Mandelas. The way we will make a difference in the world will be through working one-on-one, mentoring on a personal, heart-to-heart level. That work, with friends, family, co-workers, clients and strangers, would involve elders holding integrity and being beacons of peace, altruism, wisdom and compassion. In doing so, wise elders would provide inspiring models for younger generations to emulate.

Being Of Service

The first half of life is about, "what does the world want of me and how do I meet it's demands?" *The second half is about,* "what wants to enter the world through me?"

Jungian Analyst James Hollis

A crying child has lost its parents in a crowd, a stranger is weeping, sitting on her luggage in the train station, a young woman, looking forlorn, is standing next to her car with a flat tire, an old man has fallen and is dazed, sitting on the sidewalk. I think there is an instinctual human drive to be of help. Perhaps we see these people in need and, by empathy, feel their distress. "This could be me." We automatically reach out and offer a helping hand. Or else we purposefully quash the instinctual, empathic urge, walk by, not wanting to get involved in someone else's drama. Either way, there is a decision point—stop and be of service, or assume someone else will. And the truth is, there are no right decisions.

However, there are consequences when you offer to be of service. Gandhi said, *"The fragrance remains on the hand that offers the rose."* It's true, *in the process of giving, you receive.* When he was a teenager, our son, Jason, was self-obsessed. It seemed all he cared about was himself. We drove him nuts trying to get him to do something for other people. Finally, in exasperation, he volunteered to be a driver for Meals On Wheels, an organization that delivers food to seniors who are housebound and cannot obtain their own meals. It's been decades now that Jay has been volunteering. The two days a week he delivers are days he is sure to feel good about himself. Serving others this way has made a difference in his life as well as the lives of the many people he serves.

Being of service has no age limits. I read an article recently about an experienced businessman who had formed and run several successful companies. He wanted to share his knowledge about creating a business. He and a few buddies started a voluntary organization to help advise young people in deprived communities who wanted to start their own businesses. He was 96 years old.

As older persons, we might be retired and probably have much more free time than when we were younger. What better way to spend some of that time than to give of ourselves by helping those in need or serving in organizations that benefit the public. The needs are endless.

Retired after reaching the pinnacle as motion picture producer and director and former president of the Academy, our friend Howard "Hawk" Koch now derives great fulfillment producing and directing plays with the old actors at the retirement community for those formerly in the television and movie industry. What joy for him, the actors and for the audience of friends and family who view the plays.

Our service will likely be personal, like one-on-one mentoring of a young student who has trouble with arithmetic class, or teaching embroidery to a girl who is mentally challenged. Or it could be in small groups, like coaching an after-school basketball team, or joining a group of volunteers distributing food for the homeless.

Sometimes even small acts of kindness will make a big difference. A visit to a sick friend, a lift to an appointment, some weeds pulled, a load of laundry done, a meal prepared—these things are messages. "I care about you, your welfare is important to me, I'm willing to go out of my way to make your life a little more comfortable." The message of caring from your service is sometimes more appreciated than the service itself.

We all have areas of interest and expertise. These person-to-person and small group interactions are where your experience and wise counsel will be put to use. Maybe even more important than the particulars of what you have to give is your bearing and mature character. Your behavior will model these qualities and your wisdom will be absorbed by the people you are working with. They will be attracted to your depth like a moth is attracted to light. They will "get it" simply by being around you. You will be a model for them. And you will make a difference in their lives.

Motivation for your desire to help is key. Do you want to help in order to get Brownie Points and be seen as one of the "good guys?" Do you help because it's expected? Are you trying for a seat closer to God in heaven? Do you help in order to avoid feeling guilty? Do you expect to receive payback at some later time? Or is your offering to be of service pure and coming from a place of genuine concern, genuine generosity. Giving from your heart is the most powerful form of service. Giving from your heart in service is an expression of love in action.

Rabbi Zalman Schachter-Shalomi verbalized the ideal attitude behind the offering of service by a wise elder, *"I've learned something about life, my friend. I love you and am available to share it with you."* What an inviting invitation.

Expressing Your "Gift"

In the James Hollis quote on page 314, "what wants to enter," is a gift we have within us to give the world or give to ourselves. Let me be clearer. I believe that every person has within them some aspect of themselves that needs expression. It is a "gift"—a talent, a desire, a calling, an appreciation. It seeks expression "through" us, in other words, we are vehicles for that expression. Pursuing this gift gives our life meaning, or at the least, adds meaning to our life. It helps organize our life. Pursuing our gift gives us energy, and that energy can excite and incite energy in ourself and others.

If we cannot or will not give expression to that gift, we will have denied an important part of ourselves, and we will never quite feel complete, or feel we have done in our life all of what we have come here to do. Without giving birth to our gift, our death will leave the promise of our gift unfulfilled.

Gifts can vary widely, but they are invariably connected to what gives us passion. My gift at this point in my life is my writing. This is what holds passion for me now. Alice's gift is her art and her connection with other people and with animals. My brother Steve's is his drumming and healing work. Ellen's is her singing. Tiana's is her support of abandoned animals. Your gift doesn't have to be world-changing. If you love food, it could be cooking and sharing your meals. If you have a keen sense of humor, it could be making people laugh. If you love to nurture, your gift could be serving as a loving parent or grandparent. If your mind is at peace, your serenity is a gift that can touch everyone around you.

Your gift doesn't even have to involve others. It could be a gift to yourself, such as savoring the beauty of art or music, or of camping and taking hikes in the wilderness. Author and psychologist Carol Orsborn has wisely written, "Now I know that the culmination of this long journey is not achievement—but appreciation." Expressing your gift, to yourself or to others, brings you appreciation of that gift. And joy, to yourself and others.

The quote by James Hollis referred to the second half of life. What about the last quarter? The last quarter of our lives is different from the second half. During our middle age, we might still be building, still striving to acquire, still ego driven. As we enter the doorway of old age, however, we might tend to have less interest and less energy available to pursue our gift. Is it too late for a woman in her eighties to take up learning to play piano as she had wanted in her earlier years? (Just got off the phone with our friend Marilyn, age eighty-four. She has recently engaged a piano teacher and is learning to play piano.) Is it too late for a eighty-eight-year-old retired lawyer to begin writing a novel that had been on his mind for forty years? Is it too late for a grandmother in her seventies to return to college to study astronomy? I suspect that it is never too late, that there is no age limit for expressing a gift. It's about passion. It's about doing what you love and sharing what you've done. The fact that your passion and your love is contained in your gift should be a reminder to you—giving is always an exchange. Giving your gift involves receiving. In offering your gift you are receiving your gift in return.

Maintaining An Expectation Of Being Respected As An Elder

In many fairytales, world mythology, children's stories and fantasy movies, there is a wise elder, an old man or crone, who acts as an advisor to the main character or hero figure as they are about to embark on their dangerous adventure. This old person holds some special knowledge, or possesses a powerful secret, or key, or incantation, or protective amulet, or magic substance that will help the hero accomplish his or her goal. Because of their special knowledge and power, and their willingness to share their secrets, the elder is held in high esteem.

In past civilizations and in many cultures around the world today, elders are venerated, as gurus, as seers, as shamans, as healers, as wisdom keepers. Yet its no secret that, as a rule, the elderly are not routinely held in high regard in our society. Oh, we'll help an old lady across the street, carry heavy packages for an elderly neighbor or give up our seat in the bus to an old man, but that's courtesy. I'm speaking here about honoring and respecting one who has the experience of years. This is not common practice here. Even many of us elders have taken on for ourselves, the lack of respect for old people shown by contemporary society. We think that because we're old, and past our "productive years" we no longer are deserving of respect. However, if we don't respect ourselves for our hard won wisdom and depth of experience, who else will?

We had a friend, a Native American medicine man named Grandpa Semu Huate, an elder from the Chumash tribe. Grandpa and his wife were staying with us when we learned that a well-known African shaman named Malidoma Som'e was giving a retreat not far from us. Grandpa wanted to pay a visit. Grandpa was an impressive figure, 90 years old at the time, over six feet tall, long white hair in braids, wearing colorful full Native American regalia. We barged in as the retreat was in full swing. As soon as Malidoma saw Grandpa, he stopped the proceedings and welcomed him, making sure he was brought a chair and a glass of water. He sat on the floor at Grandpa's feet, speaking to him humbly and treating him with deference and deepest respect. This was how elders were honored in the Dagara culture that Malidoma was raised in. This honor and respect for elders is common in many cultures around the world.

Unfortunately, it is not always true here in America and in other countries influenced by our contemporary way of life. Here, youth is given preference over age, accomplishing has greater importance than being, glitter is more attractive than depth, and knowledge is sought after over wisdom. We don't display great respect for elders who have aged beyond their "productive years." They are not that useful anymore. It's a sad fact that at this point in an elder's life, when they have so much to share, our culture has marginalized them.

When an elder is shown respect, it is of benefit to both that elder and the one showing respect. When you honor an elder you are not only honoring the person, you are honoring their years of experience. Elders have the gift of perspective, and that is an invaluable gift. Their minds hold a storehouse of knowledge and experience that is worthy of respect. Yet, of what use is that knowledge and experience in a culture that does not seek answers from their previous generations? The famous quote by philosopher George Santayana, "Those who do not remember the past are condemned to repeat it," is true. Elders know the past well, they have experienced it. It is a wasted resource to not consult wise elders.

Remember this as you age. You, and the experience you have gained over the years are valuable. Your depth and wisdom is deserving of emulation. Your wrinkles are a badge of honor. You deserve to be respected. *You will be honored to the degree you honor yourself.*

Sharing Your Story

Each individual is a completely unique manifestation of nature. There has never been, nor will there ever be, anyone who resembles anyone else. There are almost 8 billion of us, each a completely different version of a human being. And every one of us who has ever lived has their unique story to tell. Anyone who is willing to listen can learn from that story.

There is a project that started in Denmark that has now spread worldwide, called Human Library. You can "check out" a living person, sit down with them for a half hour, listen to their stories and ask them questions about their life. How interesting it would be to check out a monk, a thief, a scientist, a prostitute, a politician, a very old person.

Go to an assisted-living facility and observe the residents. The old lady with the oxygen tank on her wheelchair was a well known author. The old fellow slowly making his way through the dining room was a college professor at a prestigious university. The old man watching TV in the day room is a decorated Viet Nam veteran. If we could hear their stories, these people would come alive for us, rather than just being a passing image of an old person. There is no way to tell a book by its cover. Each of these people have a story to tell. And so do you.

Often, when we're young, we don't think to ask our grandparents their stories. We're preoccupied with our present life, uninterested in the past. I was like that when I was younger. Now, I think of all the questions I should have asked and regret not asking. How did my grandparents meet and fall in love? What were my parents like when they were young? What was the family's experience of the Great Depression? What was life like when my grandparents were teenagers? The book of their lives is closed and I'll never know the answers to these fascinating questions. How I would love to speak to Grandma and Grandpa now and listen to their stories.

For years, our friend, Howard, also known by us as, How Odd, has been working on a series of books about his life and adventures, which he has been sharing in bits and pieces with his kids, grandkids, and great- grandkids. It has grown now to numerous volumes. He used to work as an artist and illustrator, and the books are full of his zany drawings. What a wonderful gift to pass down to his family. And what a joy for himself. The stories he writes are part of his life review and gives him a sense of completion as well as revealing part of his inner self to his descendants. Rather than just being a name and old photograph, the stories in his books will reveal his life to those who read them long after he is gone.

People love stories. Don't be shy. Share yours. In much of this book, I am sharing my stories with you. I hope you appreciate them as much as I've enjoyed remembering and telling them.

Leaving a Legacy

A society grows great when old men plant trees in whose shade they shall never sit.

Greek proverb

In Winter, the harvest has already been gathered. Seeds have fallen to the earth and are covered with a blanket of leaves. They rest in the moist, dark soil, waiting for the coming of Spring to waken them to aliveness. Human life is not a cycle, it is a progression from beginning to end. For all we know, there will be no Winter for us. Each of our lives ends with Winter. But there is an essence that is passed on. It is passed through your genes, but is also passed on through the life you have lived. After your death, the seeds—of your love, your generosity, your wisdom—will be planted in the hearts and minds of those you left behind, hopefully to grow and blossom in future generations.

The gophers killed our fruit tree. It was a wonderful tree that gave us delicious plums for over a decade. The gophers must have climbed over the wire barrier that was to keep them out, ate the roots, and the tree quickly died. I got another plum tree and planted it. Chances are, by the time it starts producing fruit in volume, we won't be

The best time to plant a tree was 20 years ago.
The second best time is today.

Chinese proverb

around. It doesn't matter. The tree we plant now will provide joy and nourishment for whoever will be living on our land after we've gone. Planting that tree will be a legacy we'll leave for those who come after us.

The most common form of legacy is counted in money and property, distributed by a will to your heirs. But that is a very limited definition. In truth, our financial assets are but a limited form of what we have available to leave behind.

Another form of legacy, richer than cash, stems from a desire to create good for ensuing generations. Many of us are thankful for the richness of the life we have lived or are living. We want to give back, in the form of financial support for people and groups that need it, or by the formation of a charitable organization that will live beyond us, or by volunteering our time and energy to help others in need, or through the dissemination of the knowledge and wisdom we have gained that will make the world a better place than the condition we found it. Or by planting a tree.

Everyone, rich or poor, leaves a legacy. This kind of legacy I'm referring to is a personal one. It lives in the hearts and minds of those who knew you and know you. It lives on in their memories after you have died, and in their hearts if you still live. This legacy is created by the way you are living and have lived your life, by the love you are giving and have given, or by the greed and hate you have generated by your actions. Has your life inspired others with your enthusiasm, your open-mindedness, your support, your generosity, your joy? That is your legacy.

All you have may someday be given;
Therefore give now,
that the season of giving
may be yours
and not your inheritors.

The Prophet
Khalil Gibran

There is nothing you can take to the grave with you except your dead carcass. It's best to leave your legacy to the world when you're alive. You are fortunate to have been given birth as a human being. It would be a shame to leave the world just as you found it. Do something that will make the world happier, kinder, safer, more beautiful than when you entered. That is a loving thing to leave behind. Let your legacy be love.

What kind of ancestor do you want to become? What

benefit would you want to bestow on your loved ones, your friends, the human race. The world? If you're old, there is not a lot of time. There is so much need. Why not start now?

Working With The Tendency To Fall Into Sadness And Hopelessness

I've done the math. At eighty years old, as a white male in the US, I've exceeded my life expectancy by almost three years. That makes me a "dead man walking." And I am facing a future that is very likely to have increasing debilities, increasing pain, increasing loss. That can be depressing and can lead to a sense of hopelessness. "I'm almost done. There's no future. It's downhill from here. Might as well give up on life." Many people have taken on this deadly attitude. I won't.

At different points in this book I have written very directly about the challenges we go through when aging, and also I celebrated the power those challenges have to motivate us to wake up and live our best life. I have not touched on the emotional effect those challenges might have on us, namely, sadness and depression.

Various types of depression are not uncommon among elders. Debilitating chronic illness, memory issues, decline in independence and mobility, thoughts of one's own death and the deaths of loved ones, these and other factors can contribute to persistent sadness, anxiety, confusion, tiredness, lack of motivation and thoughts of suicide. These are symptoms of depression. Depression is more common among older people than among the general population.

Added to the challenges of growing old, is the weight of the depressing times we are living in. Glance at the news and you'll see pure insanity. Children being murdered in their schools, innocent civilians bombed, pandemic, political circus, natural disasters, prejudice, senseless violence, nuclear threat, rape, mass shootings, animals being abused, environmental devastation. Today, Alice

A pessimist will never be disappointed.

Finnish saying

came home from her yoga class in tears. She had been listening to the news on the radio on the drive home and was overwhelmed by humanity's inhumanity. It's all we can do just to keep from drowning in a sea of sadness.

Those who have not experienced depression have no idea of what it feels like. It is much more than feeling "sad" or "having the blues." People who have had depression describe the following symptoms; feeling numb inside, no enjoyment, feeling alone and isolated, having no hope for the future, low energy, stuck, the world lacks color, nothing matters. These feelings are not transitory, they persist, sometimes for a lifetime.

To be honest, I have been feeling waves of sadness that come and go ever since I began writing this book. In addition to feeling the weight of despondency about the dismal state of the world, I attribute much of the heaviness I feel to the explorations I've done being immersed in the challenges of my own growing old. It's brought home to me the awareness of increasing signs of my aging, my losses, and my and Alice's impending deaths. While this recurring sense of sadness is no fun, the beneficial effect of bringing the challenges of aging to awareness has overall been a great boon. It has deepened me and helped prepare me for the coming years, whatever they may bring. But it's not easy to take in.

Depression can be serious. Medical and psychological intervention may be called for in some cases. However, there are measures that can be taken which can help "garden variety" sadness that can come on during aging. Some of the things Alice and I do to keep our head above water in the face of the losses of age and the insanity of the world are; limiting the time we spend reading and watching negativity in the news, especially the gruesome details, engaging with uplifting people and avoiding "downers," focusing on the goodness and positive things and people in our life and giving thanks for them, cultivating an attitude of acceptance, or as Riley would say, "allowing," and redefining the challenges of aging we are facing as not just misery visited upon us by fate, but as valuable opportunities to grow and learn to be more peaceful, accepting human beings. Overall, we try to approach our experience more from our heart, rather than from our mind. Though I've mentioned all these activities almost in passing, they are not to be minimized. Each one can be considered a practice, to be worked with diligently until they become part of the way we approach negativity.

All this is easier said than done. Sadness and depression is like quicksand—attempts to extricate yourself can often get you stuck more deeply. One of the worst things with depression is the strong tendency to become self-obsessed. Nothing outside yourself holds your interest. Feeling like an empty shell, you isolate and turn your energy within and resist efforts of self and others to pull you out. That, and lack of life energy, sucks you deeper, more helpless and hopeless into the quicksand. In this state, it's easy to give up and "fall in love with your bed."

When we're young, death and disability are so far away. We have so many things ahead of us to occupy us—future goals, career, growing family. But when we're old, our future is short and distractions few. The losses wrought by aging are real and immediate. It's important to be aware though, that being in a rush to cut off sadness and hopelessness is not always the best thing to do. Sometimes it's beneficial to turn inside and explore our sadness and disturbing emotions, or just allow them to be, without rushing to eradicate them. These feelings can be powerful vehicles for the growth of our wisdom, and can motivate us to prepare to meet the challenges of old age as they come. In this sense, it is possible for depression to be a rite of passage.

Developing A Practice To Clear, Quiet And Control Your Mind

Remember my experience with the air conditioning unit? I sure do. That was a classic example of a mind out of control and a mind that was suffering.

This task of attempting to gain control of your mind is one of the most important tasks of aging, if not the most. Also, one of the most difficult. (You notice I used the word "attempting.") The untethered mind is the cause of much suffering. It has been compared to a wild monkey, jumping from one thought to another. That monkey is very powerful, more like a gorilla. A big gorilla.

Calming the wild monkey mind as we get older is also a necessary task. As we age, we must deal with increasingly serious crises like health issues, life changes and deaths of loved ones. By comparison, a broken air conditioner is a minor blip. With major crises, our minds could easily careen out of control. Fears can come up and take over our consciousness. Fear is a product of a mind that looks to the future, then catastrophizes by thinking the worst and obsessively recycles the thought. A mind out of control is a mind that suffers.

OLD YOGI
Old man meditating in half lotus position

Another analogy about the mind uses the comparison to a horse-drawn chariot. The horse is the untamed mind, the chariot driver is the higher Self, the one who has the potential to control the horse. If the driver doesn't use his reins (his skill and determination) to control the horse, it will wander all over the place, and the driver will never be able to get to where he wants to go. So the driver must hone his skills and garner his determination.

There are forms of meditation that are specifically aimed at controlling, quieting and relaxing the mind. There are breathing and systematic physical relaxation techniques that can do a similar thing. There are even cutting edge technologies and electronic devices that purport to attain relaxation and meditative states in a relatively short time. For one who is willing, there's a whole smorgasbord of techniques available to hand you the reins to control your horses and calm your monkey mind. But maybe all that is needed is to schedule some time to simply go to a quiet room, turn out the light, sit comfortably, and allow the calm to gradually overtake you.

Think of your mind as the ocean. Wind and tides keep the waves roiling on the surface, while on the bottom, the water is still. The agitated surface waves are the thoughts that are constantly going on in your mind. As you dive deep below the surface, using meditative and other techniques that quiet the mind, you reach a place of stillness and peace.

Mind and body are interrelated. When you are stressed, your body tenses. When your body is relaxed, your nervous system quiets, your mind slows down and relaxes. As your mind and body relax, you are better able to intervene to slow down the monkey, control the horse and dive below the surface to a place of peace. The key is *stillness*, becoming suspended in inactivity and in silence. In stillness, the quiet body quiets the mind, the quiet mind quiets the body.

A great benefit of meditation is that it helps you to separate yourself from your monkey mind. As the mind jumps from thought to thought, sensation to sensation, we experience our thoughts and sensations as "me." But actually, the "you" that you are is separate from the experiences that are coursing through the screen of your awareness. Our language illustrates this. We use the expression "my" mind, like, "My mind is racing." Who is this "my" if not a consciousness separate from the mind. Sitting in meditation, we watch the thoughts and sensations as if we are a separate observer. Over time, we identify more with the calm consciousness who watches the thoughts, feelings and sensations. Being the "watcher" and having this distance keeps us from falling into and swallowing all the crazy stories our monkey mind spins.

As "watcher," we are able to observe our moment-by-moment truth. We are able to more accurately see and feel the contents of our experience as it happens. I cannot emphasize enough how important and necessary this is. Without this clarity of vision, we can be blind to the happenings in our mind and our life. Our blindness can cause us to create uproar and stumble into mind spaces we don't want to be.

Now is the time to learn and practice these quieting and self-observation techniques. Once your mind begins to take you for a ride, it's too late to begin to learn them. You're on the roller coaster.

If you are an elder, you probably have more free time than when you were younger. You can use this time and make it your profession to work at quieting your mind. A quiet mind is essential for sanity. A quiet mind is a supreme accomplishment. A quiet mind is the mark of a sage elder.

Cultivating Spirit

What if our religion was each other? If our practice was our life? What if the temple was the Earth? If forests were our church? If holy water—the rivers, lakes and oceans? What if meditation was our relationships? If the Teacher was life? If wisdom was knowledge? If love was the center of our being?

Ganga White

The span of a human life is usually considered to take the form of an arc. You are born, you grow in a rising arc, to be a child, an adolescent, an adult. You start off being strong and vital. In later adulthood, entropy takes over your body, and strength and energy ebbs. The trajectory of the arc turns downward. This may be a description of the body and the mind, but not the soul. The spirit is independent of years lived. In fact, as we grow older, there is greater potential for spiritual growth. The arc of spiritual growth is more likely to ascend as we age.

The material world holds attraction for us when we are younger and engaged in the ascending arc. Impressive cars, designer clothes, prestigious job, influential friends, attractive appearance, a flush bank account—for some of us, these were what was important in the earlier years of our life. But as we grow older, they lose their luster. We want to find meaning in our life beyond material possessions and sense pleasures. So we want to bring a spiritual dimension into our life.

What is spiritual? The word can conjure images of dimly lit rooms, burning incense, calming New Age music and pictures of foreign looking people in white robes on the walls. These are merely trappings. That which is spiritual is concerned with a reality greater than oneself. More particularly, spirituality is concerned with a self that is beyond the ego self. The ego self identifies with the narrow territory of the body, gender, profession, social status, life history. The function of bringing the spiritual aspect to more prominence is to loosen identity with that smaller, ego self, and develop

IN GOD'S HANDS

An old couple held, in naked innocence, in the hands of Divine protection

greater identity with a larger Self. The Self of spirituality identifies with a unitive consciousness, a vastness that is of the nature of unconditional love and abiding peace. The inner work of spirituality is to come in closer contact with the Self, and ultimately make real that experience of unconditional love, acceptance and inner peace.

Each person's experience is different, but I believe the result of years of inner practice, in addition to a growing experience of peace, acceptance and unconditional love, is a sense of appreciation of the existence of a power greater than ourselves, maybe even a connection with a Divine being, and perhaps a feeling that we are part of an immensity of incomprehensible proportions. That immensity is beyond space, beyond time, and beyond anything our mind can grasp.

Approaching the Winter of life, there commonly is a slowing down, a turning away from worldly concerns and a natural tendency to turn within. Ram Dass called this tendency, transitioning from Role to Soul. Spiritual work amplifies that tendency. Such work cannot be accomplished by occasionally attending church on Sunday, shul on Saturday, or mosque on Friday. It cannot be accomplished by meditating a few minutes or reading a few verses from the Bible, Torah or Koran. It usually requires developing a personal spiritual practice. This could be an ongoing, usually daily ritual, such as meditation, contemplation, chanting, prayer, visualization.

Cultivating spirituality may also involve active exploration, through attending workshops, contemplative retreats, study of holy texts and reading spiritual books, attendance at congregations of spiritual and religious groups, following the teachings of enlightened mentors and participation in uplifting rituals. These kinds of practices involve withdrawing your consciousness from the noise and chatter of everyday life, and turning your focus within. Withdrawal, sometimes for a protracted period of time, into a peaceful, contemplative environment, can sometimes be helpful to bring about a new way of seeing the world and your life.

Now is the season for you to know that everything you do is sacred.

Hafiz, Persian poet

While these spiritual practices may involve a temporary withdrawal from the everyday world, withdrawal is not their purpose. For the practitioner, the purpose of spiritual practice is the opposite. It is to bring the fruits of the spiritual practice into the everyday world. It is to imbue your everyday life with a sense of the sacred. Walking the dog can become a spiritual experience, washing dishes can become a spiritual experience, driving to work, making love, emptying the trash all can become a sacred experience. What is it that makes them spiritual? Your sense of what is holy is enlarged to include all of creation. And by focusing presence in the moment, and strengthening the focus, the moment reveals its holiness.

We are stardust
We are golden
We are billion-year-old carbon
And we've got to get ourselves back to
the garden

Joni Mitchell,
"Woodstock"

Then what? The sense of holiness from spiritual work is to be shared. Your patience is gifted to your children, your acceptance is gifted to your partner, your serenity is gifted to your co-workers, your forgiveness is gifted to your enemies, your expanded love is gifted to the world. You inspire in others what you have attained. You, as an elder who has turned inward and cultivated your spiritual Self, can act as a bridge for those of us in the everyday world, to help us cross over to the unseen world of spirit. In this way, one soul at a time, the world becomes more soul-full.

Never Abandoning The "Child" Part Of You

We were not born to be miserable. We were born to experience joy. Yet nothing can kill joy faster than having to be a responsible adult all the time. Worrying about the future, paying the bills, taking care of health, being an efficient employee, these are all serious and necessary responsibilities for our support and maintenance in the world. However, there is a part of us that remains joyful and alive, no matter how old we are—our "child." But many people, especially older people, have forgotten this part. We have sacrificed our innocence in order to become responsible adults.

Alice and I used to facilitate a playshop, (not a workshop). It was called Creative Expressions. We offered it on weekends in Southern California community colleges. The goal was to help people reduce mental inhibitions, overcome embarrassment and let go of self-judgment (these confining afflictions are what many adults deal with.) Our aim was to assist participants to rediscover and re-animate the childlike part of themselves. We provided them the opportunity to jump into the moment and engage in uninhibited play. Participants danced to lively music while twirling long pieces of colorful fabric, held phony intellectual conversations while wearing goofy hats and masks, went blindfolded on "trust walks," created spontaneous drawings and tried their hand at improvised acting scenes. There was lots of laughter as they gradually sloughed off their "serious" adult and came in touch with the neglected child in themselves.

We don't stop playing because we grow old. We grow old because we stop playing.

George Bernard Shaw

Who is this child? Our child is composed of our boisterous humor, insatiable curiosity, fresh innocence, surprise, creativity, spontaneity, unbridled imagination, unrestrained excitement and childlike playfulness. And laughter, lots of laughter. Our child is present in the moment, unconcerned about the future, cares nothing about the past. Our child sees everything as new, with eyes of wonder, as if to be experienced for the first time. Our child serves as a counterbalance to that adult part of us that takes everything so damn seriously. No matter how "adult" we are, no matter how old we are, our child never leaves us. *It is we who abandon our child.* Being an adult, we don't have to abandon our child. Rather, we retain, when we want to and need to, the ability to bring back the child part of us.

It takes intention to bring back your child. Put down your smart phone, turn off the TV, power down your computer. Rip off your clothes, turn up

The problem is we're looking for someone to grow old with, while the secret is to find someone to stay a child with.

Charles Bukowski

It takes a long time to become young.

Pablo Picasso

the volume of your favorite music and dance naked. Get your hands dirty and paint a picture with finger paints, wrestle with your dog, go outside and howl at the moon. Find a playmate to play with. Two frisky old kids are twice as fun as one. Schedule time in your calendar for pure childlike play. You need it for your sanity.

Remember you are a child of God or child of the universe. Love your child-self. Treat yourself as you would your grandchild.

Living a Vision Going Forward

It's early morning. I just now awoke from a dream. I was dreaming I was in a laboratory and a scientist was showing me his invention, a time machine. He was saying, "With my machine, you can travel to any time in the past." I told him, "I'm not interested. I want a machine that will show me the future." Then I woke up.

"What do you plan to do for your future, for the rest of your life?" Ask that question to some ninety-year-olds. You'd probably get a variety of responses. Most might laugh at you and think you are joking. "Nothing, of course, just to survive" would be their response. But the ninety-six-year-old retired businessman I wrote about earlier, who, with his buddies, just started a consulting business for new entrepreneurs in deprived neighborhoods, wouldn't laugh. He would sit you down and bend your ear telling you of his plans for the future.

The conception you have of your future is intimately tied to your answer to the question, "Why am I here. What is my purpose?" If you have not contemplated this question, you might be living your life, as I did when younger, drifting day-to-day, seeking one pleasant experience after another. I was untethered, except for my search for pleasure and ego satisfaction. It was an ultimately unsatisfying way of life. Therefore, I recommend contemplating this question of life purpose. If you do, it could very well lead you to your vision.

Another question that might clarify vision might be, "What gives me joy, what am I passionate about?" Ideally, your vision must be aligned with something you love, something you are excited about, something you can't wait to go to your office, your workshop, your studio, your creative space, so you can begin.

Your vision might include engaging in spiritual work, leaving a legacy, being a loving parent and grandparent, writing your memoir or the novel that has been on your mind for years, or just traveling the world and having fun. It's up to you. It's your vision.

The vision you have can give your life meaning. Dr. Victor Frankl, Holocaust survivor who spent years in Nazi concentration camps, found that often those who survived the camps had some reason to live. Frankl believed he personally survived because he needed to complete the important manuscript he had been working on. That manuscript became the basis for one of the most influential books of the last century, *Man's Search For Meaning*. He wrote, "Those who have a 'why' to live, can bear almost any 'how'." While your vision may not help you survive a concentration camp, it should provide you reason to get out of bed in the morning.

Another piece of advice about vision concerns what a necessary part of what your vision should include. I say this even though I do not know you. I'll say this because I know that, in order for anyone to live a fulfilling life, they must have this piece in their vision. No matter what you foresee for your life ahead, no matter how many days or years you have left on your plate, *your vision should include an intention to become a more loving person.* Make that part of your vision. If you don't, you will be ignoring the most important, most fulfilling aspect of human existence—to love and be loved.

With love in your vision, learn about love, value love, put yourself in the company of loving people. Above all, every day, practice giving and receiving love—with your partner, your friends, your family, your pets, yourself, with strangers, with people you despise, even with people who hate you and wish you harm. This will all encourage you to greater love and will bring your vision alive.

Now that's a worthy vision.

Being In Awe Of The Mystery

Have you gone out on a moonless night and stared up at the stars? Have you placed a stethoscope over your chest and listened to the beating of your heart? Have you seen a baby being born? And held the newborn in your arms? Have you been in a room as someone is dying? And been with the body after their death? Have you thought about your death? Have you tried to consider infinite time? Infinite space? These eye-opening moments make you think about the "Big Questions," don't they? Moments like these put you in touch with the mystery of being alive in an incomprehensible world.

There are "Big Questions" human beings tend to ask themselves as the years go by. *Who am I?*—What is my nature and what does it mean to be human? *Why am I here?*—What is my purpose in life? How shall I live my days? *Where will I go?*—Is there an afterlife or is this lifetime all there is? *Is there a god or higher power, and if so, what is its nature and how am I to relate to it?* These and other big questions have no answers. In trying to answer them, we simply bring up more questions. We are living in a mystery we will never understand. The only appropriate response is to be in awe.

> There are two ways to live:
> you can live as if nothing is a miracle;
> you can live as if everything is a miracle.
>
> Albert Einstein

Here's a horrible analogy, but I think it has some merit. Imagine a garbage can with rotting garbage. A maggot (fly larvae), wiggles it's way to the rim of the can and looks out to the street, the cars, the people and the surrounding buildings. That maggot's understanding of the world that is spread out in front of it is analogous to human beings limited understanding of the magnitude of the universe, it's unknown processes and its possible diverse inhabitants.

When I was a kid, I had a microscope. What a mind-blowing experience for me as an unseen world opened up before my young eyes. The multi colored scales of a butterfly wing, the cells in a drop of my blood, the eye of an ant, the busy life moving around in a drop of water; I was able to view the world I thought I knew in a whole new way.

I also had a telescope when I was young. I was able to view the craters on the surface of the moon, the rings of Saturn, the Milky Way, the windows of our neighbor's teenage daughter's bedroom. All these fueled my sense of wonder.

I still have a microscope and telescope. It's been years since I've unpacked them. I've intended to give them to the local school. Let unjaded eyes appreciate the wonderous worlds they reveal.

I go about my daily routine. I sleep, I wake, I wash, I eat, I shit. I live with little sense of the myriad processes that are constantly going on in my body that are keeping me alive. Lungs breathing, heart beating, food digesting, hormones secreting, all working together, automatically, without my awareness. What a miracle I am.

For most of us, as the years pass and we get older, we lose that sense of wonder. Occupied by the horrible world news, complaining about our constipation, trying to save a buck, we live out our lives, navigating around in these miraculous bodies, on this miraculous earth, in this miraculous universe, with little sense of appreciation of the miracle that it is, that we are. If only we could see again with the eyes of children, and care with the eyes of a mature adult.

Astronomer Carl Sagan saw with eyes of wonder and also deep concern when he contemplated the 1990 Hubble telescope photograph of the Earth taken from the fringes of our solar system. Our planet, with all it's diverse life, it's human hopes, dramas and dreams, appeared in the photograph as a tiny, pale blue dot. He wrote:

There is perhaps no better demonstration of the folly of human conceits than this distant image of our tiny world. To me, it underscores our responsibility to deal more kindly with one another and to preserve and cherish the pale blue dot, the only world we've ever known.

Think of what a magnificent privilege it is, to be alive, to be old, to be together with loved ones, as temporary visitors drifting on this miraculous, tiny, pale blue dot. If we could comprehend even a small fraction of the immensity of the place where we are living our tiny, tiny lives, we would be swept away by the majesty of it all.

Should I stop here on this high note? Maybe not. Now I'm rounding the final lap of the book, I am taking a second look at these tasks for the last stage of life. Granted, they are valuable. Addressing the need to come to terms with our world, our loved ones, our history, our selves, this is an important part of coming to peace with our aging self. Working through tasks like facing our mortality, completing unfinished business, forgiving ourself and others, nurturing our spirit, these seem essential in order for us to grow to our full potential. Yet, looking back, these nearly three dozen tasks for aging seem like so much hard work, so serious, so about "self-improvement." Maybe they are not for everyone.

We come from a culture where we believe there is a solution that will fix every problem. We just have to find it. And when we discover what the solution is, we have to work long and hard until we accomplish our goal. It doesn't work this way with aging. Aging is not a problem to be solved or a self-help project to be undertaken. Aging is an experience to be lived. Sometimes the solution is less about doing, and more about being, less about holding on tightly, and more about letting go lightly, less about trying to emulate some ideal, no matter how worthy, and more about simply being as much of our authentic self as we are able.

If we address our aging as another self-improvement project, we immerse ourselves in negativity, "What's wrong with me? What character defects must I get rid of? What qualities do I need to acquire that will make me a better person?" Perhaps a more gentle and fruitful path is to start by looking toward seeing our inner perfection, and appreciating and accepting ourself as we are.

A zen master offers us a conundrum when he said, "We are all perfect. But we can still use a bit of improvement." Which side of the conundrum should we choose? Perfection or improvement? I don't know.

So, with this in mind, I'm tempted to add just one more task for the last stage of life. This is one that could apply to all the other tasks. And it might modify how you approach them all. In fact, this task might well apply to the entirety of the way you live your life. This last task I suggest for the latter stages of life is…

Not Being So Hard On Yourself

Being a mature adult is a daunting undertaking. Forgiving others and self, being kind, loving everyone and showing up with your best and highest self, all day, every day. This is a full-time job. I struggle with it every day.

We're human, not saints. Even if we consider ourselves strong and masterful, at heart, we're still tender and vulnerable. Some days you'll feel dark and not want to put out the effort to be kind. Some days you'll be too hurt and angry to forgive. Some days you'll be too afraid of the consequences if you would be genuinely honest, so you bend the truth with a little white lie. Some days you'll be too out of control to maintain self-restraint, too distracted to be present, too stressed to do anything except curl up in bed and pull the covers over your head. Go ahead. "Cut yourself some slack." Take a day off. A month off. A year. You don't have to be perfect.

Truth be told, you don't have to do anything. You've lived your years. You've earned a right to live out your life any damn way you please. In fact, I think that to accept who you are without feeling guilty about your shortcomings is a far more enlightened approach than to use guilt as a crowbar to force yourself to be someone you are not. Or feeling that you're not good enough and have to suffer and work hard in order to change so you can make yourself acceptable. That's torture. Forgive yourself for not being perfect. You don't have to be the hero. Do what you want, how you want. You're the boss. And you're OK as you are. Have compassion for yourself. Relax. Be gentle. Accept. Respect. Be who you are now. Release who you were then. Give up what you cannot be.

It's hard being human. Humans are a strange breed. We're all a little weird, every one of us. Maybe more than a little weird. Just think if our private thoughts were broadcast out loud so that other people could hear them. Would you be horrified to have others know the craziness and stupidity that goes on in your unhinged mind? I would. And so would probably everyone else. No matter how holy we are, our poop still stinks.

Life would be so much easier if we would be more inclined to accept ourselves more for the goofy, imperfect beings we are and sit back and enjoy the show. If you desire change, it might be easier to give yourself permission to allow change to happen in its own way and its own time. The desire you have for change is itself a powerful factor that will effect the change you desire.

But if you feel the call and decide to put in the effort to work at being a mature adult, put in the effort. Rise to the occasion and try the best you can. If you want, make it part of your life's movie. When you fall down—and you will—pick yourself up, dust yourself off, and continue to try the best you can to be the best that you are. Failure is a part, an important part, of the process of learning to be your best self. Take your fall as an opportunity to learn, then recommit to keep on the path. As Alcoholics Anonymous recommends, "Progress rather than perfection." You don't have to be perfect. You just have to show up.

The immortal words of Leonard Cohen's song, *Anthem,* says it.

Ring the bells that still can ring
Forget your perfect offering
There's a crack in everything
That's how the light gets in.

Each one of us is a unique work of art. Up until the moment of our death, the masterpiece we are remains unfinished. You are, I am, we all are, works in progress. So do the best you can at living the life you want. And if you need to, don't be reluctant to cut yourself some slack. Then go on, ring the bells you can still ring, and celebrate your perfectly imperfect offering.

❧ ❧ ❧

The contemplations about love and time, relationship and aging, life and death throughout the book, and the tasks for the last stage of life described above, are all preparations we can make in our encounter with time. They can all be powerful remedies that can help as we approach the challenges of growing old in the Winter of life. If you put in the time and effort to work with them, you'll find that they can contain healing medicine. They are prescriptions that can enhance wisdom, vision and perspective. And they can help to alleviate some of the suffering that inevitably comes if you are fortunate enough to be the occupant of an aging human body.

More than healing medicine for mind and body, these contemplations of love and time hold potential for joy. We're here for a reason. We were born to celebrate and learn and share love, not weep and sleepwalk through our life. Embracing our aging and embracing our loving heart is a way we can receive and enjoy the gift of life we've been given. Feel the preciousness of that gift and celebrate, celebrate, celebrate! Then step into the great adventure that awaits you in your renewed, elder life.

CLOSING—LOVE AND TIME

COUSIN SATYA HAD GIVEN BIRTH a week earlier. After a short, easy labor, Deia entered the world. At this evening gathering of family and friends, a party welcoming her arrival, Deia is being passed around, person to person, to waiting arms, a delicate pink bundle, wrapped in a soft blanket. Now, it is my turn, for a minute, to hold her. She is gently placed in my arms. Cradling her tiny body, I look down at her. Deia looks up, and for a moment, our eyes lock. In that instant, my mind is transported into a fantasy, a dream vision of her growing into her future.

Infancy…Childhood…School…Adolescence…Loves…Work…

Children…Family…Joy…Heartbreak…Loss…Old age—A life.

Sadly, I'll never know the story of that life. Long before her life is complete, I will have turned to dust.

In an instant, this reverie abruptly evaporates and I am shockingly brought to the present moment, staring into a pair of unfocused, uncomprehending brown eyes. Slightly dazed, I pass Deia on to the next set of waiting arms.

Shakespeare famously wrote:

"All the world's a stage,

And all the men and women merely players;

They all have their exits and their entrances."

341

Eight decades ago, I was like Deia, a brand new consciousness, recently entered the stage, about to play my role in the theater of life. Maybe in eighty years or so, Deia will be like me, an old consciousness, having played her part, soon to exit stage left, leaving the theater to other newborn actors to play their parts.

During our short appearance on life's stage, we humans are affected by the changing scenes, changing dramas of our unfolding life. We follow the scripts that are written for us and those we ourselves write. We grow and are altered through the impact of the occurrences, the characters we meet and encounters we go through as we live out the days of our lives. These ever-changing scenes constitute the contents of our lifetime. Most of those experiences won't retain meaning for us. They lack the power to change us. They are just passing sense impressions—experienced and then forgotten. But some experiences are so profound, touch us so deeply, that we absorb them into our very being. They have the ability to shake up our complacent world and create transformation in our life. One such powerful experience is of those moments when our heart opens in loving awareness to a person, a child, even to a pet…and we are able to give and receive love as never before. Another powerful experience is the profound realization of the passage of time…observing, with a mixture of terror and curiosity, the reality of ourselves, our loved ones, and our own body becoming frail and withering away as we grow older. The experience of awakening to love, and the experience of awakening to the passage of time. Love and Time.

Alice and I give talks and workshops about aging and about our art. We usually end by showing a short video that encapsulates, in about a minute, the whole span of a human life. It came from an advertisement for Xbox, a video game format. The scene opens in a hospital maternity room where a woman is giving birth. At her last push, the baby shoots out from between her legs and, to everyone's horror, is propelled out through an open window. As he continues flying in a rising trajectory, the infant boy changes to a toddler, to a young child, a teenager, an adult man. As he comes on to middle age, the arc begins to turn downward. The man keeps getting older, grayer and more wrinkled as he rapidly approaches the ground. The final scene shows the moment the now aged man crashes into an open grave, kicking up a cloud of dust. Silence as the dust settles. Black screen. Then, in bold white letters, the words appear, LIFE IS SHORT. Next come the words, PLAY MORE.

Wise words. So true. They should never be erased from the blackboard of the School For Love.

Life *is* short. Don't waste your valuable time crying and being miserable. See the positive. Appreciate what you have. Enjoy beauty. Enjoy laughter. Look for what gives you vitality and joy. Follow your bliss...*Play More.*

Life *is* short. You have been born for a reason. Whether you're young or old, search inside your heart and mind and discover your life's meaning, your life's passion and purpose. Find you wisdom... *Look Within More.*

Life *is* short. Change is the nature of the world. Joy and pain will come. Joy and pain will go. Don't hold on. Don't declare war on reality...*Accept Life As It Comes More.*

Life *is* short. All around you people are suffering. Our earth is suffering. Greed, hate and evil abound. Be good. Do good. Be kind. Don't add to the pain. Wherever and whenever you can... *Cultivate Goodness More.*

Life *is* short. You have so little time, and as you grow older, with each passing moment, the time you have remaining becomes more precious. Spend that limited time loving, which is the one single thing in your life that will give you the most joy, provide you the most meaning, help you embrace change, and do the most good in the world. Open your heart, to yourself, to others, to the world.... *Love More.*

There is no better way for you to spend your limited time on Earth.

Our human lifespan is minuscule. Even if you are one of those persons who are fortunate enough to live an entire cycle of the seasons, from early Spring to late Winter, your life is but a fleeting dream, a shooting star, a bubble in a stream. You are here for an infinitesimal moment. Living in that moment, you may consider the dramas of your individual life to be of great importance, more significant than anything and everything else in the universe. So important you believe you are, so demanding your needs, so impressive your accomplishments, so consequential your actions. Yet, to all the rest of the world, your individual life is as insignificant as a flea—of no more importance than a grain of earth, a flake of ash, a speck of dust. That will be your eventual destination; a return of *"earth to earth, ashes to ashes, dust to dust."*

But while you're here, celebrate. Your life is a gift. Time has been gifted to you. Your ability to think, to feel and to love is a blessing. Celebrate this late season, this Winter of your life. Celebrate the incredible honor and miracle it is to be alive, to be a conscious being, to have lived long in this miraculous body. You are a tourist, cruising for a short, short while, a sojourner among the stars, aboard this beautiful, tiny, pale blue dot.

Enjoy the journey.

APPENDIX 1. THE LOVING PROMISES

THE LOVING PROMISES are a way of life, a set of goals you want to live by. They are 39 vows, statements of intention you make to yourself, not your partner, as to how you will behave in your relationship. Here is a summary of the Promises. They can be found in detail in my book, LOVING PROMISES: *The Master Class For Creating Magnificent Relationship.*

I WILL STAND STEADFASTLY BY YOU. I am wholeheartedly committed to the permanence of our relationship. I will not leave or threaten to leave, even during times of great difficulty.

I WILL REMAIN PRESENT WITH YOU. I will abide with you in mind and body, and will not cut myself off from you by withdrawing physically, mentally or emotionally.

I WILL BE AWAKE TO YOU. I will receive you with an open heart and mind, trying to intuit the feelings and decipher the meanings that lie beneath your words and actions.

I WILL SERVE YOUR BEST INTERESTS. I want the best for you and will take care of you, comfort you, encourage you and protect you from harm in ways that empower you and not interfere with you growing into your perfection.

I WILL BE UNSELFISH WITH YOU. I will make it my practice to attempt to give to you unconditionally. When our needs are in conflict, I will seek solutions only in terms of our mutual benefit.

LOVE AND TIME

I WILL PARTICIPATE IN YOUR LIFE. I will make the ongoing decision to extend myself and choose to participate with you in the interests and activities that you find important and enjoyable.

I WILL BE FLEXIBLE WITH YOU. I will always remain open to relinquishing my stance and altering my behavior when it is appropriate. I will do so graciously, without regret or expectation of compensation.

I WILL BE ACCEPTING OF YOU. I will not expect perfection from you. I will seek to recognize and appreciate your individual uniqueness and acknowledge your human frailty. I will not attempt to change you into my idea of who you should be.

I WILL REGARD YOU AS MY EQUAL. I will immediately cease when I become aware I am judging you to be inferior or superior to myself, believe that my needs are more important than yours, assume that I cannot learn from you, or expect that I am entitled to better treatment than you.

I WILL EMPHASIZE YOUR POSITIVE SIDE. I will applaud your admirable qualities, activities and accomplishments, and refrain from focusing on your feelings and imperfections.

I WILL INSPIRE YOU TO BE YOUR BEST. I will persistently urge you to strive to be the very best person you can be. I would encourage you to pursue your dreams.

I WILL CHALLENGE YOU WHEN NECESSARY. I will not shrink from asserting my power in order to influence you for your benefit. I will confront you and offer constructive criticism when I recognize you are in need of guidance.

I WILL BE GRATEFUL FOR YOUR GIFTS TO ME. I will be mindful of the things you do and have done for my benefit. I will not take these things for granted or automatically expect them from you. I will receive graciously.

I WILL APPRECIATE YOU. I will honor the miracle, mystery and beauty of who you are. I will keep alive a sense of appreciation of how your presence has enhanced my life. I will not hesitate to express that appreciation.

I WILL EXPRESS MY FEELINGS OF LOVE FOR YOU. I will demonstrate my love for you through my words, my touch, my giving, and especially through my conduct.

I WILL BE FORGIVING OF YOU. I will look upon you with compassion and strive to let go of my anger, blame and judgments when I feel you have wronged me. I will never engage in any form of retaliation.

I WILL BE DEPENDABLE WITH YOU. I will try to the best of my ability to identify and accomplish the things that need to be done for our mutual well-being. I will attempt to always follow through with what I say I will do, and will perform my tasks with care.

I WILL BE TRUTHFUL WITH YOU. I will not tell you anything I know to be false, nor will I omit telling you what I know to be true. I will not bend the truth in order to gain advantage, protect myself, or keep peace.

I WILL BE TRANSPARENT WITH YOU. I will allow you to know the real me. I will not attempt to protect myself by maintaining a false façade and by withholding my true feelings, thoughts and motives from you, especially when I feel vulnerable.

I WILL SPEAK TO YOU WITH CARE. My words hold power for you, so I will take care to honor your feelings and your dignity, not only with what I say to you, but also how and when I say it.

I WILL NOT MANIPULATE YOU. I will not exploit your vulnerabilities in order to control you. I will not belittle you, blame you, threaten you, deliberately hurt you with words, or intentionally withhold money, favors, information or affection from you in order to get my way.

I WILL PROTECT OUR CONFIDENTIALITY. I will not share anything with others, about you, me, or us that you would not want other people to know.

I WILL RESPECT OUR INDEPENDENCE. You are not my possession. I will honor your freedom to think, say and do what seems right to you— even if I do not agree or understand. I will foster my independence so that I can be free and autonomous with you.

I WILL BE CONSIDERATE OF YOUR DESIRE FOR PRIVACY AND SOLITUDE. Periods of interior time are necessary and healing. I recognize your occasional need for privacy, silence and alone time, and will abide by your wishes.

I WILL TOUCH YOU AND WELCOME YOUR TOUCH. I understand that touch is a gift and a healing. I will welcome physical expression of our love for each other through loving caress, in ways that are reciprocally appreciated and at times that are mutually desired.

I WILL REMAIN FAITHFUL TO YOU. Sexual fidelity is a bulwark of our relationship. I will consider you my exclusive sexual partner and reserve intimate caress for you alone.

I WILL PLAY WITH YOU. I will do what I can to make humor, entertainment, curiosity, surprise, creativity, imagination, romance, excitement and childlike playfulness—vital elements in our relationship.

I WILL VITALIZE OUR RELATIONSHIP. A partnership that does not continually grow can stagnate. I will instigate and participate in uplifting activities, learning and adventures that inspire us to evolve physically, socially, intellectually, emotionally and spiritually.

I WILL HONOR YOUR FAMILY. Family ties are complex and binding. I will treat your family with respect and graciousness, ever mindful that my first loyalty is to you.

I WILL BE ALERT TO NEGATIVITY IN OUR RELATIONSHIP. I will not allow harmful feelings and destructive situations to persist and fester. I will attend to the first indications of disharmony between us.

I WILL ASSUME RESPONSIBILITY FOR MY DETRIMENTAL BEHAVIOR. When there is discord, I will take impartial account of my part and do what is necessary to make things right.

I WILL INVOKE THE LOVING PROMISES WHEN WE ARE IN CRISIS. During stressful circumstances, our relationship requires greater loving from me. At those trying times, I will attempt to apply the Loving Promises to the best of my ability.

I WILL HONOR MY OWN NEEDS AND MY OWN FEELINGS. When trying to uphold these Loving Promises, I will attend to the way I feel, and will not disregard my needs and desires, compromise my values, or allow others to overstep my boundaries.

I WILL NURTURE MYSELF FOR BOTH OF US. My well-being affects you as well as myself. I will strive to choose wholesome alternatives in my life to keep my body healthy, my mind positive, and my spirit uplifted.

I WILL MAINTAIN THE AWARENESS OF THE SPIRITUAL NATURE OF OUR RELATIONSHIP. You, our love, and the bond we share are sacred gifts. It is an essential aspect of my spiritual path. That understanding will inform all choices I make.

I WILL REMIND MYSELF OF THE FLEETING NATURE OF OUR TIME TOGETHER. At some point, one of us will be alone. I will endeavor to keep this in my mind and savor the preciousness of each moment I have with you.

I WILL DEEPEN MY LOVE FOR MYSELF. If I do not love me, I cannot give love to you, nor can I be available to receive your love. I will aspire to acknowledge myself as unconditionally lovable.

I WILL EXPAND MY LOVE INTO THE WORLD. My love will wither if it is reserved only for you. I will extend my love, respect and care to family and friends, acquaintances and strangers, to nature and all creation.

This final Promise is not a vow you make. It is a realization you come to over time, through practicing the Loving Promises. I WILL EMBRACE LOVE AS THE GUIDING LIGHT OF MY LIFE. My ultimate goal is to think more loving thoughts, feel more loving feelings, speak more loving words, act in more loving ways—at all times, in any situation, with every person—including myself. My intention is to bring more goodness into my life, into your life, into our relationship, and into the world.

APPENDIX 2. METTA

METTA IS AN ANCIENT Buddhist lovingkindness practice. It begins by wishing goodness to self, then loved ones, and gradually extends that wish for well-being and happiness to strangers.

Begin by getting into a comfortable position. After a few deep breaths, take some time to allow your body to relax. You will be repeating several short phrases. There are many variations. The following is the wording that was taught to me over fifty years ago.

We start with goodwill toward ourself, because we cannot extend love to others without first feeling love toward ourselves. Sit quietly, and slowly, silently repeat the phrase to yourself, "May I be happy." Repeat this phrase until the intention for your happiness feels real, and you sense a warmth and friendliness arising. Do the same with the next phrase, "May I be peaceful." Feel that desire for serenity. The next phrase you repeat is, "May I be free from suffering." This is a desire for physical and mental health. The final phrase of this series is, "May I Love and be loved." (I added this to the phrases I was taught. It felt right for me and may feel right for you.)

The next series concerns extending the wish for goodness toward friends, family and those you care about. The words are, "May————be happy, May ————be peaceful," etc. If you are up for a challenge, try repeating these Metta phrases for those who have hurt you or who wish you harm. The benefit is multiplied if you do this.

The final series for Metta extends lovingkindness toward the whole world. The phrases are, "May all beings be happy. May all beings be peaceful. May all beings be free of suffering. May all beings love and be loved."

Sometimes the opposite feelings may arise and you will feel angry, sad or unkind toward others and yourself. Not to worry. Don't judge. This is part of the process and shows you that Metta is working. Keep on practicing.

AUTHOR

RICHARD MATZKIN, MA, has a magnificent, four decade long relationship with his wife, Alice. He is an award winning author of books on aging, relationships and men's issues. He is a former men's group leader, director of a domestic violence program, meditation teacher, and program director of a psychiatric hospital. He is also an accomplished sculptor and jazz drummer. He lives with Alice, and 4 chickens, on an acre at the end of a road in the hills above the small hamlet of Ojai, California.

www.ingramcontent.com/pod-product-compliance
Lightning Source LLC
Chambersburg PA
CBHW080835120626
46553CB00009B/2442